Splendor of God

The life of Adoniram Judson

Splendor of God

Honoré Willsie Morrow

BAKER BOOK HOUSE
Grand Rapids, Michigan 49506

Copyright 1929 by
Honoré Willsie Morrow

Paperback edition issued 1982 by
Baker Book House Company
with permission of copyright owner

ISBN: 0-8010-6129-6

Printed in the United States of America

CONTENTS

CHAPTER		PAGE
I	THE SAD, SILLY TOWN	1
II	THE IRON MAUL	12
III	FELIX CAREY	21
IV	NIAGARA FALLS	33
V	THE GAING-ÔK	42
VI	THE NOVICE IN AFFLICTION	54
VII	DISCIPLINE	61
VIII	THE "FLYING SQUIRREL"	74
IX	COMMON ANCESTRY	83
X	THE ZAYAT	92
XI	JESUS CHRIST'S MAN	105
XII	THE LOTUS LAKE	114
XIII	THE KING	124
XIV	THE LITTLE CHURCH	137
XV	THE WITCH WOMAN	148
XVI	JONATHAN DAVID PRICE	157
XVII	SURGEON TO THE KING	164
XVIII	THE INWARD SILENCE	181
XIX	HONEYMOON	192
XX	HAND, SHRINK NOT!	204
XXI	ORDEAL	214
XXII	BANDULA	224
XXIII	UNBROKEN OF HEART	232
XXIV	THE SENSE OF HONOR	242

CHAPTER		PAGE
XXV	AVA AT BAY	258
XXVI	SIR ARCHIBALD CAMPBELL	270
XXVII	JOHN CRAWFURD	280
XXVIII	ANN	291
XXIX	BARE TO THE BUFF	297
XXX	DESIRE SHALL FAIL	309
XXXI	SARAH BOARDMAN	322
XXXII	AFTER THE EARTHQUAKE, A FIRE	334
XXXIII	AT THE FRONT AGAIN	343
XXXIV	RAIN IF THOU WILT, O SKY!	355
XXXV	SPLENDOR OF GOD	368
	PARTIAL LIST OF BOOKS CONSULTED	375

Splendor of God

CHAPTER I

THE SAD, SILLY TOWN

LATE in the afternoon of July 13, 1813, the ruinous old coasting vessel, *Georgiana,* dropped anchor before Rangoon.

Ann and Adoniram Judson had arrived in Burma.

Ann had been very ill during the three weeks' stormy voyage from Madras. She had lost her baby prematurely and had almost lost her life during the dreadful trip. There had been only Adoniram to help her in her hour of need and Adoniram was little more than a boy. The Judsons were the only passengers. The crew was a miscellany of Orientals, the captain alone speaking English. There were no cabins; only a canvas shelter for Ann's sake. And she was a New England girl, reared in the meticulous modesty, the chaste orderliness of a Puritan home. She was twenty-one years old. Adoniram was twenty-five.

From the moment the ship had entered the Rangoon River, Adoniram had stood just without the shelter, his eyes strained toward the shore.

He looked very much younger than his years for his face was unlined and he had not yet lost the high coloring and the rounded cheeks that had made a pretty child of him. He was a trifle over medium height with thick black hair touched by ruddy tones and hazel eyes that looked brown in a half light. His features, the shape of his head were of the type we have come to associate with the finest of our New England scholars. Emerson had such a head and Whittier and Hawthorne; high domed and broad across the brows, with large ears set close to the skull. He had a rather long, straight nose, wide, delicately turned mouth, the underlip a little full and a strong jaw line, ending in a firmly rounded but dimpled chin. The dimple counter-acted somewhat the over-determination of the lower part of the face. Adoniram's eyes were his most beautiful feature. They were set under the full upper lid of the linguist and were very large and filled with a wistful and searching fire.

He wore black, as became a missionary; breeches and coat of broadcloth, stockings of white cotton and white cambric neckerchief. He didn't know as yet how to dress for the Burmese climate.

It was the rainy season. All day long the southwest wind had driven slanting lines of gray drizzle over the mangroves that fringed the river and across an immense expanse of flat lands now flooded by many waters.

Hour after hour, Adoniram had watched for signs of civilization, but it was noon before he had his reward. Then there suddenly emerged from the clouds to the north a tremulous, perpendicular line of gold. It remained but a moment. Lavender mists covered it almost at once and although it appeared occasionally during the afternoon, it was not until the *Georgiana* was dropping her anchor that it came into full view. Then the clouds definitely lifted, the westering sun flamed across the paddy fields and Adoniram gasped in admiration.

From a green hill to the north rose an exquisitely proportioned spire of gold, broadly round where it left the trees and tapering to a point where it touched the crimsoned heavens. That enormous love of beauty which was to so complicate Adoniram's tremendous experiences in Burma responded overwhelmingly to this his first view of the Buddha's greatest shrine. This was no concept of barbarity! This was an expression of minds both intelligent and spiritual. His folded arms stiffened. His pulse raced. If this glorious monument was a true symbol of the Burman's spiritual aspirations, what a glorious battle waited

THE SAD, SILLY TOWN

for Christ in Burma! Here was a struggle worthy of any man's intellect!

He was smiling happily when his eye dropped to the town which lay between the golden pagoda and the shore. As far as Adoniram knew, he and Ann were destined to spend the remainder of their lives in this spot and he began to examine its outlines with eager curiosity. He saw, a stone's throw from the *Georgiana*, a sandy beach, dotted with small boats, and above this a line of thatched huts on stilts. Behind the huts, a tall log stockade, stretching perhaps a mile along the beach. Behind the stockade, trees sloped up to the pagoda hill. An occasional clump of palms towered above the general level of foliage.

Somewhere behind that stockade was a shelter for Ann and him. He peered under the canvas. Ann was still asleep. She had slept, poor dear, from the moment they had left behind the rough waters of the Bay of Bengal. Adoniram dropped the curtain and asked the captain to set him ashore. Ten minutes later, he crossed the beach and walked through the south gate of the stockade.

Before him opened a tree-shaded street, rudely paved with brick, the gutters running flush with dirty water. On either side stood a row of thatched huts on stilts, pigs and chickens messing in the muck beneath or if the water were deep, rooting and scratching on the highway.

Half-clad men and women went to and fro or squatted on the verandas. Naked little children shared the labors of the pigs and chickens. Dogs rushed at Adoniram from everywhere, snarling and barking. People stared at him and a few followed him along with the dogs. But the appearance of a white man in Rangoon was, he knew, not unprecedented. There were half a dozen Europeans in the town. The captain of the *Georgiana* had directed him to the house of the collector of the Port, a Spaniard, in the Burmese king's employ. So he followed the street until it widened into a bazaar, with stalls closed for the day, crossed the bazaar and halted before a small brick house, painted red. The young missionary splashed on stepping stones from the bamboo gate to the veranda steps. Here sat a darkly bearded man of perhaps fifty, in a crumpled linen suit. He took a huge cheroot from his mouth and invited Adoniram very graciously in French to come up on the veranda.

Adoniram complying, said in the same tongue, "M. Lanciego, my name is Adoniram Judson. I have just arrived on the *Georgiana* and wish to land to-morrow."

"So the old tub has made it once more!" smiled the collector. "Will you be seated, M. Judson, on what I believe is one of the three chairs in Rangoon? Tell me what I may do for you, other than in my official capacity."

"I suppose there must be a good many things that I'm too ignorant to ask you for, monsieur," replied Adoniram with his ingenuous smile. "My first problem is shelter. But I think that's already solved. I'm to live at the Baptist Mission house."

Lanciego shook his head.

Adoniram, a little troubled, went on eagerly, "But there *is* one, you know. It was built several years ago by an Englishman named Chaytor. I believe he has left Burma but a M. Felix Carey remains."

The collector eyed Adoniram in silence for a long moment before he replied, "Officially, monsieur, I mustn't know of a mission house because I'm employed by the king who's a Buddhist. I do know of a house belonging to M. Carey. But he is no longer here. He's in Amarapura, the capital, employed by the king. Are you another English missionary?"

"I'm an American missionary. But I have a letter from M. Carey's father, the famous English missionary in Serampore to his son here in Rangoon. I'm to work with M. Felix."

The Spaniard's dark eyes were not unkindly as he leaned

THE SAD, SILLY TOWN

toward Adoniram, confidentially. The rank smell of his cheroot cut wholesomely through the sickening miasma of flooded Rangoon.

"My dear young sir, let an older man advise you. And a man who knows his Burma. My wife is sister to one of the queens and his majesty has honored me with his confidence for many years. I know what I'm talking about when I say to you, Go back to America! Go back to-night! There's nothing for you here but heart-ache. These people have a fine, strong religion of their own. I tell you that, though I'm a Catholic. They'll resent you. And while they're the kindest, pleasantest people in the world they're also the most passionate and cruel. Go back while you're still a youth full of the fire of your faith!"

Adoniram listened, his gaze wandering from the collector's earnest face to the gloomy cavern of the tree-enclosed bazaar. Not since leaving Salem had he been so profoundly depressed, not even when, three months before, he'd become convinced that the British authorities would not permit him to remain in India. There was something in the filthy, tree-darkened town of Rangoon that was tomblike and ghoulish. It gave him a feeling of fear. But no trace of doubt as to his course crossed the boy's mind.

"My wife and I have come to stay," he said, simply.

"Wife!" roared Lanciego. "Wife? Another babe like yourself, I suppose! So you plan to add murder to suicide!" He sank back in his bamboo chair with a grunt of disgust.

"Madame Judson's as eager to work here as I am. She is a very remarkable person, my wife. You'll see what I mean when you meet her," declared Adoniram, very earnestly. "M. Lanciego, we've been coming to Rangoon by God's devious path ever since February of last year. Every known device of Satan has been used to turn us back. But we're here! When we left America, we supposed we were to work in India. But the East India Company wouldn't have it. We went to Madras, then to the Isle of France. Still we were not allowed to rest. Then the *Georgiana* agreed to take us to Rangoon. And here we are. God has sent us to save the Burmans from hell and no warning can unseat that purpose."

The Spaniard gasped but for several moments was silent. By the lines between his brows and the prominence of his lower lip he would appear to be a man of choleric temper. But after a deliberate study of Adoniram's face, something there must have convinced him that petulance would have no effect and that his protests were pitted against a force he did not understand. This was only a boy and yet—! Lanciego shrugged his shoulders.

"Carey's house," he said, "is north of the town, outside the stockade and near the hill on which the Shwé Dagôn pagoda stands. Madame Carey is there with their children. I suppose you know she's a native woman?"

Adoniram had not known and this really was a hard blow, when added to the news of Carey's having left the mission. The young American had a horror of mixed marriage and more than this, Ann had counted heavily on having a friend in Felix Carey's wife. For just a moment a great blast of homesickness made him speechless. He smiled a little pathetically at Lanciego. "I suppose we've got a good many things to unlearn," he murmured. Then he asked, firmly, "If you'll be so kind as to set me on the road, I'll go out to see Madame Carey."

"She speaks only Burmese," warned the collector, a little maliciously, "and I cannot call there with you because of my official position."

But Adoniram's nerves were steadying. He rose. "You've been very patient, monsieur. Tell me the Burmese words for missionary and wife, and I'll be off."

"There's no native word for missionary," grunted Lanciego. "You address the lady as Ma Carey, while your lady will be Ma Judson and you're Maung Judson."

THE SAD, SILLY TOWN 7

Adoniram chuckled. "*Ma* Judson! How my wife will laugh! And now for the directions, monsieur."

They were simple enough. He was to follow the street beyond the bazaar to a stockade gate. Beyond the gate, the road led through the jungle to the Shwé Dagôn pagoda. If he followed this for half a mile, he'd come to the execution ground which he'd recognize by the smell and other matters. Just beyond this unsavory spot was Carey's house.

Adoniram thanked the Spaniard and went slowly down the steps. When he reached the gate, Lanciego called after him, "Be sure to take your shoes off before you enter their houses. It's very offensive to them, if you don't. And don't try to shake hands with any woman. No man must touch a woman but a relative." Adoniram waved his hand and set off on his journey.

The shade was deep, pierced but lightly by the setting sun. He recognized only a few of the trees, the palms, the plantains and the fig nor did the gorgeous chorus of birds speak a single homely word to him. The way was constantly intersected by little creeks over which bamboo bridges were thrown. Ducks floated and guzzled from ditch to creek and from creek to street. People stared at him. But only a few followed him. It was the supper hour. Little fires twinkled on the verandas.

He passed through a wide gate, over a moat, and northwest along a broad, well-paved road, built high enough to throw off the rainfall. Little and big pagodas and innumerable shrines heaped with flower and food offerings lined the way under magnificent trees. The air was filled with the deep notes of gongs while clear above them and silver sweet, sounded the desultory tinkling of many bells.

It was very beautiful. Adoniram, whose nerves had been jumping, suddenly felt soothed, almost happy. He strode along with growing assurance in every step, new beauties of tree and vine and bursting flowers opening on him as he went. He forgot the execution place and it was inexpressibly shocking at the end of a half mile of sheer loveliness to meet by the roadside a man stretched on upright bamboos, naked and disemboweled!

Adoniram jerked backward, his heart racing. Then he clapped his hand to his nose to shut out the unspeakable stench and broke into a run. Almost immediately he came to a bamboo gate opening on a yard in which stood a larger house than any he'd seen. It was set on stilts and well roofed with split bamboo. He hurried along the stepping stones to the veranda. The house door was open. Adoniram slipped off his shoes.

Within, there glowed a little fire in a shallow box of sand. An earthen pot was propped over the coals and squatting before it was a woman, naked to the waist. She was smoking an enormous cheroot, and another was stuck through a hole in her ear lobe.

"Ma Carey?" asked Adoniram, uncertainly.

With a startled cry, the woman jumped to her feet. She wore a beautiful, rose-striped petticoat that trailed on the ground. Adoniram thought her very ugly with her flat nose and blackened teeth and as he took the elder Carey's letter of introduction from his pocket, he wondered more than ever at Felix Carey. He offered her the letter, at the same time pointing to himself and saying, "Maung Judson!" She gave him an uneasy look. Then he added with a gesture toward the town, "Ma Judson."

This she understood for she smiled and took the letter. Adoniram put his finger on the address. "Maung Carey," he said.

"Amarapura," returned Ma Carey, promptly.

Adoniram laughed delightedly and beckoned to the two brown babies hiding in the shadow. But they turned their little bare backs on him. Adoniram nodded to their mother, touched his breast, pointed to the children, and measured with his hands the length of the tiny son he had committed

THE SAD, SILLY TOWN 9

to the waves, two weeks before. Then he wiped his eyes.

Ma Carey understood. She gave a little cry of grief, "Amé!" and from that moment the sign language between them became fluent. Adoniram told her that Ann was ill and that he would like to bring her to the mission. Ma Carey pattered in bare brown feet and trailing rose skirt across the room and through an open door. Adoniram followed her into a dim room with windows on the veranda. There was a bed in it and some fine black reed mats.

"Ma Judson," said Ma Carey.

"Yes! Yes! O wonderful! Thank you! Thank you!" cried Adoniram. He forgot and would have taken her hand had she not drawn back with a frown. But she accepted a very gallant bow from him cheerfully and Adoniram hurried out into the dusk.

It was an eerie walk back to the stockade. Rain had begun to fall again. It was so dark when he rushed past the execution place that he recognized it only by the dreadful stench. One thing was certain, he'd not let Ann see this horror, on the morrow. He reached the beach breathless and depressed. Rangoon in the night and the rain were funereal.

But when he clambered aboard the *Georgiana,* the canvas shelter glowed with light and his heart rose. Ann must be awake and watching for him. And so she was.

Curious how sweet and homelike the shelter seemed, set as it was on the squalid deck with rain washing over the floor and only a pallet and their sea chests for furnishings. Yet, though during the three weeks' passage he'd loathed it for what Ann had suffered behind its walls, he now entered it with a thrill of relief and pleasure. One would, seeing that it contained Ann!

Even in her long-sleeved, high-necked nightgown, she was lovely. Even after her illness, her grief and the frightful voyage, her beauty was unimpaired. Her face was oval, with rather pronounced cheek bones and a high forehead round which her dark brown hair fell in curls. Her mouth was small and full with sensitive corners and extraordinarily tender for a mere girl. Her eyes, large, full and a deep brown, dominated her face, giving it its look of intelligence and self-control.

She sat up in bed and held out her hands. "Adoniram, *darling!*"

He rushed to her and kissed her a dozen times. "Lovely, lovely Nancy! I've been touring the metropolis of Rangoon. And as a metropolis, my sweet wife, it's the saddest, silliest spot on earth."

Ann laughed. "Sit down and tell me every single *unimportant* thing. O Adoniram! You're sopping wet!"

"Don't bother about that, Ann. We're Burmans now and amphibian. These clothes are all wrong for this climate, anyhow. And, O Nancy, it's a world of dirty water yonder, I assure you!"

He gave her a vivid picture of his experiences, eliminating only that crucified figure in the shadow of the mission. Ann was fascinated.

"I'm stronger already, just at the thought of a house and a woman friend, though we can't talk together," she declared. "Did you see her children, 'Don?"

"Only vaguely. Pretty brown shadows in corners," replied her husband, soberly. His spirits whipped up for Ann's edification drooped again. Children! To attempt a family life in such a spot! His shoulders drooped.

"The sad, silly town's depressed you," exclaimed Ann, quickly.

"A little," he admitted. Then looking at her with renewed consciousness of her sufferings and their loss, he whispered, "O my dearest wife, what have I done to you? Who am I to have brought your bright beauty to this rotting jungle?"

"You had very little to do with it, 'Don, darling, except to make the trip with me," returned Ann in a matter-of-fact tone. "God planned it, you know." But she closed her eyes to hide the tears in them and for a moment neither spoke.

Then Adoniram went off to the cook's galley to prepare their evening meal.

The clouds of mosquitoes so tormented them that immediately after supper Adoniram went to bed. It was very hot behind the mosquito curtains. And his deep dejection finally had infected Ann. She cried a little for homesickness, she said, on Adoniram's shoulder. He comforted her with caresses and finally they both lay quietly listening to the thunder of the tropical rain on the canvas, their thoughts in far-away New England.

CHAPTER II

THE IRON MAUL

THE problem of moving Ann to the mission house was solved by the captain of the *Georgiana*. No wheeled vehicles were permitted on the streets of Rangoon and Ann couldn't sit on a pony in her weak condition. So the captain loaned an armchair in which Ann was set ashore and in which four native sailors carried her out to the mission. Adoniram was not ungrateful for the rain which fell during the entire trip. It enabled him to hold an umbrella between Ann and the execution place.

Ma Carey met them at the gate, all smiles and staccato exclamations. She wore a white jacket now over her gay tamein or skirt and a great red hibiscus in her hair. She directed the men in business-like tones and they carried Ann gently over the porch, into her room. When Adoniram returned from paying the sailors, Ma Carey already was helping Ann to undress, accompanying the process by cries of wonder over the unheard-of fact of underwear. He paused in the doorway, chuckled and went out to inspect the premises.

The house contained five rooms, unceiled and with walls of mats. Tiny lizards ran in and out of cracks in the teakwood floor and up the walls to the roof beams where they disturbed festoons of bats. The only furniture in the house beside the bed in the Judsons' room consisted of a table and chair in the room that contained the cooking box. One or two earthen pots and some red- and black-lacquered trays and bowls were stacked beside the box. A huge water jar stood beside the veranda door. There were many beautiful mats, some spread on the floors, others rolled up against the walls. Evidently Felix Carey was content to live native fashion.

Adoniram wandered out to the wide porch which encircled the house. The rain had ceased for a moment and he descended to the yard. It was full of fine trees and back of the house was a vegetable garden, badly kept but, at that, containing enough garden stuff to feed half his own town of Plymouth. Excepting for potatoes and onions and peppers, he recognized none of the vegetables.

The jungle pressed to the very fence at the rear of the yard. To the north, the great pagoda gleamed. To the south were mango and palm trees, thick grown with ropes of smilax. Beyond these, he heard pigs grunting. Adoniram parted the vines and stared over the bamboo palings. The pigs were rooting in what was apparently the city dump. On the farther edge of the dump were scattered a dozen corpses in various attitudes of horror and in varied degrees of putrefaction. Adoniram forced himself to gaze for a full minute. It was absolutely necessary that he learn to control his sense of loathing if this was the Burmese attitude toward death and the human body.

A huge kite with a mighty beating of wings dropped among the rooting hogs. Adoniram turned away with an ungovernable shudder.

Ann was delighted with her new quarters and her new friend. Somehow, it had been agreed between the two women that the Judsons would live on native food of Ma Carey's preparation until Ann was strong enough and sufficiently familiar with words and customs to make other arrangements. So they dined on fish and rice with vegetable curry and mangoes, served in red lacquer bowls, and while they ate they discussed immediate plans.

Obviously everything must be subservient to the learning of the language. To this end, a good teacher must be found. So as soon as he had finished the meal, Adoniram set off to call again on M. Lanciego. He found the Spaniard in the customs house, a dilapidated building near the south gate, arguing with the captain of the *Georgiana.* It was the custom of the collector, it seemed, to confiscate the rudders of vessels visiting Rangoon harbor until certain more or less personal fees had been paid him. The captain was not flattering in his comments on the collector's preailection for handsome presents and the collector shouted that the English were more grasping than the Armenians. But in five minutes the matter was adjusted and Lanciego turned to Adoniram and said:

"If you'll walk back to my house with me, monsieur, we may talk at ease. The confusion of enormous business here is wearing."

The customs house and the wharf beyond were quite empty, with the captain of the *Georgiana* disappearing down the ladder to his boat. But Adoniram tactfully made no comment. He talked instead on the short walk about the chance of picking up a few pieces of European furniture in Rangoon. Lanciego was certain he could supply the missions' needs if the Judsons' tastes were simple and became quite affable at the prospect of a little lucrative trading. Adoniram then made his second request.

"A teacher," repeated Lanciego thoughtfully as he seated himself on his own veranda and ordered tea. "That'll be more difficult than furniture, monsieur, and furniture's as scarce as beautiful women in Burma. Many of the citizens of Rangoon can read and write their own tongue but not one of them knows a word of French or English. All the real teachers are monks and a monk can no more associate with a heretic than with a snake, or half as much. I think your only hope is to find a renegade monk. Some of these are real scholars but the vows were too hard for them to keep."

"What are their vows?" asked Adoniram.

"The one which they find the hardest to keep is continence," grinned the collector.

Adoniram flushed and the Spaniard went on ruminating.

THE IRON MAUL

"There's Maung Shway-gnong. He was in a monastery up the river near Prome until about ten years ago when he left and married. His uncle used to be the viceroy at Rangoon. The Burmese word for viceroy means 'Eater.' That's what the viceroy does, devours everything he can get away from the people. I hear that Maung Shway-gnong has the family talent for 'eating' but the best job he's been able to get is one of tax collecting. He's looked on with a good deal of respect by the people of Rangoon because he's good at expounding the doctrines of Buddha. I often see him sitting in a zayat laying down the law to a group. I think Maung Shway-gnong for one reason and another may consent to being your teacher, M. Judson."

"He doesn't sound especially attractive," murmured Adoniram.

"You're in no position to be critical," snapped Lanciego. "You're only a boy and you've no more idea than a girl fresh from a convent what you're facing. Supposing that by a miracle you do beguile some Burman to turn Christian? I don't think you can, but I admit that you have something very beguiling about you. Suppose you do make a convert? Do you realize that when the authorities hear of it, that convert'll be tortured to death? You can get some idea, monsieur, of what Burman torture means from the shambles near the mission."

Adoniram gasped. "But you can't mean that!"

"Do you think I'm a liar, M. Judson?" shouted Lanciego. "You're ignorant. There was a Portuguese priest here a number of years ago like you, who thought to circumvent Buddha. He sent a very intelligent Burman, who'd been a monk, to Rome where a good Catholic was made of him. But as soon as he put foot in Burma again, he was denounced and by his own nephew! The king ordered him to be tortured till he recanted. They used the torture of the iron maul. He was beaten from the soles of his feet to his breast. But with every blow, the poor fool screamed,

'Christ!' so the king concluded he was a madman and when he was nearly dead he ordered him turned into the jungle. He was rescued by the priest before the tigers or the pigs got him and was sent back to Rome. That was the last effort of the Catholics to proselyte! I would further call your attention, my friend, to the fact that the nephew who put his uncle under the iron maul is now the highest official in the kingdom, second only to the king's golden presence."

Adoniram bit at his thumb and stared out at the bazaar where under dripping umbrellas the devotees of Buddha haggled over the price of pineapples and jackfruit.— Could Adoniram Judson send men to the iron maul? What would Christ Himself do, in Burma?—He wiped the moisture from his forehead, and became aware that the collector was smiling a little contemptuously at him.

Adoniram flung back his dark hair and said clearly, "God sent me here. I can only do what He tells me to do."

"It must be pleasant to know the Almighty's mind," growled Lanciego. "However, until you learn the tongue, Buddha's in no danger of being routed by Christ. So I'll send Maung Shway-gnong to you. Mind you, monsieur, I vouch for nothing save his knowledge. He may prove to be another nephew who'll denounce you to the king."

"I'll make a Christian of him!" declared Adoniram stoutly.

The collector gave a sardonic laugh and Adoniram rose with dignity and took his departure. He was very young and he could not bear that the cloth should not be reverenced.

That the Spaniard took Adoniram's commission seriously was not to be doubted, however, for the very next morning, Maung Shway-gnong appeared. Adoniram was sitting on the front porch eyeing the green mold on his leather-bound Bible a little disconsolately and trying not to think about a New England breakfast of codfish cakes and corn muffins, when two natives turned in at the gate. Both were naked to the waist and wore their pasos or skirts well kilted

THE IRON MAUL

up out of the mud, showing the elaborate tattooing on their thighs. One was a servant for he held a long-handled green umbrella over the other's head.

They made their way sedately across the flooded yard and up the veranda steps. Adoniram bowed. The taller Burman eyed him with interest and offered him a note. It was from Lanciego who said that this was Maung Shway-gnong who would require five rupees a month from Adoniram for daily instruction.

Adoniram raised his eyes from the note to the Burman. He was above the average height of his race, standing perhaps five feet eight inches in his bare feet. His black eyes were deep and unhappy, set in an emaciated face. His lower lip was heavy and his chin receded slightly. But the forehead beneath the white turban, twisted like a tourniquet about his hair, was high and fine and the shape of his head, magnificent. In spite of its unattractive points it was the physiognomy of an intellectual man and Adoniram smiled at him in eager welcome.

Maung Shway-gnong returned the smile showing betel-blackened teeth and seated himself on one of the mats. Adoniram did likewise. The servant took a palm leaf book from the lacquered box, presented it to his master and departed.

And thus Adoniram's struggle with the most difficult of the Oriental languages was begun.

Ann's health returned rapidly and as soon as she was on her feet, Adoniram insisted that she must not be content with Ma Carey's casual instructions, but share his lessons with Maung Shway-gnong. She could give only a part of her day to study because housekeeping engrossed much of her time. But she actually learned more of the vernacular than Adoniram, in her contacts with tradespeople, though he, studying fourteen hours a day, soon far surpassed her in a solid foundation of Pali, the classical language in which Burmese literature was written.

They were very busy and very lonely. The rains made

sight-seeing impractical and they formed no acquaintances outside the tradespeople in the bazaar. Lanciego would not prejudice his own position by any social intercourse with them. Even the apparent friendliness of Maung Shwaygnong could be only a phantom thing for many months because of the language barrier which yielded with exasperating slowness to Adoniram's attacks. For the same reason, the life of the town reached them only in pantomime and this, dimly, through mists and torrential downpours. It was very lonely.

Their routine continued uninterrupted until one morning in late August. Then the dawn songs of nightingales and orioles were cut across by a sound of shocking discord. Ann and Adoniram jerked up from their pillows and stared at each other in sick dismay. They needed no explanation. A human being was in process of crucifixion, beyond the curtain of smilax.

"I can't lie here and listen to that!" gasped Ann.

"Nor I!" Adoniram steadied his voice with difficulty. "It's not raining. Let's dress and walk up the Pagoda Road out of ear-shot."

"You have your practical moments, 'Don!" Ann tried to smile while she began to pull on her stockings with unsteady hands.

The sun was only beginning to glimmer when they reached the gate and paused to allow a procession of monks go by with their begging bowls. Two little boys led the way, banging on a bronze gong which effectually covered the sounds proceeding from the execution place. The long rays of the sun slanted beneath the mighty trees and turned the yellow robes of the monks to brilliant orange.

"I wish I could speak the tongue well enough to ask them how their food looks to them as they pass there," said Adoniram, nodding toward the shambles.

"If they're as indifferent as Ma Carey they'll keep excellent appetites," was Ann's comment. "Let's get away quickly, dear," as the last yellow robe fluttered past.

THE IRON MAUL

They stepped into the road, joining the straggling line of worshipers which moved toward the great pagoda. People stared at them and made comments of which they understood little and shortly they reached the foot of the hill on which the Shwé-Dagôn stood. Here they paused and watched the folk remove their sandals before ascending the long, covered stairway. Every one bore an offering, a flower, a bit of food. Little spots of light from candles carried by the worshipers twinkled in the twilight of the arcade. Gayly beautiful pasos and tameins fluttered remotely at the top like butterflies' wings.

"Shall we take off our shoes?" whispered Ann.

"Certainly not," replied Adoniram sternly, lifting his young chin above his collar and glaring disapprovingly at a woman who prostrated herself before a monk.

Ann was not too much impressed by her husband's manner. "But you take them off for Ma Carey and for M. Lanciego's wife. Why not be diplomatic here, my dear?"

"That's mere meaningless politeness," replied Adoniram. "I refuse to make a single gesture of respect toward the Buddha Gautama. After all, I *am* a priest of God. You mustn't forget that, Ann, merely because I lack a church."

"I don't," replied Ann with meekness. "But so long as the gesture means nothing to a Christian why object to making it if it will smooth our way to their hearts?"

"I object because it would mean to these Burmans that I respect their god. It's nonsense for Maung Shway-gnong to keep insisting Gautama was a man and that they don't worship him. Just look, Ann!" nodding toward the bowed heads and the offerings of the Burmans. "Come along, my dear!" He took her hand and began to ascend the stairs.

Immediately people called out angrily and at the third or fourth step a monk pushed in front of the two missionaries.

"Go back, foreign animals," he ordered.

Adoniram, holding Ann's hand firmly, would not allow her to retreat. The monk was an old man, wrinkled over the whole of his shaved head but his black eyes were young and fiery.

"Depart!" he repeated. "No one may wear head or foot covering here. Have you no respect for the Blessed One?"

Adoniram understood as much from the monk's manner as from his language. He longed inexpressibly to declare himself. But a scant six weeks in a tongue that knew not God had given him no words for this particular need. He could only stand his ground, saying slowly, "I will not remove my foot covering."

The crowd which now blocked the stairway muttered angrily.

"We'd better go, Adoniram!" exclaimed Ann.

"We'll go," agreed Adoniram, "because I don't want you to get hurt, and because I've done what I've been aching to do, declare myself. I hate the feeling of skulking there in the mission." He led the way back toward the road.

"I don't think any one will ever accuse you of skulking, darling," said Ann, drily. "But I think after what M. Lanciego told you, a little diplomacy is essential. You may have started endless trouble." She shook her head, then smiled up into his sober face. "I'm proud of your courage, 'Don, but you are so very young!"

Her husband returned the smile. "Indeed! Dear grandmother, what great eyes you have!"

"The better to see you with, my dear," retorted Ann.

They both laughed, then Adoniram said: "Sometimes I'm afraid you see me too well! I have to keep reminding you that I'm a preacher and I wouldn't have to if I weren't so faulty."

"Not faulty, but hasty," corrected Ann. "But you'll do very well after I've calmed you down a trifle."

Again they laughed.

All was silent, when they regained the mission. And in spite of the implications of this morning walk they were able to make a hearty breakfast.

CHAPTER III

FELIX CAREY

THEY told no one of the episode on the Shwé-Dagôn stairway. But a few days later when Adoniram called at the customs house to learn whether or not Lanciego had found him a desk, the Spaniard said to him grimly: "You've made yourself an important enemy, M. Judson. If you're not more careful, you'll soon be where a desk will be of no service to you. You affronted the gaing-ôk the other morning at the great pagoda."

"And who is that?" asked Adoniram. "I spoke only to a monk!"

"Yes, he was a monk, but a monk at the head of all the monasteries hereabouts—a sort of bishop and a very powerful and much-loved one in lower Burma. You ought to keep away from their pagodas unless you conform to their habits, my foolish young friend."

"Look here, M. Lanciego," exclaimed Adoniram. "I'm in Burma to war on the Buddha Gautama. Why try to conceal the fact?"

"Why?" shouted Lanciego, pulling at his grizzled black beard with one hand and shaking his finger at the young missionary with the other. "Why? Because you've no business to war on Gautama. You have a right, if you want to be so silly, to come here and tell them about your God. Do you perceive the difference?"

"Yes, monsieur, I do!" replied Adoniram impatiently. "But I can't act on it when I see all Burma sinking into hell and when I realize that I'm the only person on earth bent on saving the Burmans from that fate."

"Bah! You're an ignorant child thrusting his hand into

the coils of a cobra to see what happens! I can't control my temper and listen to you. You're of too fine stuff to waste yourself in this way." Lanciego stared at Adoniram and his gaze softened. "Too fine!" he repeated. "Go back, for God's sake, to some quiet church in your own land where the folk will appreciate a scholar and a gentleman!"

A thought of a beautiful white spire and of church bells ringing lashed Adoniram's memory with quick pain. But he crowded it back and said gently to the Spaniard, "I'm sorry to have seemed impatient, monsieur. Won't you believe me when I tell you that I *know* that God has fixed my life here in Burma for better or for worse?"

There was a pause, with the sound of waves running up on the beach.

Then, "I wish it were otherwise," said Lanciego, and he turned back to his accounts.

Adoniram made his way home slowly. He was troubled in spite of his conviction of destiny and wished that he understood the language well enough to question Maung Shway-gnong more about the organization of Buddhism in Burma.

But a week later some one arrived at the mission who could answer all his questions; a slender, dark man in European clothing on whom Ma Carey threw herself with a sob of joy. It was Felix Carey.

He was frankly dumbfounded at the presence of the missionaries in his house. "Europeans!" he gasped as he disengaged himself from his wife and crossed the veranda to bow over Ann's hand.

"But, Mr. Carey, didn't you receive your father's letter?" asked Adoniram as he introduced himself and Ann. "Ma Carey sent it early in July."

"I've been in Arracan for the king," replied Felix, shaking his handsome head and staring at Ann. "You can't think what it means to see a white lady in Burma.—But you must not, you dare not remain!"

FELIX CAREY

"Oh, but I must and I dare!" replied Ann, smiling. "We're American missionaries, Mr. Carey!"

"Ah," he returned the smile. "But even American ladies—no, let me have the story before I make more comments."

"We won't trouble you with our affairs until Ma Carey and your babies have visited with you," suggested Ann.

"Quite so!" Carey nodded, and turned to pick up his small ivory-colored daughter and devour her with kisses. Then he followed his smiling wife into the house.

Later, when the Judsons had eaten their supper of tough fowl and plantains and were sitting on the veranda fighting mosquitoes, Felix joined them.

"You can do nothing against the pests unless you smoke," he said, "or keep a greenwood fire going. You'll get used to them after a time." He asked Ann's permission to light a cheroot and then showed them how to kindle a smudge in the veranda firebox. When they were a little less uncomfortable, he puffed vigorously at his cheroot and remarked:

"In spite of my wife's explanations, I still can't understand your being here in Burma."

"It's really very simple," smiled Adoniram. "A few years ago there were several of us theological students at Andover in America who agreed it was time to change the shameful fact that our country had no foreign missions. We were very young but very persistent and by the grace of God, out of our efforts came the founding by the fathers of the Congregationalist and the Presbyterian churches, of a foreign mission board. Mrs. Judson and I were among the first group sent to the Orient by this board. We expected to begin our work in India under the advice of your father, at Serampore. It's a long voyage out, you know, Mr. Carey, and among other matters which my wife and I were able to study deeply was that of baptism. We were Congregationalists. Your father is Baptist. We wished to be prepared to defend our creed against the clever English Baptists of whom your father is the most distinguished. And so we went deep into the matter of infant baptism."

Adoniram paused, trying to observe through the flickering light the effect his story was having on Felix. But the Englishman's face was in shadow.

"Go on, my dear," urged Ann.

Adoniram picked up the tale, obediently. "There's not much further to go. We convinced ourselves that the Baptists were correct and when we reached Serampore we were baptized into their faith!"

The end of Felix Carey's cheroot glowed. "Quite so!" murmured Felix. "And what did my father say?"

"He said the most heartening things in the world," said Ann, briskly, as Adoniram fell silent, utterly dashed by this cool reception of what had been to the two young Judsons a matter of stupendous importance. "And more than that, he is helping us with funds until we hear from America."

"It's like him!" Felix nodded. Then he said slowly, "I'm afraid that from a worldly point of view you haven't bettered yourself, sir. I've heard that the American Baptists are even poorer in this world's goods than the English."

"That's true!" exclaimed Adoniram. "And they're only loosely organized, I fear, with no provision for missionaries. However, I wrote them a letter that may stir them to unity of action—either for me or against me!" he chuckled. "I sent an account of my change of creed to a Baptist minister in Boston and told him that it was the most distressing event that ever had befallen me!"

Ann and Carey both laughed.

Adoniram laughed too but went on earnestly. "It really was distressing! To leave the faith of our childhood of which my father is a clergyman, to desert the organization that with prayers and in personal confidence, sent us out, to know that relatives and friends would be shocked and alienated—not daring to believe that the Baptist churches of America would compassionate us— Well, Mr. Carey,

I wrote all this to Dr. Baldwin and told him that if a Baptist society for the support of a mission in these parts should be formed, I was ready to consider myself their missionary. I wrote that letter just about a year ago and I don't know when I'll receive an answer. In the meantime, your father is helping us and we have a little money of our own." He paused and then said hesitatingly, "Dr. Carey was sure you'd welcome us."

"I can't welcome you to a land accurst," was Felix Carey's suddenly passionate reply. "Mr. Judson, the Burman king literally owns every one of his subjects, body and soul. They're his slaves, his cattle. He robs them, tortures them, murders them, at will. No Burmese king is going to admit to his empire any other religion so long as Buddhism keeps his slaves submissive to his will."

"Your every word proves how they need Christianity!" exclaimed Adoniram.

"A dead Christian can't minister to that need," retorted Felix. "Nor can a dead Christian keep his wife out of the king's harem, and Mrs. Judson is beautiful."

The Judsons gasped, but before they could speak, Felix went on.

"And as if you would hasten your fate, my wife tells me you've taken Maung Shway-gnong for a teacher. That man's hated by the viceroy. Your association with him is bound to prejudice the viceroy against you. It was very mean of Lanciego to recommend him. If you insist on remaining here, as I fear in your ignorance and fervor you will, I'll try to find you some one more trustworthy before I leave."

"No, I thank you, Mr. Carey," said Adoniram, decidedly. "I like Maung Shway-gnong. I have faith he'll be my first convert. As for the rest, I'd gathered from Lanciego pretty clearly what to expect. We are here for all time, Mr. Carey. . . . And you will not remain with us?"

"The king has given me my choice," replied Felix, "of

leaving Burma for good or taking a position with the court at Amarapura. No Burmese woman ever may leave the country. So unless I wish to give up my wife, I must go into the king's service, and I've done so. I have built a house in Amarapura and will remove my family there as soon as I return from a trip to Bengal in which his majesty is sending me."

"This is a hard blow!" exclaimed Adoniram.

"And have you no regrets, Mr. Carey?" asked Ann. "It seems a dreadful decision to have had to make."

"I'll be frank," replied Felix. "I was very much discouraged about the mission work, Mrs. Judson, quite convinced that it was hopeless. And I love my wife."

"But your dear father!" cried Ann.

"Quite so!" The dry voice effectively stilled Ann's protests and it was a relief to have Ma Carey appear in the doorway and call her husband into the house.

The Judsons talked for a long time before they slept that night. They were much disturbed by Felix's desertion of the mission. Both of them had counted more heavily on his return than they had admitted to each other. In spite of the statement made by Lanciego about him, Adoniram had been very sure he could win Felix back. But there was an aloofness in Carey's manner that precluded any attempts to discuss the matter.

Felix was very affable and helpful the next day. He gave them some much-needed instructions about the food resources of Rangoon, warning them particularly not to buy meat in the bazaar. The Burmans would not kill an animal and ate meat only from one that had died of disease or by accident. He promised to find them a Bengalese cook whose religion would not prevent his killing a fowl for them when a fowl was to be had. And he told them that Lanciego was a great favorite of the old tyrant on the "golden throne" at Amarapura and that they must keep on the Spaniard's good side by making him an occasional handsome present.

"Nothing is accomplished in Burma save by purchase," he declared, with more earnestness than he'd shown on any other topic. "You could buy the king's soul if you possessed enough flowered silver. They have no understanding of the word honor. The best thing about the Burmans is their women. They're intelligent and devoted and they have the rarest quality in the amiable world of females, keen humor."

"I thought all Burmans had that," said Ann.

"Quite so. But especially the women. My wife is a charming exemplar of them all." He bowed to Ma Carey who was listening with a puzzled, eager smile on her brown face.

Altogether, Felix was amusing although disappointing and in nothing perhaps, quite so amusing as in his departure. A huge gray elephant arrived at the mission gate, late in the afternoon. Felix bade them all good-by and, barefooted, walked up the elephant's great flank with all the nonchalance of a native. Then with a servant kneeling behind his shoulders holding an umbrella, he gave a cryptic order to the mountainous beast and quietly disappeared beyond the bamboo hedges.

The Judsons watched him go, speechless with varied emotions.

Felix did not forget the matter of the cook. The very evening of his departure, a Bengalese in a white turban, jacket and breechcloth appeared at the mission and introduced himself as Koo-chil, a Mohammedan. He could speak the Burmese tongue and had great scorn for the Burmese inconsistencies in the matter of their willingness to eat but unwillingness to kill animals. His wages would be ten ticals, or five dollars a month and he would find his own food. He would wish to build his own house in the mission yard. He was middle-aged, grave and courteous and Ann almost sobbed with joy over him.

The rains were growing less now and Rangoon was heavy with a spring-like beauty. Adoniram was able to take a before-breakfast walk with considerable regularity and to begin to make himself acquainted with the environs of his new home. He did not again venture to investigate the Shwé-Dagôn but he was always conscious of its presence like a living thing brooding over the quiet activities of the mission. Some day when he could speak more fluently, he planned to fight the matter of removing the shoes to a finish. For now, he contented himself with examining a neighboring monastery which Maung Shway-gnong had told him was the store-house of priceless manuscripts.

Adoniram's heart yearned over those manuscripts. As often as he took his morning walk, he prowled around the teakwood fence of the monastery, gazed through the gates at the curving roofs and spires, and wished that his conscience would permit him to enter and talk with the old librarian-monk whom Maung Shway-gnong had assured him was a scholar of great attainments.

One morning he saw the gaing-ôk march out of the gate with his brethren of the begging bowls and something like a vague regret passed through Adoniram's mind. If only the question of religion didn't enter, he believed he could be friends with that old man. Perhaps the gaing-ôk was Maung Shway-gnong's librarian! Perhaps—

Adoniram brought himself up with a jolt. This was a spiritual infidelity of which he had not supposed himself capable. Was Burma going to corrupt Adoniram Judson as well as Felix Carey? He turned his back on the monastery and strode along the road toward the town, berating and warning himself as he went.

It was a seductive sort of day, warm and sweet-scented with the early rising Burmans already crowding the bazaar. Adoniram, mingling with the chattering crowd, shortly forgot his chagrin with himself in amusement at the maneuvers of a little old woman who insisted on his buying a gay cherry-colored tamein. He was airing his vocabulary for her benefit when some one took him firmly by the arm. He turned quickly, to face a Burmese soldier in a red paso and green jacket, an ugly fellow scarred by smallpox.

"The viceroy has sent for you, foreign animal," said the soldier gruffly.

"You needn't hold me, I'll not try to run away," protested Adoniram, whose fastidious nose was offended by the fellow's unwashed condition.

"Don't chatter like a monkey," twisting Adoniram's arm a bit, "but move rapidly."

They were only a step from one of the larger thatched huts, known grandiloquently as the Hall of Justice. Adoniram paused at the steps with his guard and stooped to remove his shoes as the soldier kicked off his sandals.

"I see you're beginning to get civilized," growled the Burman.

"Thank you," murmured Adoniram as he followed the soldier into the courtroom. It was large and bare of furniture save for a low platform at one end. A great number of Burmans, men and women, were squatting below the dais on which sat the viceroy, a huge Burman in a white robe. Adoniram made a creditable sheeko; that is he dropped to his knees and in that position essayed to bow. Then, still half sitting, half kneeling, he waited to learn why he was wanted.

The viceroy did not leave him long in doubt. He listened to a prisoner in chains make a plea for a pardon and after a moment's thought, ordered the alleged culprit to be trampled by elephants. The doomed man raised a great outcry and a servant came running into the room carrying a red velvet bag. At an order from the prisoner, the servant crawled on his hands and knees to the dais and emptied a quantity of coins at the viceroy's feet. His lordship gave the pile a careless glance.

"Free the prisoner," he grunted. Then he turned to an old man who groveled near the doorway. "As for you," he shouted, "it's time you joined your friends in hell!" He flung his spear and it impaled the old man through the buttocks to a doorpost. "And now," demanded the viceroy, glaring at Adoniram, "what are you doing in the golden empire?"

"I am learning to speak the golden tongue, your lordship," replied Adoniram, trying to put into his deep voice a meekness he did not feel.

"For what purpose?" The Burman's black eyes were searching.

"In order to tell the Burman people about my religion," replied Adoniram.

The viceroy gave a snort of surprise and looked Adoniram over more carefully. "Listen, foreign animal," he said finally. "On the day you begin to try to persuade any Burman even to think of the name of your religion, on that day that Burman will be tortured and you will be sent out of the country. What do you say to that, my beautiful white monkey?"

"I say that I hope no Burman will be tortured through me," answered Adoniram, "but that only God can keep me from spreading His word."

"Take warning!" urged the viceroy. Then he added: "You speak well for one who has been here so short a time. Who is your teacher?"

Felix Carey's warning! Adoniram felt an inward trembling, but he made his reply stoutly. "Maung Shway-gnong, your lordship!"

"That buffalo!" exclaimed the viceroy. Adoniram waited for a further outburst but none came forth. The viceroy gave him a vicious look and suddenly rose and stalked out of the room.

This was the signal for every one to depart and Adoniram followed the crowd which passed the old man imprisoned by the spear without a glance. It was more than the young American could bear.

"Let me pull it out?" he whispered.

The old Burman was crouched motionless and after a

FELIX CAREY

moment Adoniram saw that he was either unconscious or dead. He did not make a sign when the missionary pulled out the spear and laid it on the floor. Feeling a little sick, Adoniram moved on out into the early sunlight.

He was unmolested as he made his way back to the house where Ann was awaiting him with growing anxiety.

"My dear, where have you been?" she cried as he seated himself at the breakfast table.

"Darling Nancy!" he exclaimed. "I've been arrested, convicted and freed, all since dawn. And I'm badly in need of advice from the most amiable of wives, as our English friends called you."

"Do you mean you've really been in trouble?" gasped Ann.

He nodded and told his story.

"Do you think you'd better give up Maung Shway-gnong?" asked his young wife anxiously when he'd finished.

"No, indeed I don't!" declared Adoniram. "I refuse to let these pagans dictate to me. Where would be the end if I gave in on this point? They'd be telling me next that Koo-chil is an arch-traitor and to send him off."

"And that's where I'd make a stand," Ann smiled but with a very firm nod of the head. "Very well, my liege, your wife approves. She also makes this suggestion. Why not give the viceroy a present?"

"I hate bribery," Adoniram's stern young jaw was set. But Ann went on, eagerly.

"So do I, dear 'Don, but I think we ought to give in where we can and if a little gift will leave you free to learn how to teach these people, why not give it?"

"A *little* gift would do no good, Nancy," protested Adoniram.

"That depends, 'Don! Ma Carey and I've been talking and she insists that if I take the viceroy that little painting of Niagara Falls that was Elnathan's wedding present to us, he'll be our friend for many months."

"*You* take it, Ann?" looking at her with disapproval.

"Yes, Mr. Judson! You see there's nothing very remarkable about you. The Burmans have seen dozens of European men. But your *wife!* My dear, she's the eighth wonder of the world, the only white woman in Burma. So do let me call on the vicereine with Niagara Falls under my arm for her husband!"

Adoniram chuckled. "What a scene you suggest! I will go with you, of course and—"

"But you can't! Ma Carey says that won't do and that I'll be quite safe, alone. Do let me go, Adoniram."

He was uneasy about it and yet he had great confidence in Ann's diplomatic powers. Finally he gave his consent and Ann flew to Ma Carey for a further conference.

CHAPTER IV

NIAGARA FALLS

THAT afternoon, Ann appeared on the veranda in her best frock. It was a high-waisted white muslin, ankle length, with dainty ruffles at neck and skirt edge. She wore with this, a white straw skuttle bonnet with a pink rosebud under the brim.

Adoniram, who had left his studies to see her off, looked at her with an adoring smile.

"I think I appear very frivolous for a missionary's wife," said Ann anxiously. "Especially the rosebud. But you remember, I wore this bonnet before I graduated from Bradford Academy and I feel a little sentimental about it. And if I take off the rosebud, the straw will show a discoloration."

"You know, my darling, that no one loves beauty more than God. Look at the flowers He's made!" Adoniram kissed the delicate face under the rosebud. "I'm sure He must love to look at you and your adornments."

Ann's brown eyes twinkled. "Did you or did you not tell me a little while ago that the beauty of Burma covered a whited sepulcher? You must learn to be consistent, 'Don!'"

"Your beauty has no source in Burma!" retorted Adoniram, "and I'll elucidate still further, if you wish."

Ann threw up her small white hands. "No! No! I'll never reach the vicereine if you begin!"

He laughed. "Very well, Nancy! But if my wife won't listen to my sermons, who will?"

They stood for a moment, smiling at each other; both beautiful, both young, both surcharged with love and faith and hope. Then with Koo-chil bearing the little painting, wrapped in a fine piece of red Bangkok silk, Ann set off on her errand.

She was gone about two hours. Adoniram was pacing up and down in front of the "palace" when she emerged.

"I was just going to burst into the house, shoes and all!" he exclaimed as he pulled her arm within his. "What did detain you, Nancy? Really, I could almost wish you weren't quite so charming!"

"I'm not really quite so, you know," smiled Ann. "But listen to my story, Adoniram."

So pacing slowly homeward under the glory of the golden Mohur and the pink acacia she described her experience.

The vicereine was in bed when she arrived but the several inferior wives were charmed to receive the white woman. They conducted her to a mat and squatted in a circle about her. They offered her pickled tea which she ate though she loathed it and they begged leave to try on her bonnet, her mitts, her slippers. Ann laughed and obligingly shared what she could of her clothing.

Here Adoniram interrupted with a shudder. "They all have lice, you know, my dear!"

"Well, I didn't see any traces," said Ann, "and anyhow, I suppose it's *lèse-majesté* to refuse to loan your clothes to a queen even if she is—er—verminous!" She chuckled and went on with her tale.

The wives tried on the clothes and screamed with pleasure and amusement. In the midst of this the vicereine entered.

She was of a very pale yellow complexion, made paler still by sandalwood powder. As she entered, the lesser wives returned Ann's possessions and retired to the rear of the room. The vicereine apologized for not appearing earlier. She had been ill. One of the other wives brought hibiscus blossoms which she fastened in Ann's hair and dak blossoms for the vicereine. And the vicereine began to question Ann.

How many wives had her husband? Had she children? How long would the Judsons remain in Rangoon? Ann found herself chatting in the gayest and easiest possible manner, wondering all the time how to ask for the viceroy, when that gentleman himself stalked into the room. He wore, Ann said, a white robe, a spear and a savage scowl. She was startled by his size and his saturnine expression.

He looked his wives over, scowling more and more until his eye alighted on the visitor. Then his heavy lips parted in a delighted smile and he stood gaping at her like a child entranced before a new toy. No one spoke until the viceroy gasped:

"Amé! How beautiful is your skin. A wife of the foreign animal! Will you take a cup of rum as all foreigners do?"

Ann assured him that she never indulged. The viceroy was not at all offended.

"No true Buddhist drinks, either. Then what may I give you, O white-skinned foreigner?"

Ann rose from her mat and to the curiosity and delight of her audience, made a deep courtesy. Then she presented the gift to his lordship.

He undid the silk, then stood holding the picture at arm's length, his eyes fairly blazing with excitement.

"How was this made? Did you make it? Where is this fall of water? Can all Americans paint thus? Burmans can carve and lacquer but they can't make pictures. Look! Look! It's as if one heard the rush of deep waters! Amé! Look!"

Ma Carey had known her viceroy!

After a time, his lordship again and with increased emphasis, demanded, "O lovely stranger, what may I do for you?"

"Your highness, allow my husband and me to live in peace in our house and our yard in the jungle," replied Ann.

"But how can that be?" ejaculated his lordship. "You're open to every band of robbers that pass your way. You're near the execution place where tigers call frequently. The thirty-seven nats of Burma couldn't safeguard you where you live. But come within the stockade and I'll take care of you." And before Ann could say a word in protest, he called in his writer and dictated the order she now gave to Adoniram.

He seized the bit of oiled palm leaf on which was stenciled a message commanding the provincial treasurer to "sell to the foreign animal the deserted property of the Portuguese priest near the old water tank."

"But we haven't the least reason for moving!" protested Adoniram.

They were on their own veranda now and he looked with the pride of possession on the new orderliness of the garden, the mended fence, the new fruit trees.

"What of the execution grounds?" asked Ann. "I live in dread of the next torturing."

"Do you, poor Ann? Why didn't you tell me?" exclaimed Adoniram.

"Because I knew you felt the same way," replied his wife, "and what could you do to relieve the situation? But now"—she nodded toward the viceroy's order—"now I'll never have to smell— Oh, Adoniram!" She twisted her delicate fingers together and gave a little dry sob.

Adoniram clasped her in his arms. "Nancy, you poor, poor lamb!" He held her close then laughed softly. "Ann, I'm so glad you've hated the smell! It's all wrong for a man to have to feel that he's less strong-minded than his wife! And you know, my dear, sometimes, I'm afraid I'm a little finicky."

Ann released herself and said with a note of amusement, "Well, that's one characteristic I can safely leave to Burma to cure."

"I'm afraid you can," agreed Adoniram, ruefully.

They went before supper to investigate the property designated. It lay within the stockade, on a lane which led east from the Pagoda Road. There were no buildings left on the land but there were two acres of neglected fruit trees and a magnificent fig tree in the center of the three-acre plot under which they decided that their house must be built.

Both were a little troubled about money. They had an almost perfect faith that the American Baptists would see God in all that had happened but they did not want to go more into debt with Dr. Carey. And their personal funds were less than a thousand dollars. But after a long evening of discussion in which Ma Carey gave them building prices, they decided to draw on their own moneys for the new venture.

The very next day, accompanied by Maung Shway-gnong as adviser, Adoniram purchased the plot for fifty rupees and made a contract with a builder to put up a house like the Careys' for two hundred rupees, making a total of about one hundred and twenty-five dollars.

Adoniram had his first argument with his teacher a few moments after closing the bargain with the builder. The young missionary insisted that he himself would choose the teakwood posts for the foundation of the house.

"I want them symmetrical," he explained, "not bulbous in spots like all the houses one sees here."

"But the bulbs are most important, O pupil!" said Maung Shway-gnong. "Look!" He walked across the builder's yard to a pile of logs. "Each post has its function. Male posts are symmetrical. They're easy-going but one is enough under your house. The female posts are larger at the base. They bring good luck. Use three of those. Neuter posts swell in the middle and should be used only under conditions you wouldn't understand."

"I won't countenance such nonsense!" exclaimed Adoniram. "I'll choose my own posts."

"Then choose them according to Burmese ideas or no Burman will enter your dwelling," warned the teacher.

Adoniram looked at the emaciated face. "And you're the

man whose intellect I've admired! Don't you know that's mere nonsense, my teacher?"

The Burman drew himself up huffily. "Perhaps you'd better find a teacher who is not nonsensical," he said and turned on his heel.

Adoniram, face flushed angrily for a moment, watched the brown skeleton back disappearing across the yard and then with a little exclamation of remorse, he ran after Maung Shway-gnong and caught his arm.

"O teacher! I'm sorry! You mustn't forsake me. You're the only friend I have in Burma!"

Maung Shway-gnong looked from the missionary's white linen suit to his pleading hazel eyes and said, very gently, "I cannot come, my pupil, unless you allow the builder to choose the posts under my supervision."

"Very well," said Adoniram reluctantly and he returned to the mission house, leaving the teacher and the builder examining logs with much abstruse and acrimonious conversation.

Adoniram, as has been said, was not a patient soul. And this first contact with the Burman way of working was very trying to him. Although his house was ordered in November and could easily have been finished in two weeks' time, varied superstitions combined to delay the workmen and when all appeared to have been smoothed away, December turned out to be the builder's unlucky month and he dared not begin a piece of work in that period. So it was mid-January before the house was ready for them.

It was quite a cavalcade that moved into the new quarters. Ma Carey had insisted on living with them until her husband's return. There was, of course, Koo-chil, and also the gardener and his cross-eyed wife, recently acquired. It was a pretty spot, full of peace and color. The fig tree was gay with green pigeons. Koo-chil's chickens clucked contentedly under the house.

Ma Carey rushed ahead of the rest of the family as it

turned into the yard from the lane and, running quickly up the steps, took from the folds of her tamein a cocoanut shell which was covered with strips of yellow cloth. This she hung under the eaves at the south corner of the veranda. Adoniram at once asked what was the purpose of the curious ornament.

"It's a nat house," replied Ma Carey, a little defiantly. "It's to be hoped a pleasant nat will come to dwell in it, O foreign friend, for this house will need protection of magic, I assure you. We must give it cooked rice and an occasional silver tical and all will be well."

"I suppose this is the result of compromising on the logs," said Adoniram grimly.

"Don't forget you have a sense of humor, 'Don," and Ann, her arms full of books, passed on into the house.

Adoniram followed her. "My sense of humor shall not make me give in on this point," he said. "I'll not argue about it, though. I'll act."

And that night, after the house and yard were quiet, he carried out his threat. He bore the cocoanut shell back into the jungle and dropped it gingerly under a palm tree. Then he went to bed.

The next morning, when the two missionaries appeared on the veranda where they had told Koo-chil to serve their breakfast, there was no Koo-chil and no breakfast. Ann investigated and returned to report that the place was completely deserted.

"The nat house!" exclaimed Adoniram.

"I told you there'd be trouble," said Ann. "Even Koo-chil who despises the Burmans wouldn't dare to work for foreign savages who insult the Burmese spirits."

"Ann!" exploded Adoniram. "Do you expect me to preach Christ with a spirit house hanging over my head? Do be reasonable, my dear wife!"

"That's what I'm trying to be, 'Don!" Ann began peeling a banana. "In the first place, you're a long way from preaching. You say yourself it will be two or three years before you'll speak well enough not to make your faith ridiculous. In the second place, you can't take away their nats until you can give them God, the Father. They're human and they must have something above themselves to cling to."

"They have Buddha!" exclaimed Adoniram, staring unseeingly at the banana Ann placed on his plate. Ann did not reply and he went on thinking aloud. "But as I've been saying for months, Buddha is cold. He's the embodiment of the eye for an eye and the tooth for a tooth philosophy. He offers nothing of hope or consolation— But, Ann, it is absurd and I'm not sure but what it's actually wrong to have that thing on our porch."

"True," agreed Ann. "But I can't do without a cook and you can't do without Maung Shway-gnong."

Adoniram sighed deeply. "Well, I suppose I can add this as well as many other offenses to the enormous load I already carry on my conscience. . . . I'm a poor excuse for a man of God, Ann." He rose and went slowly down the steps.

"You'll make a very great man of God, some day," Ann said softly to his retreating back. "Greater in spirit than I can hope to be."

He shook his head dismally and went on down the yard to the rear gate which let into the jungle path to the water tank. It was very gay in the jungle this morning. Sambur belled from the bamboo thickets. The dancing song of finch and oriole adorned the day like golden beads on a vivid garment.

Adoniram lifted the nat house from under the palm tree, gingerly, and strode back to the veranda where he hung it on its peg with a jerk. Then he hastened to Koo-chil's cook house to help Ann prepare breakfast.

"I shall certainly have to apologize to any Europeans who may call on us," he said as he began to kindle the fire.

"Let's hope that the nat that moves in will appreciate the sacrifice to your feelings," smiled Ann.

"He's much more apt to take advantage of my weakness and bring a whole family of nats in with him," said Adoniram. "And here comes one of his adherents."

Koo-chil was hurrying across the garden with an armful of fruit and vegetables as if he had just come from the bazaar. Ma Baik, the gardener's wife, was unconcernedly sweeping her own veranda and Ma Carey appeared around the corner of the house with the two babies, mother and babies each smoking a nonchalant cheroot. It was in an atmosphere of brisk approval that Ann and Adoniram settled to their breakfast an hour later.

The matter was not referred to again except that night when Ma Carey dropped some cooked rice into the hole at the top of the cocoanut and after leaning a listening ear against the shell for several seconds, reported to Ann that a cousin of the king nat had moved in.

"What does one call him?" asked Ann solemnly.

"*You* give him a name," replied Ma Carey, evasively.

"Mr. Beg Everybody's Pardon," suggested Ann.

Ma Carey struggled with the English sounds and at last achieved an approximation and Mr. Beg Pardon entered the mission family as a member of rather less than good standing.

CHAPTER V

THE GAING-ÔK

THE water tank back of the new mission was a place of great loveliness and loneliness. It was an oblong, sunken pool of red brick with the steps descending into it along one side, quite overgrown with moss and creeper. Bamboo and mango bent above it and turtles and frogs crowded one another along its brim. The Judsons examined the pool several times with the idea of bathing in it. Ann finally gave out the opinion that its green depths held too much terror for her, but Adoniram, who suffered very much from the heat, bathed on the steps one morning and found it delightful. Thereafter, for nearly a week, he ended his early morning walk there.

On the seventh morning, as he finished his ablutions and began to dress, a monk ran along the path which led from the town and bade him, angrily, to leave the place.

Adoniram, buttoning his white cambric shirt, smiled. "It seems sad, O gaing-ôk," he said, "that we meet only for you to order me away from your presence. Maung Shway-gnong tells me you're a great scholar and it would be a wonderful privilege for a young foreigner who dreams of scholarship to sit at your feet."

The gaing-ôk stared at the young man as if puzzled. Adoniram returned the look with wistful eagerness. The old man had no aspect of decrepitude. He wore his years mellowly. The deep furrows across his forehead and from nostril to lip only added to the benignity of expression with which his harsh orders to Adoniram were hard to reconcile.

"Maung Shway-gnong does ill to speak of us together," the monk said, finally.

THE GAING-ÔK 43

"The teacher loves you," said Adoniram.

"He shows it well, living in carnal passion like a buffalo! I shall question him about his instructing you. It must stop. And you, foreign animal, must cease polluting this water. It is sacred to our monastery."

"I had no idea of that," returned Adoniram, earnestly. "I'll give up bathing here, of course. But I urge you, O gaing-ôk, let me keep my teacher."

"Will you assure me that you will do nothing to win him to that God of whom you told the viceroy?" The Burman spoke sternly but no longer with anger.

"I can't assure you of that, O gaing-ôk," replied Adoniram sadly. "My God has sent me to Burma for that very purpose."

"Then you will not be permitted to remain in Burma," declared the monk. "It will be my duty to speak to those in authority the moment you begin to teach Maung Shway-gnong or any one else."

"It will be useless." Adoniram drew on his white linen coat and ascended the moss-grown steps to stand before the old man. "Speak to whatever authority you please, Christ and God, His Father, have come to Burma to stay. You may kill me or send me away. But I have brought Them here and once They have entered a land they never leave it."

"That cannot be," was the gaing-ôk's flat denial.

"You are old," returned Adoniram, "but not so old that you won't live to believe what I say," and with this he bowed and went back along the jungle path to the house regretfully, for the old gaing-ôk had a real fascination for the young preacher.

He told Maung Shway-gnong about the interview and the teacher looked much perturbed.

"You didn't seem to mind when the viceroy made threats about you," said Adoniram, half sorry he had spoken. "Why should the gaing-ôk, who has no secular power, bother you?"

"He doesn't need secular power any more than a centipede needs an extra leg, O pupil," muttered Maung Shway-gnong. "It would be best for me to call on him, soon."

He finished the day's lesson but was obviously uneasy and when the day was over he hurried northward, toward the monastery.

The next day he did not appear, nor the next. The Judsons were certain that fear of the gaing-ôk was in some way responsible for the Burman's absence, but his wife on whom Adoniram called claimed complete ignorance of his whereabouts and of the reason for his departure. And when two weeks had gone by, Adoniram decided to seek another teacher. M. Lanciego was absent in Amarapura and Ann made the suggestion that the viceroy be asked to send a teacher.

The request was accompanied by the gift of a pair of opera glasses and brought immediate results in the shape of an old man who had been a writer for the viceroy. The writer as he was called was not as able a man as Maung Shway-gnong, but he worked very industriously with Adoniram on the Burmese grammar and dictionary which the missionary was preparing and was affable and full of amusing stories. He and the vicereine who was a regular caller on Ann made the Judsons' one vivid contact with Burmese social life.

Adoniram was, however, beginning to feel at home with the spiritual life of the Burmans. He could now read Pali readily and was studying the teachings of Gautama with extraordinary interest. The Buddha had had a very great philosophy which at some points, as in its moral code, harmonized completely with Christianity. And the Buddha Gautama had had a great and tender soul. So great and so tender that no thoughtful Christian could scorn him nor could fail to realize that it would be a task of extreme difficulty to win his adherents away from him.

Adoniram tried frequently to acquaint the writer with

THE GAING-ÔK

some of the basic ideas of Christianity but the old man always laughed at him. "What! Would you play the harp to a buffalo, O pupil? I have no brain for speculation. The doctrine of the karma is good enough for me. And," he would invariably add with an amiable grin, "karma will always be too good for your success!"

"The doctrine of karma," Adoniram would retort, "has no attraction for a man who knows there's an eternal heaven."

The writer would never respond to this bait. And Adoniram would think longingly of Maung Shway-gnong who loved to speculate.

The second rainy season settled in with still no word from America and with a growing anxiety regarding Ann's health. She was losing her charming whiteness of skin and turning more yellow than a powdered Burmese beauty. There was, of course, no European doctor in the golden kingdom. But Adoniram dosed her with mercury for her liver's sake and sweated her to get rid of the mercury until the poor girl became a mere saffron-colored shadow. But the fever and ague persisted.

At last, in the fall, Adoniram fought a hard battle with the selfishness that is ineradicable in the best of human nature and announced that Ann was to leave him for three months and go to the doctor in Serampore. Ann was as stricken as though he had decreed their permanent separation. There was a long day of protest and defiance, but she yielded at last. And having yielded she planned the trip with all her usual practical good sense. Even the Rangoon fever could not shake Ann's hold on realities.

She arranged to go on the *Georgiana* with Ma Baik, the cross-eyed, as maid and companion. She gave Ma Carey strict orders with regard to her husband's linen, about which he was a bit fussy and she made Adoniram promise that each night when the evening star rose, he would sit on the veranda and think of her as she would be thinking of him.

That nightly communion of their spirits, via the star, was an unbelievable comfort to Adoniram, as Ann had known it would be. Even more than she had known. For a week after Ann's departure, the viceroy and vicereine were called up to Amarapura and they took the old writer with them. The aged Burman seemed genuinely sorry to leave his pupil, and Adoniram, from the veranda, watched the old fellow's gay purple umbrella bob down the lane to the road with a sense of desolation he found it hard to control.

"I suppose I'm the loneliest human being in Burma," he thought.

It was early twilight. The casuarina tree by the gate sighed sympathetic melancholy and from its mysterious depths came the moving notes of the nightingale. A pale blue chameleon ran over Adoniram's foot. A python moved like a dread shadow across the path, disappearing into the shadows of the jungle beyond Ma Baik's hut. Ma Carey passed on noiseless bare feet and dropped a coin into Mr. Beg Pardon's house.

"There's a shadow on the place," she murmured. "It's sky closing time. You should come in and shut the door. Now that the viceroy's gone, all the wild Karens from the jungle will be creeping by."

Adoniram did not respond and, after waiting for a moment, she went into the house and shortly he heard her crooning to her babies. The sound belonged to the twilight. He sat motionless, his back against the wall, his feet drawn under him Burmese fashion. For a long time, he was conscious only of his aching loneliness. He did not believe that he could endure it. He had prayed to be relieved of it, had asked God so to fill him with zeal for the Burmans that his own yearnings and uneasinesses could find no abiding place within him. And no relief had come. Loneliness, he told himself, had its seat in the brain. One who did not think couldn't be lonely. Oh, for a soporific

THE GAING-ŌK 47

that would overpower his senses until Ann's return! If only he could sit as the monks did in a meditation so deep that their foolish, demanding minds were merged with the profundities of the Universe and they knew peace!

He experimented, tried to wipe the exquisite twilight from his consciousness.—The low notes of the nightingale continued, heart-breakingly sweet. Far in the jungle a tiger howled. The smell of young figs—almost—almost he attained—almost he touched the unknowable, the unattainable—then as in a dream, he saw a red globe of light sail slowly above the top of the casuarina tree and tried to thrust it from his attention. It would not go. It hung firmly above the branches—disturbed him, beckoned him, urged him—

Suddenly he started as though a hand had touched him. "Ann!" he ejaculated. It was the evening star! Ann was praying for him. Adoniram clasped his hands and lifted his young face to the flaming heavens.

"God," he prayed, "make me worthy of her! Amen."

It was not difficult after this to obey Ma Carey's earlier command. He went into the house and closed the door. And as if Ann's wholesome presence were with him, he made no difficulty over the supper he had previously refused but ate a sound meal of Koo-chil's curried chicken and good wheat bread. And afterward instead of returning to the veranda he went into the little room he used as a study.

Some one was sitting at his desk; the desk so meticulously arranged that even Ann was not allowed to touch it. Adoniram carried the earth oil lamp indignantly around to face the interloper. Then he set it down quickly and held out both hands. "Maung Shway-gnong! What a pleasant trick! Best of teachers, where have you been?"

Maung Shway-gnong rose, grinning broadly. "You wondered who was taking liberties with your sacred manuscripts, best of pupils?"

"I was going to throw some one out bodily!" laughed Adoniram. "But why have you neglected me so, Maung Shway-gnong?"

"I had a long illness, O pupil, and I was obliged, finally, to take a sea voyage to cure me."

"But you might have told me," insisted Adoniram, reproachfully. "I would have brought you here and cared for you; gaing-ôk or no!"

Maung Shway-gnong gave him a queer glance. Adoniram was instantly sure that the teacher's disappearance had, as he had suspected, been connected with the gaing-ôk's threats. So when the teacher said, "The matter was not so simple as that," he was willing to cease his inquiries.

"Shall we go on where we left off with the story of Queen Shin-saw-bu?" asked Maung Shway-gnong after a pause during which he eyed the neat piles of papers and lacquered books on the desk.

"Oh, that was finished long ago with my other teacher!" replied Adoniram.

"I heard of the writer," said Maung Shway-gnong. "What mischief did he do you?"

"None, my teacher," smiled Adoniram. "He was no such scholar as you so I let go many things and gave all my time to the attempt to tell the story of Christ in Burmese. Look!" He lifted a little sheaf of papers, tenderly, and handed them to the Burman who bent his cadaverous face over them eagerly.

Adoniram watched him with acute interest. He had attempted to translate the Gospel according to Matthew from the Greek into the Burmese vernacular. It had been a very difficult task. Maung Shway-gnong read rapidly. At first his face expressed only keen curiosity. Then, he laughed, immoderately, and instantly Adoniram put out an outraged hand and took the manuscript from the teacher, the look on his thin tanned face one of speechless indignation.

The teacher quickly became serious. "I beg your pardon,

my pupil! But you have used a vile expression there that makes your first verses ridiculous."

"Vile!" gasped Adoniram. "But that was examined by the writer and he congratulated me on the beauty of my choice of words."

"Undoubtedly!" Maung Shway-gnong nodded his head. "The word which made me laugh has two meanings, one of them beautiful. But used in the relation you've put it, the word becomes vile. I believe the writer has deliberately led you astray. Don't be angry with me, my pupil. Let us inquire further."

"It doesn't seem possible!" groaned Adoniram. But he took his place beside the teacher, and read the verses slowly aloud.

There could be no doubt that the writer had played him a scurvy trick and that the translation was filled with words having foolish and obscene interpretations.

For a little while Adoniram was bewildered. "But I can't see what satisfaction the writer got out of such low knavery," he insisted.

"Can't you?" grunted Maung Shway-gnong. "Can't you see either how cleverly the viceroy considers the way he's managed to make your teachings, your Christ, ridiculous? No wonder he has left you in peace all this time! I have fallen so low as to collect taxes but not even for the king would I have done so vile a thing as this, my pupil!"

Adoniram jumped to his feet and paced the floor, face flushed, hazel eyes blazing. "And I believed that I was almost ready to preach!—It's not the affront to myself I mind, Maung Shway-gnong. But the fellow has desecrated Christ. Suppose a Christian had done this thing to the Buddha Gautama?"

"I know! I know!" The teacher chewed furiously at the end of his cheroot.

Adoniram continued to pace the floor for several minutes thinking as he had said, not of the priceless months of work so meanly lost but of the slime flung upon a sacred thing. Still he was not long in recovering his poise.

"After all," he said, with a little smile, "I suppose this is God's way of bringing you to His thought, my teacher. Shall we begin to undo the mischief now?"

"To-morrow," replied Maung Shway-gnong. "One doesn't go about the streets of Rangoon late at night with the chief authority at Amarapura. I will get home now and come to you at sunrise. It will be a most interesting task, this of purging your vocabulary. I am going, my pupil!"

"Well, go then," return Adoniram in the Burmese formula for farewell.

It was a blow, of course, but at least with this task on hand there was no temptation to long and lonely meditations and Adoniram pushed Maung Shway-gnong hard. He feared that with the return of the viceroy from the north the teacher would have more reason than ever for disappearing and, excepting for his daily walk at dawn and his meals, Adoniram never left his work.

It seemed to him as the weeks slipped on, that the teacher was only too glad for the shelter he found in the mission house. More than once Adoniram had it on the tip of his tongue to ask if some one was dogging the Burman's steps, he skuttled so furtively in and out of the rear gate, never moving except when the dawn or the dusk was full of shadows. But he was sure that the teacher would only lie to him and so asked no questions.

By the time Ann was due from Serampore, the work of purging was completed and Adoniram urged Maung Shway-gnong to undertake the job of making several copies of the translation to distribute.

"You say yourself it's the most moving story you've ever heard," said Adoniram. "Why keep the pleasure to yourself?"

"Because the gaing-ôk will have me disemboweled if I don't keep it to myself," replied the teacher succinctly.

THE GAING-ÔK

"Aren't you over-timid?" asked the missionary. "A monk won't even kill a fly."

"But he'll allow some one else to do so," retorted the Burman. "The gaing-ôk and the viceroy have a complete understanding of each other's thoughts about you and me and while they both are in Amarapura, one of their tasks undoubtedly will be to give his majesty a share of the understanding. I think, though I'm not able to make sure, that both of us are regularly spied upon."

"By a member of my household?" asked Adoniram, quickly.

"I can't be sure," replied Maung Shway-gnong, "and I shall name no name till I am."

"That's a happy suggestion!" ejaculated Adoniram with a grim smile. "However, I'm not going to worry over this bug-a-boo that's been held over me for two years but which never really appears."

"The time for it to appear is when you begin to win their subjects away from Buddha," said Maung Shway-gnong, earnestly. "They don't care how you or any other foreigner worships, so long as you don't propagate your faith."

"The gaing-ôk isn't the gentle soul his Buddha Gautama was." Adoniram's lips were a little scornful.

"He's consistently a monk. If he protects the Buddha as well as keeping his vows, his karma will be complete and he'll emerge from this life straight into nigban."

"Do you believe that?" This time Adoniram carefully kept contempt out of his voice.

"Do you believe you'll go to your heaven if you keep your religious teachings?" countered the teacher.

"Yes, but my teachings were inspired by God Himself and are a religion of hope and consolation for sinners. I don't wonder that you Burmans are always doing things with the idea of finishing with rebirths or karma as you call it. It's a dreadful idea."

"You don't understand life yet, my pupil," eyeing the

young face half sadly. "You'll live to realize that Buddhists and Christians alike spend the best part of their days in an attempt to escape the consequences of their own lusts. And you'll grow to believe that one life is not enough in which to slough off all these lusts. We require many lives to make us fit for the eternal peace."

Adoniram listened thoughtfully. There seemed to him to be a certain unanswerable logic in the Burman's words, yet his own faith was undisturbed. He shifted his attack slightly.

"I'm not so fond of myself that I wish to appear again and again; bear with myself during innumerable new body existences," he declared.

"Still you don't understand! When I die the component parts of my personality, which is made up of all my deeds, fall apart. A new personality is formed of these parts whose kind depends on what sort of life I've lived, good or bad. So my future self is really the son of my acts in this life. Isn't this more just than your doctrine of soft forgiveness?"

"I'm not sure that it's just, God being Almighty God," replied Adoniram.

The Burman shook his head. "Some day, you'll understand. When you've suffered. When one you love lies cold and you desire madly that the loved one may live again within the very purviews of your own life."

Adoniram stirred uneasily. "You make me wish that my dear wife were safe at home with me."

"May she soon be so!" Maung Shway-gnong smiled with sympathy. "But you evade my reasoning."

"I cannot answer you except by proclaiming my own faith," said Adoniram, honestly. "And that, you, in your turn, aren't ready to understand."

The two men exchanged a look of mutual respect and liking and as the shadows had crept from the jungle to the veranda, the Burman slipped quietly away. But the conversation remained vivid in Adoniram's mind; remained colored by an extraordinary sense of apprehension. He took Ma Baik's husband, Maung Nau, away for a week from his gardening and posted him on the beach with the offer of a silver tical when he brought him tidings of the *Georgiana*. And when on a hot April afternoon, Maung Nau came panting up the veranda steps with the news that the old ship was anchored, his trembling legs would hardly bear Adoniram to the wharf. Yet when he had folded Ann in his arms and had kissed the dear face so tinged again with health, the sense of apprehension though appeased, lingered in the shadows of his mind.

CHAPTER VI

THE NOVICE IN AFFLICTION

ANN brought with her the long-looked-for letter to Adoniram from the American Baptists.

It was a supremely satisfying epistle.

Scattered and feeble in organization as was the denomination, the news that the much-heralded missionaries to India had turned to the Baptist faith had electrified it to sudden cohesion. It had required time and patience to gather a representative conference. But this had been achieved in Philadelphia. A foreign missionary society had been formed and an income pledged to the Judsons, with the fervent gratitude of the men and women who had made the income possible.

It is difficult to describe the depth to which Ann and Adoniram were heartened by this word of approval and backing. For a time it made everything seem not only possible but simple—even the conversion of Maung Shway-gnong.

Ann's interest in the language study slipped a good deal during the next few months and she became engrossed in sewing. And Adoniram's conscience entirely deserted its task of admonishing him to keep Ann on her intellectual tiptoes. Even when she deserted Maung Shway-gnong entirely, Adoniram did not murmur. For a baby was coming to the mission! Ma Carey was excited and as fussy as a little hen, in her attempts to make Ann eat the food thought proper in Burma for coming motherhood. Ma Baik, the thin and cross-eyed and short of temper, called an astrologer and out of her own pocket paid for a forecast of the new-

THE NOVICE IN AFFLICTION

comer's sex. It was to be a girl. Koo-chil forgot caste, and waited on Ann like a well-trained nurse. And Maung Shway-gnong wrote her a lullaby, set to music that Ann couldn't learn. Adoniram was keenly anxious about the actual delivery of the baby. There was no medical aid to be had and he had a most unhappy recollection of the details of the early tragedy aboard the *Georgiana*. But Ann had been well instructed by the Serampore doctor and she put in many hours during the summer training Ma Carey in Anglo-Saxon methods of mid-wifery.

It was a great trial to both the Judsons therefore when Felix Carey appeared late in August and being under the king's orders, carried his wife and children at once aboard a boat for the long journey up the river Irrawaddy to Amarapura, and they had not yet adjusted themselves to the little Burman woman's absence, when tragic news reached the mission regarding her. The Careys' boat had been on the river about ten days when it upset and went down immediately. Mrs. Carey and the children were lost. Felix tried desperately, he wrote, to save his three-year-old son, but finding himself going down was obliged to let the child go and save himself.

Adoniram feared for the effect of the shock of this on Ann but Ann's concern for the coming baby was an adequate counterweight to her grief for dear little Ma Carey and her tiny ivory-tinted children. And a few days after they learned of the drownings, on September 15, 1815, to be exact, little Roger Williams Judson made a safe and not too agonizing arrival at the mission.

Adoniram was the doctor. The profound experience was in some ways more ghastly for him than for Ann and he was as much exhausted as his wife when it was over. It was Koo-chil who dressed the baby for he would obey orders while Ma Baik could not be trusted not to inaugurate some of her own outrageous ideas. And it was Koo-chil, his pockmarked face dripping sweat, who as soon as Adoniram had seen Ann and the baby sink into slumber, gave Adoniram a cup of hot tea and put him to bed.

Blue-eyed Roger interfered seriously at times with Adoniram's study of Pali literature and translations of the New Testament. The child filled an unnaturally large part in both their lives. As a matter of fact they were starved for play, for mental relaxation, for their own people. Adoniram, as Ann knew, had gone stale from overstudy. And deliberately tempted by the wise young wife, he spent hours of every day with his son.

In his great bass voice, he sang Maung Shway-gnong's lullabys to Roger or walking up and down the veranda would warble the gayest hymn tunes he could recall and complained to Ann that they all were too sad. He made a delightful wagon for the little fellow, a quaint replica of the two-wheeled buffalo cart of the country. And he made a rare excursion to show Roger to the vicereine immediately on her return to Rangoon.

That lady, who, of course, never had seen a white baby, was so excited that she sent for the viceroy. He was sitting in court but, far from being resentful of the unseemly interruption, was as pleased and excited as his chief wife and, although he ignored Adoniram, he whistled and talked to the baby and made him a present of a bright red woven wicker ball. The vicereine's gift, which she brought herself the next day to the mission, was a finely carved Burmese cradle. She made sure that it would be used by herself ordering the gardener to hang it from the rafters and waiting to see the child placed within the pretty nest.

Maung Shway-gnong took an austere interest in the baby which manifested itself in a formal visit each day to Roger's cradle during which he stood chin in palm and talked to the child as though he were exchanging opinions with a fellow philosopher.

And little Roger, though he was a delicate baby, was a

THE NOVICE IN AFFLICTION 57

joyful one and was friendly to all the brown and yellow faces that bent above his little swinging bed.

He was eight months old when he took the jungle fever. The battle was very short with every one in the mission family doing his own peculiar best to save the baby. Each of the Burmans dropped a rupee into Mr. Beg Pardon's house. Koo-chil made a charm of hair and cardamom seed and sesamun oil and what-not and hid it under the baby's pillow. The teacher braved the mysterious fear that shadowed him and in broad daylight brought in a famous wizard doctor. But little Roger died before there could be even the beginning of an argument about the wizard's ministrations.

Ann was prostrated. After they had buried the baby under the casuarina tree, she lay on her bed in a coma from which Adoniram tried in vain to rouse her.

He was forlorn, indeed! He attended to the necessary duties of death, wrote to Bradford and Plymouth telling the sad news, concealing from his mother and Ann's any hint of his despair. But to Dr. Carey in Serampore he divulged something of his wretchedness.

"Our little Roger died last Saturday morning, May 16, 1816. We looked at him through the day and on the approach of night, laid him in his grave. Perhaps I am a novice in affliction. Had I lost a wife I might not thus lament for a little child eight months old. Nothing but experience can teach us what feelings agonize the soul of a parent when he puts his face to that of his dear, his only child to ascertain whether there may not be one breath more! And when satisfied of the truth, when hope expires with life, he tries to raise the bursting prayer, 'O Lord, receive the spirit!'—Where has that spirit fled? Into what strange scenes? Who supports and guides its trembling feet across the dark valley?—Might not this have been spared? He was almost all our comfort and amusement in this dreary place. Pray for us—"

Adoniram sealed this letter to Carey and was staring unseeing into the rain-drenched yard when Ann crossed his line of vision. She was wringing her hands and as Adoniram sprang to his feet, she threw herself face down on Roger's grave. Ann needed spiritual help!

It was the first time in his relationship to her that the priest had risen above the lover, though never could the lover be entirely separated from any communication between them. He rushed down the steps and across the yard to kneel beside her.

"Ann! Ann!"

She did not heed him.

"Ann!" pleadingly, "darling Ann!"

She did not raise her head. He was slight himself, but Ann's little body was as fragile as an empty chrysalis. He lifted her in his arms and she beat her hands wildly against his breast.

"Go away! Oh, let me die, let me die!"

He bore her under the dripping plantains, across the yard, up the veranda steps and into their room where he laid her on the bed. Then he stood looking at her, sternly. This was the clergyman. But the husband choked with tears and whispered to himself that on his soul lay the fact that it was he who had beguiled the happy, the lovely Ann Hasseltine away from the New England where she belonged to this alien, poisonous jungle which was sapping her vitality and had killed her child.

He was responsible for this as her husband and as her clergyman he was responsible for her breaking under grief.

He was twenty-eight years old now. The round pink cheeks were gaunt and brown. The hazel eyes were deeper set and hungrier than ever, but the sensitive mouth was firmer. Twenty-eight years old, he reminded himself and six years out of divinity school, yet only now about to begin his ministry!

He choked back his tears and began to speak in a voice

THE NOVICE IN AFFLICTION 59

that could not be heard at first above Ann's sobbing. "Jesus said, 'Whosoever drinketh of the water I shall give him shall never thirst, but the water I shall give him shall be a well of water springing up into eternal life.' Ann, darling Ann, I am holding His perfect cup to your lips and you *must* drink!"

His remarkable voice, full and deep, was infinitely tender, yet filled with an arresting confidence. Slowly Ann turned from her face to her side, away from him but with shaking fingers pressed hard to her lips as though she fought back her sobs.

"Jesus said, 'He that believeth in Him that sent me, hath everlasting life. The hour is coming, and now is, when the dead shall hear the voice of the Son of God and they that hear shall live.'"

He would not touch her. The mighty words must be her only help.

"Ann, dear, our little son lives. There is no death. Only new forms, new life. The essence of little Roger is imperishable."

Ann turned on her back and lifted her brown eyes all blind with weeping to the rapt face at her bedside. The gray evening light shadowed the room, the house lizard called "taktu" from the bedfoot. The sunset gongs rang softly from the monastery.

"'Verily I say unto you, he that believeth in me hath everlasting life. This is the bread that cometh down from heaven that a man may eat thereof and not die.'—Oh, God, heavenly Father, look down on this mother and comfort her for the sake of the mother who in pain and hardship bore Thy Son for Thee. Let her know that there is no death, that the soul of little Roger is born again to life more joyful. Give her, O God, another little child for the sake of Thy Son's deep understanding of every woman's pain—"

Ann sat slowly erect, still gazing into Adoniram's face.

She had ceased to weep and the frenzy had gone from her eyes. Adoniram wiped her poor cheeks gently with his cambric handkerchief and smoothed her curls back from her forehead. After a short silence Ann said:

"Where is Roger now, Adoniram? Oh, where is my baby now?"

Adoniram's face went slowly white. His faith to feed Ann's! His spiritual knowledge to supplement hers! No speculating now, but truth. *And what was truth? Where was Roger now?*—A cold sweat broke out on his lips as he whipped his spiritual vision to try to pierce the black beyond.—Slowly and with infinite difficulty he struggled to put into words that for which there are no words.

"Roger's soul," he said, "has merged with God's. If God wills it, Roger may be born again. But only if God wills it."

He ceased speaking for he had told all that he knew.

Faint through the rain tinkled the pagoda bells.

Where was God?

Ann, looking up into the face that was now the whole of life to her, suddenly caught Adoniram's hand to her heart. His lips quivered. But he laid his free hand on her soft hair and blessed her.

CHAPTER VII

DISCIPLINE

MAUNG SHWAY-GNONG insisted that Adoniram go on with his work. "I am old in the ways of grief, my pupil," he said three days after Roger's funeral, "and I know that the desire for our dead is soonest lost in work of the mind. We'll take up one of the loveliest tales of the Buddhist, the dialogue between the Blessed One and the herdsman."

He had found Adoniram beside Roger's grave. He put a bony hand on the missionary's arm and led him firmly back to the little study, talking as he moved.

"There are many intricate threads in the garment of life; threads impossible to break without rending the garment," he said as he wiped the rain from his glistening ribs and prepared a chew of betel by wrapping the lime-smeared nut and tobacco in a betel leaf. He stowed the quid in his cheek and went on. "I am reminded of that when I speak of the dialogue of the Buddha and the herdsman. It was first read to me by the gaing-ôk when I was in high favor with him. It was his favorite piece shared with his favorite pupil—Amé—how far afield the flesh can lead us!"

He opened a beautiful book, bound in wooden covers carved in high relief, with pages of silk and bade Adoniram read. The young missionary obeyed in a voice that shook at first but steadied after the opening sentence.

"I have boiled the rice, I have milked the kine—so said the herdsman Dhaniya—I am living with my comrades near the banks of the great Mahi River: the house is roofed, the fire is lighted—then rain if thou wilt, O sky!"

"Now I will read the words of Gautama," said the

teacher. "'I am free from anger, free from stubbornness—so said the Blessed One. I am abiding for one night near the banks of the great Mahi River; my house has no cover, the fire of passion is extinguished—then rain if thou wilt, O sky!'"

Adoniram's tired face kindled. He turned the page of the book and read the herdsman's reply with ringing voice. Ann, pausing at the door caught the teacher's eye, smiled and nodded at him. She suspected Maung Shway-gnong of being a bit of a coward but in her estimation his devotion to her husband more than covered that frailty. And he could minister to Adoniram's needs better now than she could, although Adoniram had given her command of herself the day before.

And yet it was Ann who, when their grief had eased a few weeks later to a point where they could speak of Roger without tears, gave Adoniram the one solacing word that came to him out of the tragedy.

"The most unsupportable aspect of our baby's death," he said, one evening after they had gone to bed, "is that one can see no possible purpose in it."

"Ah, but we can," returned Ann, quickly. "I am convinced that God will pursue you relentlessly until you so understand human suffering that every man you meet must melt to you."

"Oh, Ann, but little Roger—and you—!" exclaimed Adoniram.

"Nothing matters to God, of that sort. All that matters is that you are disciplined until you save Burma."

"It's an awful thought," whispered her husband, gazing into the darkness with his heart beating suffocatingly.

"A glorious thought, if one can gaze at it without being blinded," said Ann, gently.

Her words stayed with him all night.

The next day Adoniram attacked his work of translating

DISCIPLINE

with renewed vigor and when in early July a letter reached them from the Baptist Missionary society saying that they were sending a missionary printer, one George Hough and his wife to Rangoon, it looked like a direct notice from God that He approved of the work. All Burmese men could read. As soon as his Gospel translations and tracts were printed, Adoniram would be speaking with a thousand tongues. He wrote the wonderful news to Dr. Carey and that great man hurried a letter back to Rangoon saying that when the Houghs arrived at Serampore, on their way to Burma, he would present them with a printing press and Burmese type!

"Now," said Adoniram, "I see the beginning of my real task. A year hence, I'll no longer be an onlooker but an actual fisher of men. Ann, isn't it strange that so impatient a man as I should have learned to acquiesce with at least partial cheerfulness to this long, dull period of preparation?"

"Nothing in your growth upward astonishes me," was Ann's reply.

"You're not so strict in your discipline as you used to be," chuckled her husband. "You sugar-coat a good deal of your training, now."

"I didn't want you to turn against the school mistress, my dear—I'm afraid I'm really getting to look like one! 'Don, was I so vain about my appearance that I needed this yellow skin to check me?"

"Your skin's *not* yellow any more!" cried Adoniram indignantly.

Ann looked at him with brown eyes that were tenderly amused. "Darling, I shall wash your mouth out with soap if you keep on telling such fibs. Where are your eyes?"

"To tell the truth but not to contradict what I've just stated," said Adoniram, a little ruefully, "my eyes are very painful, Ann. I wonder if there's anything we can do for them?"

"I've been afraid of the effect of all this study!" exclaimed his wife. "Let's try hot bathing and a darkened room, dear."

"I have no time for coddling," protested Adoniram.

"You may have to take more time for it later, if you neglect the pain now," warned Ann.

But Adoniram kept on with his work for another week before pain claimed him for its own. Suddenly he could not bear light and for many days could not bear even to have Maung Shway-gnong read to him. He lay in his bed twisting in silent agony.

Ma Baik as usual when there was sickness became very brisk and attentive. Ann had found her amusing and helpful on her trip to Serampore. But Ann had not been in severe pain. Ordinarily, Adoniram was very much amused by the wasp-like little woman, but now, the mere smell of her cheroot as she swept his floor made him half frantic and one morning he ordered her out.

She was deeply offended and sought Ann. "If that were my husband," she shrilled, "I'd beat him."

"But he's already in such pain, Ma Baik!" protested Ann. "If we could stop the pain, he'd be begging you to return to your care of him."

"There are ways to stop the pain, if one consults the proper source," said the Burmese woman. "But, of course, you foreign savages are not willing to give money to the proper source."

Ann was willing to do anything to silence and solace Ma Baik. She gave her a tical, which Ma Baik secreted in the inner citadel of her tamein and immediately hurried out of the house. Ann forgot the incident in her anxiety over Adoniram.

The next day, however, she was forcibly reminded of it. Just at sunset, there burst forth from the yard an anarchy of sound and Ann rushed to the veranda to discover its origin. This was not far to seek. Grouped on Ma Baik's porch was a Burmese orchestra: drums, flute, cymbals and the gong harmonicon, working with might and main. And on the ground just below Adoniram's window, an old woman gyrated and postured while Ma Baik urged her on.

When Ann appeared, Ma Baik ran up the steps and shook an admonishing finger. "Don't speak, foreign friend! A tical's worth lasts only a third of a betel chew. And the dancing woman promises the demon will be out of your husband and into her in that time."

Ann gasped. But happily she was spared a protest for the dancing woman at that moment obligingly fell down in a fit and the musicians promptly wrapped up their instruments. Ann fled back to her husband expecting to find him beside himself. But Adoniram was laughing feebly!

"Tell Ma Baik I give up!" he said. "I actually do feel better! She threatened a week ago to give me the music cure."

And he did mend from that day forth; not rapidly for the swamps of Rangoon were steadily depleting his strength, and the pain gave way only reluctantly. He was confined to the darkened bedroom for the remainder of the rainy season, with only Maung Shway-gnong as an occasional visitor. He felt sometimes, so great was their solitude, as if the jungle was actually overgrowing the mission, and he had at this time his greatest bout with homesickness. But at last October came and with it a glorious sun which drank up the floods and burst the lotus in the tanks to swooning sweetness. The nightingale and the cuckoo appeared and Maung Nau, the gardener, borrowed a water buffalo for the plowing.

The end of the rains meant the end of the long Burmese lent and brought the great festival that celebrates the return to joy. Each morning Adoniram crept to his chair on the veranda and while Maung Shway-gnong read to him, he watched the throngs passing up the road to the Shwé Dagôn. It seemed to him that there could not be anywhere a prettier sight than these singing, laughing people in their purple, green, rose or flame-colored skirts, flower decked, bearing their offerings of fruit or blossoms. He interrupted the teacher one morning to say:

"I'd like to follow them and see them at their worship."

"Why?" asked Maung Shway-gnong, keen eyed.

"Because my resolution's at low ebb," admitted Adoniram, "and I'm always tempted by beauty in any form."

The teacher grunted as if disappointed and went on with his reading.

It was late in the afternoon of the last day of the celebration that the Houghs arrived. They were solid New Hampshire folk. Hough was a small man, with a sharp gray eye and a face smooth shaven save for a tiny brown chin beard at which he was always tugging. Mrs. Hough was plump and blonde—a silent woman whose comment on every problem was, "ask father." They were a familiar Yankee type to the Judsons. There could not be a great deal of intellectual companionship between the two families but the Houghs could be depended on for common sense and industry and Ann and Adoniram after four years of exile were in no critical mood. They welcomed the newcomers as the Israelites had welcomed the manna.

The time of their arrival was in a way unfortunate. Nothing that the Judsons had written home or that the Houghs had been told at Serampore harmonized in the least with Rangoon in the midst of the end of lent festivity. Sitting on the veranda after their luggage had been stowed away and an early tea finished, the newcomers stared at the passing throngs.

"But we understood Rangoon was a dreary, lonely place with tigers prowling in the streets!" exclaimed Hough, twisting his brown goatee and looking at Ann reproachfully.

Ann smiled. "But Rangoon of the lenten season is utterly

unlike Rangoon of the rest of the year. Usually we're quite deserted out here."

"My land, what pretty colors, like fireflies in a hollyhock bed!" ejaculated Mrs. Hough.

Hundreds of candles were passing, borne by worshipers, each lighting a brown, happy face, a flower-twisted braid, a fluttering bit of silk.

"You mustn't be so charmed that the real Rangoon will shock you too much," warned Ann.

"I tell you what prepares me for the seamy side of this place," said Hough suddenly, "it's the look of you folks. My gracious, you look as if you'd been kept in the root cellar and forgotten till the next season."

"They look as if they'd been in torment, you mean!" exclaimed Mrs. Hough. "I—I can hardly keep the tears back."

"You mustn't be too frank," laughed Adoniram. "You might make us vain."

"We aren't being very polite, father," said Mrs. Hough contritely.

"I suppose we aren't," admitted Hough. "You'll have to excuse us. You know I'm just a printer—"

"Just a printer!" ejaculated Adoniram. "My dear Brother Hough, nothing God could send to Burma right now could look as handsome or as well mannered as a printer! You are welcome to say what you please of Mrs. Judson and me, if you'll just print our books!"

Every one laughed. Then Ann tried to describe for their benefit Burma gasping for air and water in the burning months of April and May. But again words were wasted for even as she spoke the palm trees along the road were suddenly thrown into unearthly silhouette by a tremulous crimson the harbinger of such a moon as no untraveled Yankee ever had seen. It was a moon of molten fire that turned the palms, the mangoes and the feathery bamboos in the mission yard to dancing flame and that, most moving of all, gave the Houghs a transcendent view of the dome of the Shwé Dagôn, iridescent, enchanted, yearning toward the skies.

Adoniram cleared his throat preparatory to warning the newcomers against the snares hidden in the beauty of that heaven-kissing spire. But the impulse did not survive the influence of the night. He found himself instead telling them the intriguing story of the Buddha Gautama's leaving wife and child to discover the way to peace. And as far as he and Ann could tell, the Houghs went to bed, a little later, quite convinced that their previous conception of the Judsons' environment and work was entirely erroneous and their sympathy much misplaced.

The printing press was a surpassing wonder to Maung Shway-gnong and he deserted his teaching for a week to study its fascinations. During this week, Hough set up and printed the Gospel according to Matthew. Maung Shway-gnong took the first copy as it came from the press and rushed with it to Adoniram's study.

"Our child, O pupil!" cried the teacher.

Adoniram took the tract tenderly and after gazing at it thoughtfully to savor the moment to the full, he took up his quill and wrote the teacher's name upon it.

Maung Shway-gnong received the precious pages with trembling fingers. "Our child," he murmured again. Then with a look of deep sadness he laid it back on Adoniram's desk. "I dare not take it. If it is found in my possession, I'll be separated from you, forever."

Adoniram eyed the tragic, emaciated face, the brow of the scholar, the chin of the weakling. The moment was approaching, he felt, when Christ could hold out a hand to this Burman.

"O faint of heart and foolish!" Adoniram softened his deep voice. "Don't you realize that having worked for a year with me on the contents of this little book every word of it is printed on your brain from which no man may tear

DISCIPLINE

it? You need not take the book with you, if you are afraid. But I would admire you more if you dared to show to the world what you have already in your mind."

Maung Shway-gnong rubbed his chin, laid the tract on the desk, picked it up and fingered it lovingly, put it down on the desk and looking at Adoniram, muttered:

"The iron maul!"

"You mean that you believe Matthew's words and would feel obliged to speak out for Christ if questioned?" demanded Adoniram, eagerly.

"I don't believe one word of it," cried the teacher, vehemently.

"Then leave it where it is—coward!" boomed Adoniram.

The teacher drew himself to his skeleton height and stalked out. Adoniram leaned his head on his thin brown hand and gazed mournfully at the Gospel. Three years ... it was a long, long road, the road in Burma to Christ. And yet it was Adoniram Judson's job and no one else's in all the world to lead the way along it.

The tract lay on the desk all that day. But on the next, it disappeared and Adoniram never asked who had taken it.

The history of the second copy was only a little less shrouded in mystery.

The day after the first printing when Adoniram took his morning walk, he gave this second copy to the first Burman he met. This happened to be a middle-aged man accompanied by a servant. The man took the booklet with a stare of surprise but without a word. Adoniram watched him continue on his way toward the Shwé Dagôn and uttered a silent prayer.

That noon, after dinner, as Adoniram sat on the veranda for a few moments' recess before returning to work, the man and his servant made their way over the stepping stones to the veranda and the master seated himself on a mat. The missionary waited in silence. The caller deliberately prepared a chew of betel, inserted it in his cheek, waved away the servant and the betel box, placed his brass spittoon carefully, then looked up at Adoniram.

"Who is this Jesus, O foreign writer?"

Adoniram's heart gave a great twist. His eyes filled. But, in a moment, he left his chair and seated himself on the mat beside his caller.

"He is the Son of God who, pitying human creatures, came into this world and suffered death in their stead."

"Who is God?"

"He is a Being without beginning or end, Who is not subject to age and death but always is."

There was a long silence during which the servant who had gone no further than the steps leaned toward Adoniram, breathing heavily, and the master worked on his betel cud, eyes on the ground.

Finally he asked in a low voice, "How long will it take me to learn the religion of Jesus?"

"If God gives you wisdom," answered Adoniram, his pale cheeks beginning to burn, "the religion of Jesus is soon learned."

"I have your little book. Have you another that you'll graciously give me? Not the same but another story."

Adoniram shook his head. "Not yet. In time. But, friend, you need no other book to teach you Jesus Christ's religion. It's all in the one I gave you. Let us converse about it."

"Not now," said the visitor. "What you have already told me about your God requires much thought. It's not a religion for fools, one can see." He rose as he spoke. "I am going, foreign teacher."

"Well, go then," murmured Adoniram wistfully. He dared not urge the Burman. It would be like using force on a butterfly. He watched the servant acquire the spittoon and raise the umbrella and although every desire within him cried out to him to run after this his first inquirer, catch his hand and hold him, he did not do so.

DISCIPLINE

Maung Shway-gnong was uneasy over the episode. The man was a famous wood carver, he said, who wouldn't dare, for the sake of his craft, show any interest in any foreign gods. He must be a spy.

"The viceroy is back," added the teacher. "Aren't you afraid that he'll destroy you or at least your printing press?"

"My foolish body is afraid," answered Adoniram, "but my spirit isn't, I suppose, because that belongs to God. I tell you, Maung Shway-gnong, let's you and I settle all these tremblings. Let's go together to the viceroy and ask his protection."

"You're mad!" exclaimed the teacher. He bit his finger nails and stared at the plantain trees that edged the garden.

Adoniram was sorry for him and sympathetic though a little contemptuous; perhaps, he admitted inwardly and grimly, because he found it so difficult himself not to live in fear of the explosion the issuing of the Gospel would probably set off.

"I feel like going up the Irrawaddy to visit my brother, near Prome," muttered Maung Shway-gnong.

"How far is Prome from Amarapura?" asked Adoniram, eagerly.

"It lies half way between here and the capital," replied the teacher.

Adoniram's cheeks flushed and his heart began to beat heavily. He had conceived a sudden idea which he believed was nothing less than inspiration.

"Maung Shway-gnong, I'm going up the Irrawaddy with you but not to stay at Prome. I'm going on to Amarapura to visit the king. I am going to Burma's fountain head of authority and ask permission to teach my religion. Then all these fears will cease."

Maung Shway-gnong's sunken eyes seemed about to start from their sockets. "You would go into the golden presence with such a request after all you've heard? You rave!"

"But do I?" began Adoniram.

The teacher rose angrily. "I cannot listen to you."

"Very well," contemptuously from Adoniram. "Let us return to a safe and harmless topic."

With compressed lips, the Burman sat back on his mat and took up the book Adoniram was studying at the moment.

But the idea so impulsively conceived remained with Adoniram and that night he broached it to the mission family. The Houghs could not pretend to give advice but Hough said that he felt that he and his wife as yet were too new to the country to be left at the mission.

"My wife and I were new to the country in a way you can't picture, Brother Hough!" exclaimed Adoniram, "and no harm befell us."

"Well, I can't help that," insisted the printer. "It won't pay to have me murdered by some of those wild Karens we see passing in the jungle, now would it. That's not printing books!" He laughed but Adoniram felt a little sinking of heart. This wasn't the kind of zeal with which to conquer Burma. He turned to Ann.

"And you, my dear?"

"What will you do if he refuses your request and orders you not to preach?" asked Ann.

"He won't do that. I have a conviction that he will listen with eagerness," replied Adoniram. "You see, no one has gone about it with open honesty before. I want to do it that way. I'm so weary of keeping Christ hidden. I want to begin my work, now, and openly."

"My dear husband," said Ann, leaning toward him and putting her hand on his knee as if they were alone together, her sweet face very grave and earnest in the lamplight, "preach your first sermon before you go to Amarapura. You may never have a chance to preach another."

Adoniram drew a quick breath. Bats circled noisily in the rafters and one suddenly fluttered across the lamp wick and extinguished the light.

"There!" whispered Mrs. Hough.

Mr. Hough relighted the wick. Adoniram did not stir, had not noted the loss of light. The shattering sense of destiny that lately had seemed to desert him was on him now. He put his hand over Ann's.

"I shall preach my first sermon, next Sunday," he said.

CHAPTER VIII

THE FLYING SQUIRREL

THAT night, the pains returned full force to Adoniram's eyes. And when Sunday came, he was lying on his bed, dazed with misery, every desire stripped from him save that for relief from agony.

Hough, who was something of a rule-of-thumb doctor gave it as his opinion that it was the gas rising from the stinking marshes of Rangoon that caused Adoniram's "neuralgia." Ann agreed with him and they laid plans to persuade Adoniram to visit Serampore as soon as he was better.

After two weeks, the turn for the better began and when Adoniram, weak but glad that this attack had lasted so much less time than the first, was able to sit again on the veranda with the teacher, the others put the plan to him.

He vetoed it without hesitation. Burma, always and forever Burma was his place, he said.

"You must love this hole, Brother Judson," exclaimed poor Mrs. Hough whose first delight in Rangoon had changed to homesick horror.

"I hate Rangoon," replied Adoniram. "And I'm not trying to play the martyr either. But as a matter of plain fact, I'm the only person in the world at present equipped to preach Christ to the Burmans. That is the one qualification that makes my life valuable. Shall I risk that life on a mere trip for health?"

"Aren't you ever homesick, Brother Judson?" asked Hough, wistfully.

"Yes," replied Adoniram and closed his eyes—the summer of Plymouth—the white meeting house at Salem—

THE FLYING SQUIRREL 75

He did not speak again and the Houghs, a little disgruntled, went back to their struggle with the language. Ann, who was their teacher, lingered to press a kiss on her husband's lips—compressed she knew with a pain that was not physical.

"It's hard to be wise, isn't it, Adoniram," she said, softly. "O my dear, I can't think of Burma when I see you looking so! I love you so much. Don't you think my love ought to be considered in God's scheme of things?"

Adoniram opened his eyes. "Does my going mean that much to you, Nancy?" Then without waiting for her to reply, he pleaded, "Dearest, don't appeal to my love for you. I'm helpless in your hands when you use that plea. This must be decided outside our feeling for each other." He clung to her hands, looking up into her delicate face with all his old boyish passion in his eyes. "Help me, Nancy!" he whispered.

They looked at each other for a long moment: a look that told of all that the four years of their marriage had meant to them. Then Ann smiled.

"Will you *let* me help you, 'Don?"

"Gladly, O most gladly!"

"Then here's my suggestion. If you go to Amarapura, when you get well, I shall stay here, of course, with the Houghs. Yet, even if he knew the language, it's obvious that George Hough is a printer, not a missionary. And if anything should happen to you, your work here would be lost, largely. Now, do you remember what Dr. Carey told us about the work their mission accomplished in that place called Chittagong, northwest of Burma, on the Bengal coast?"

"Yes," replied Adoniram, quickly. "Before they gave up the mission there, they had made several converts, among them one native who qualified for a preacher."

Ann nodded. "Felix Carey told me that he saw that native on his last errand to Chittagong. He was trying to carry on the work but was terribly discouraged because of his ignorance. Now here's my suggestion, 'Don. Those natives speak Burmese. If you go to Amarapura, and leave a native preacher here, he and I together could bring about some real results, I'm certain, during your absence—or if— Well, anyhow, we'd try to make converts and it's certain a native preacher would have more effect than a white. You refuse to take a voyage to Serampore for your health. 'Don, take the three weeks' sailing trip to Chittagong and back and fetch that native preacher to Rangoon. Will that satisfy your conscience?"

Adoniram's lips twitched and a slow smile brought youth to his face. "Ann! Ann! If you'd been a man you'd have talked Benjamin Franklin into bewilderment! They'd have found you far more efficacious in Paris than the old Quaker. Chittagong! I could go up there and back in less than a month! It's a perfectly sound suggestion. When do you think I could be strong enough to go?"

"The sooner you can get out of Rangoon the better," replied Ann. "We'll call on Maung Nau's old experience as a fisherman and have him nose out a native ship, making that trip."

"What a wife!" sighed Adoniram.

"Am I not!" chuckled Ann and went off to send the gardener to her husband.

Once the decision was made, Adoniram was all impatience to be gone. But it took several days to find a boat which not only was making the required trip but which was blessed with even a crude cabin. It was the cold season and though this meant little in the New England sense, it meant discomfort and danger to a man in Adoniram's condition.

While Maung Nau carried on the search, the teacher was in a state of mind bordering on hysteria. He had a great desire to accompany Adoniram, partly from affection and partly because he wanted to get out of the country before

THE FLYING SQUIRREL

the viceroy or the gaing-ôk took notice of the product of the printing press. On the other hand, he feared being identified with the missionary any further now that the moment had come for actual mission activities. Adoniram would have been delighted to have the teacher take the trip with him. He dreaded going alone. But he insisted that Maung Shway-gnong make his own decision.

He continued in his hysterical state of indecision until the very day that Maung Nau found a suitable coasting vessel. Then he announced that he would cast in his lot with his favorite of all pupils and went off to pack up his belongings. But at the time set for him to join Adoniram on the beach, a little boy thrust a palm leaf note into the missionary's hand and scampered away. The note was without greeting or signature but was in the teacher's hand. "The gaing-ôk has received a copy of the Gospel. He has sent for the one who taught the foreign animal to write such beautiful Burmese. That one will not see the favorite pupil for a long time, if ever."

Adoniram, leaning on George Hough's arm, read the note aloud and sighed, "Poor fellow! I've brought him nothing but trouble and he won't let me exchange the trouble for joy."

"I guess you've given him a whole lot more than you realize, Brother Judson," said Hough. "Come, I've got to have plenty of time to settle you in that hen's nest of a cabin or else Mrs. Judson will be in my hair." And they clambered aboard the boat.

It was Christmas day, 1816, and the first time Adoniram had left Rangoon since he had entered it four years before. He had little idea of the contrast between the pink-cheeked boy who from the deck of the *Georgiana* had thrilled to the beauty of the lotus spire of Dagôn and this gaunt, disease-ravished man who now gazed upon it with an awe bred of knowledge.

The vessel hung in mid-stream waiting for the tide to

serve. It was a small craft with the high Burmese prow and stern, only half decked and without a name. An extraordinarily fine wood carving of a great squirrel ornamented the prow and Hough with an unusual flight of fancy had spoken of the boat as the *Flying Squirrel*. Adoniram squatting weakly on the deck among the great earthen jars of ngapi thought with a quiet grin that the little creature might well be pictured as escaping from the unspeakable smell which issued from the ngapi, a preserved fish much loved by the Burman.

Adoniram, himself, had become hardened to this and many other stenches characteristic of Rangoon. He crouched contentedly on the coil of rope, watching the crowded river. It had a strong interest to one so long immured in the jungle. Rice boats, ngapi boats and the gilded war boats and dispatch canoes of the king with their singing crews made a holiday of the twilight. He ate with actual appetite the supper Koo-chil had packed in a rush basket and when the mosquitoes grew unendurable went to his tiny cabin.

The next morning when he came on deck, he found that they had crossed the great sand bar and were well into the Gulf of Martaban. The air was gloriously invigorating. Adoniram drew deep draughts of it into his lungs and felt his blood quicken and his brain clear. All that day he lay on deck in the shadow of the lateen sail, reading or talking to members of the crew and at night felt as if ten years had dropped from his shoulders.

Their course lay west, then north along the coast of Arakan. By noon of the third day they had caught their first glimpse of the Arakan mountains to the west of which lay Burma. They were making a record voyage. If he had good luck in locating his converts Adoniram told himself he'd be back in Rangoon in nearer two weeks than three.

But on the fifth day, a northeaster struck them. The Arakan hills were hidden by clouds. For twenty-four hours

THE FLYING SQUIRREL

there was neither sun nor star and the little craft could only run before the storm! Whither, the captain confided to Adoniram, he knew not. The Burmans were river men and coasters and had no skill at deep-sea sailing. Adoniram tried his utmost to give what he had of knowledge to the captain. He drew him a map of the Bay of Bengal and tried to induce him to steer by compass for what might prove to be Madras. It was no use. This storm was to be. This confusion of wind and wave, this violence of the ship's roll and pitch, this desperate danger was a part of the karma of all on board. Why worry?

Why, indeed?

For seven days they tossed at the mercy of the storm. The food Adoniram had brought from home gave out and he was obliged to fall back on the ship's provisions of moldy rice and the disgusting rotted salt fish they called ngapi. Three or four days of this food combined, with the constant wetting from sea and cloud, to put Adoniram to bed with a high fever and the old head pains.

The captain was entirely kind when he thought of Adoniram, which was not often. The missionary lay on his berth of boards and matting alone, hour after hour. Sometimes with mind curiously alert to his situation: to the uproar of the storm, the wild fall of the waves, the booming of the close-rigged sails. Sometimes reality faded and he fought the demon of pain until mercifully delirium took him.

Their twelfth day at sea found them in a burning calm. With the quiet and the heat, Adoniram recovered his senses, but was too weak to move. The captain who after a long time gave him a drink of rain water was of the opinion that they were on the outer edge of the world's great sea, that this experience was a part of the stern moving of the Law. One repeated praises of Buddha's wisdom, chewed betel and waited.

For two weeks more the calm persisted. Then just a

month after they had left Rangoon a keen wind suddenly rose from the east. Adoniram, lying in a stupor in his cabin, was roused by the sudden rush of waters past his window. The captain a few moments later put his black top-knot in at the door to say that they were on their way to Calcutta!

They were on their way a long, long time. They should have reached the east coast of India in five or six days. But for seven weeks more, Adoniram lay half dying in the *Flying Squirrel*. He was conscious only at odd moments. It percolated through his delirium that when they came within sight of the Coromandel coast they were unable to make shore because of the combined hostility of wind and current. He knew that from an occasional native boat they obtained rice and a few buckets of water. For the rest, starvation, filth and pain claimed Adoniram for their own.

In his lucid intervals, he prayed; prayed as he never had prayed before, not only for succor, not only for surcease from pain but for greater faith in the goodness of God's mysterious purposes. And he prayed for physical strength enough to take advantage of this rare opportunity to work unhindered on the hearts of the Burmans; for strength to place the cross on every brown forehead in the *Flying Squirrel*. But his weakness only increased. His illness would not lose its grip.

Why? Staring out of the window at the bronze blue sea, he asked this—why? His only desire was to obey the command of Christ, to carry His teachings to all lands. Had he misinterpreted the command? Was Adoniram only an overwrought egoist and not at all under the direction of God? Was he usurping some one's place, some one better fitted for the task and was Adoniram being punished for presumption? Where was God, that he might go to Him and ask? *Where was God?*

A terrible question—the most terrible in man's experience. In his less lucid intervals, Buddha Gautama intruded on

THE FLYING SQUIRREL

moments of prayer; the calmly beautiful face, that had become as familiar as his own, would appear at the bed foot or in the window, shutting out moonlight or starlight to say softly, "Unwisely does one consider, Have I existed in ages past, shall I exist in ages yet to be, do I exist at all, am I, how am I; this is a being, whence is it come, whither will it go? Unwise! Unwise!"

For hours, Adoniram would struggle with this admonition—would repeat it to the shadow of the naked captain bending over him with a gourd of water, would whisper it to the squirrel perched on the heaving prow. "Whence is it come? Whither will it go?"

And then quite without his volition, Budáha Gautama would reappear and set him a task. "These are the things one should consider. 'This is suffering, this is the origin of suffering, this is the cessation of suffering, this is the way that leads to the cessation of suffering.'"

"Where is the way!" shouted Adoniram.

There was no answer. But one hot night when Buddha had been more persistent than usual, some thought of the gaing-ôk came to Adoniram's assistance. Curious that it should have been the gaing-ôk and not Maung Shway-gnong, for it was a verse that belonged to the dialogue between the Blessed One and the herdsman which came to release Adoniram from the grip of the question.

"Then the rain poured down and filled both sea and land. And hearing the sky raining Dhaniya said: 'Not small to us the gain that we have seen the Blessed One; in Thee we take refuge, Thou endowed with wisdom's eye; be thou our Master, O great sage!'"

To take refuge in Buddha, in the peace of nothingness. Was that the answer?

And then, with long heroic effort, he put out feeble fingers and clutched at something—Christ's blood-stained robe—

One day, after many weeks, he realized that the persistent clawing at his shoulder was not a tiger seeking to tear him from the bamboo on which he was being crucified but that it was the captain asking him repeatedly if he wished to be put ashore!

It was not until he had been helped by the first adequate drink of water he had received in a month that his mind cleared and he took in the blessed fact that the ship had found anchorage off the town of Masulipatam in upper Madras.

"Will you land, O foreigner?" urged the captain for the hundredth time.

"I must land," murmured Adoniram. "I must land so that my wife may find my grave. Give me writing materials, captain."

After long and broken effort, Adoniram accomplished a scrawl.

"To any English resident of Masulipatam: I am an American missionary desperately ill on a native boat. I beg you in the name of our common ancestry to help me to find a place on shore where I may die and be buried in decency. A. Judson."

The captain disappeared with the piece of paper.

Long later, a sailor came below and made him understand that actually an English boat was approaching. Adoniram turned his head to look from the window. The ship was at anchor some two or three miles off a low, uninviting beach. Within Adoniram's line of vision appeared a rowboat in which he could distinguish the red coat of the military and the white coat of the civilian Englishman. Adoniram stared as one would stare at the approach of messengers from heaven. And when he heard the precious sound of the English tongue, "Ship Ahoy! Mr. Judson!" it was too much. He dropped back on his mat in tears.

CHAPTER IX

COMMON ANCESTRY

BUT Adoniram was calm when the Englishmen entered his cabin. From the expression of pitying horror on their faces, he realized that he must be a loathsome object and he begged them to send a sick-orderly to clean him up before they tried to move him. But they would have none of it. Very tenderly they lifted him to a clean mat and with as little jarring as possible of his wracked body, lowered him into their boat and took him ashore.

There the army officer, Captain Leigh, placed him in a palanquin and carried him to his own bungalow and put him to bed, procured a doctor and a nurse and supplied him with clothing from his own wardrobe.

In a few days Adoniram's brain had cleared and when, after a week, his dysentery began to yield to treatment, the pains left his head and he started to gain strength rapidly.

It was heavenly, at first, to be in this well-ordered house, with the perfectly trained servants, the nourishing English-cooked food, and with reveille and taps each day assuring one that a strong hand held back the protesting Orient. It was good too, to be in touch once more with world events. He heard the story of Europe reëntangled by the Congress of Vienna and of Napoleon's last stand at Waterloo, and of the United States thrilled into nationalism by the Treaty of Ghent. It was not until the wide-flung gossip touched on Burmese affairs that the full significance of his own position returned to Adoniram.

His host told him that the old king of Burma claimed sovereignty over Bengal, far beyond Calcutta and was threatening that unless the English acknowledged that sovereignty, he would dispatch forces by land and sea which would capture and destroy the whole of the British possessions there.

"But does England want war with Burma?" exclaimed Adoniram.

"Heaven forbid!" ejaculated the captain. "The government here and at home are doing all possible to prevent it. The cost of subduing Burma and keeping it subdued is unthinkable. But frankly, Judson, I'm afraid war must come, any moment. After all, we can't permit the Burmans to march across Bengal, destroying in their devilish manner as they go!"

Something clicked in Adoniram's brain. Ann! Not that she'd been absent from his mind or heart one moment since he'd left Rangoon, yet although he'd longed for her unspeakably, he'd thought of her as comparatively safe under the protection of the hard-headed George Hough. But, Rangoon would be the first object of attack if the British felt obliged to send a fleet to Burma. And twenty George Houghs in that case could not protect Ann.

From that moment his peace of mind was gone. In vain the captain assured him that no such attack was imminent and that every precaution would be taken if the town were bombarded to give the Europeans opportunity to escape.

"You don't know the Burmans," insisted Adoniram. "Has the *Flying Squirrel* started back as yet?"

Captain Leigh smiled comically. "Fortunately for you, my dear Judson, she sailed from here several days ago and so far as I have been able to ascertain, there'll be no more boats leaving here for many months. You are forced, you see, by every circumstance to remain and recover your strength."

But it was not alone the Burmans whom Captain Leigh did not know. His knowledge didn't include Adoniram!

"I have a little money, captain, perhaps three hundred rupees. Would that be enough to hire a palanquin to take me to Madras?" Adoniram raised himself on one elbow and looked beseechingly into the Englishman's face. "Don't try to dissuade me, sir. You have been the perfect Samaritan. Add to my already heaped-up obligations by making it possible for me to start at once for Madras."

"But, Judson, what protection will a dead husband be to your wife?"

"I'm not to die, captain! I'm merely doomed to suffer until I'm fit for use! My wife— Captain, she's such a little thing, with hands like a delicate child's. I think of them so often—such small, warm fingers—I—" Adoniram dropped back on his pillow, his throat filled up.

Leigh cleared his own throat. "I'll see what I can do about the palanquin, Judson," he said gruffly and went out.

On the tenth day after his arrival at Masulipatam, that fine gentleman, Captain Leigh, helped Adoniram settle himself into a four-bearer palanquin, which he had stored with little comforts, and started him off on the three-hundred-mile journey to Madras.

Actually on the way home, much of Adoniram's nervousness left him. The palanquin was very comfortable indeed. It really was an enclosed bed, eight feet long and four feet wide with shutters that admitted air and shut out some of the heat and dust. Adoniram, for the three weeks required for the journey, gave himself over to getting well. His eyes would not permit him to read or to take pleasure in watching the world of the Indian seacoast through which he was passing. So he slept and ate and thrust disturbing thoughts out of his mind. The litter was his lodging house by night, as well as his coach by day. The bearers who belonged to Captain Leigh were decent fellows. And when at last, the palanquin was set down in the yard of the British mission at Madras, excepting for the weakness of his eyes, Adoniram was in fair health again.

This was the 8th of April, 1818.

The very day of his arrival he began to look for passage

to Rangoon. But he was told that nobody was going to Rangoon, these days; there was too much danger of being caught by war. Even the quietly efficient Englishmen of the mission were not able to help him and the government chose to ignore the American missionary's pleas. As day after day slipped by in vain endeavor, Adoniram's never too abundant patience deserted him and he became obsessed with the idea that Ann was in trouble. His usual love for intellectual intercourse—that for which he had starved so long—could not counteract his increasing anxiety. He haunted the harbor from daylight to dark, talking to seamen until there was not a native or foreign captain between Madras and Calcutta who was unaware of the fact that Adoniram Judson was frantic to reach Rangoon.

Only once did his normal interest in things of the mind and spirit get the better of his impatience to be gone. One afternoon, late in July, when the heat and discomfort on the waterfront had driven him back earlier than his wont to the mission, he found his hosts, Mr. Thompson and Mr. Loveless, in acrimonious debate at the tea table.

Adoniram slipped dejectedly into his place and as he sipped a refreshing cup, listened at first with only half an ear, then with awakening eagerness.

"She was French to the core, insane and blasphemous!" ejaculated Chaplain Thompson.

"No! No!" protested Loveless, the missionary, "you do her an injustice, indeed you do, my dear chaplain! She was a rare spirit, a soul caught up by the rapture of God."

"Twaddle! Fiddle-dee-dee!" spluttered Thompson, his round red face redder than ever. "She was a poor wisp of a French thing, full of lust and too cracked for any man to marry her after she'd killed her husband. So she committed as indecent a sacrilege as any it's been my painful privilege to observe. She declared Jesus Christ to be her lover, her bridegroom! Bah! The enormity of it, the—"

"Her spiritual lover, spiritual, chaplain!" shouted Love-

COMMON ANCESTRY

less, wiping his drooping brown mustache. "Be as near fair as it's possible for an established Church-man to be when speaking of a Catholic."

Thompson leaned toward Loveless, choking. Adoniram, keenly interested and a little bit amused, leaped to the rescue.

"My dear hosts, what or who on earth has upset the entente cordiale of the mission? I'm consumed with curiosity."

"Madame Guyon, Mr. Judson, only poor innocent Madame Guyon!" replied Loveless.

"Innocent! She was a medieval hussy, sir," gasped Thompson.

"You mean she is dead?" asked Adoniram. "Do cease quarreling and tell me, one of you."

The two Englishmen glared at each other. Adoniram suddenly burst into delighted laughter. "What would your church members say if they heard their two shepherds quarreling over a woman? Come, Mr. Thompson, you begin the tale and when you've finished, permit Loveless to contradict all you've said!"

Both his hosts were cooler now and smiling a little, though grimly. Thompson poured himself a scalding cup of tea and said gruffly, "Madame Guyon was a French woman who died about a hundred years ago. She didn't like the ritualism of the Catholic church although I notice she always kept a father confessor hanging about and so she evolved a very difficult method of placing herself in direct communion with the Almighty. She called the method Quietism, and wrote a lot of tosh—I beg your pardon, Loveless—she wrote a great deal on the subject, among other things an autobiography. A very handsome copy of the biography was sent here from home lately, and my fellow shepherd and I've both read it. Hence these tears." The chaplain had talked himself into his usual state of good humor. "Have I stated the case honestly, Loveless?" he added, urbanely.

"Quite," replied Loveless. Then he turned to Adoniram. "She is extreme and a bit hysterical, at times, but nevertheless, to my mind, she preached a great doctrine. Here, I'll let her speak for herself."

He took a leather-bound book from the window ledge and turned the pages rapidly. "Here's the point where she tells of the beginning of her conception of a different way of worship. She was seeking by prayer to place herself in contact with God and she couldn't compass it. She suffered a great despair and at last went to a priest, newly come out of a five years' solitude, to whom she described her difficulties. She says, 'He presently replied, It is, madame, because you seek without, what you have within. Accustom yourself to seek God in your heart and you will find Him there. Having said these words, he left me. They were to me like the stroke of a dart which penetrated through my heart. I felt at this instant a very deep wound, a wound so delightful that I desired not to be cured.—O my Lord, thou wast in my heart and demanded only a simple turning of my heart inward to make me perceive Thy presence. O Infinite Goodness! How was I running hither and thither to seek Thee, how was my life a burden to me although my happiness was within myself.—O Beauty, ancient and new, why have I known Thee so late?—Thou becamest my King and my heart Thy kingdom, wherein Thou didst reign supreme and performed all Thy sacred will.'"

Loveless closed the book. "I ask you, friend Judson, as an unprejudiced man, does that sound like the words of a hussy?"

"No!" As Adoniram made this emphatic reply he put out his hand for the autobiography. But the chaplain forestalled him.

"Wait a bit! I don't like to be called a scandalmonger! Allow me to read an extract." He in turn paged through the book. "Ha! Listen to this! Madame Guyon urged this priest who had given her the excellent advice, to become her spiritual director and confessor. Wisely, he demurred, but finally agreed to pray over the matter. And did so only to have, he reported, God say to him, 'Fear not that charge. She is My spouse!'—He thereupon went to Madame Guyon and agreed to take charge of her. She was, naturally, overpowered. 'What (said I to myself), a frightful monster of iniquity who has done so much to offend my God, now to be declared His spouse! My husband was out of humor with my devotion. What, said he, you love Christ so much that you love me no longer!—So little did he comprehend that the true conjugal love is that which the Lord forms Himself in the heart that loves Him.'"

The chaplain tossed the book to the floor. "Offensive! Very offensive!"

"You interpret too literally, perhaps, chaplain," protested Adoniram. "I don't endorse what you've read but frankly what Mr. Loveless quoted struck a great chord in me. I wish that I might read the book."

"You may have my share in it and welcome," replied Thompson, pouring a fourth cup of tea for himself and looking more than ever to be on the verge of a stroke of apoplexy. "I hope Mrs. Judson won't object to having the French woman in the house!"

Adoniram smiled. "And you, Loveless?"

"Of course, Judson! with one proviso, that the next time we meet you tell me frankly what you receive from the lady in the way of spiritual comfort. I received a great deal."

The chaplain snorted. "Let me pour you more tea, Loveless. It's the sovereign remedy for a rush of blood to the head. And you too, dear Judson, have another as a preventive!"

"Unfortunately my eyes won't let me read for a while but I'll take the preventive anyhow," chuckled Adoniram.

The tea party ended with a hearty laugh and Adoniram

tucked "Madame Guyon" away in the little sandalwood chest he was taking back to Ann. He was convinced that an unguessed treasure lay waiting for him within these leather covers and he prayed that he and Ann might be spared to seek the treasure together.

He would have persuaded Loveless to talk further to him about Quietism the next day, had not the long-sought-for, the much-prayed-for passage to Rangoon been found. The English captain of a little trading boat came to the mission for morning prayers and after the service Adoniram seized upon him.

The skipper was not in the Oriental trade for his health! He told Adoniram that he'd give him passage for the exorbitant sum of 167 rupees. Adoniram did not even think of wincing. He instantly counted out half the passage money and rushed into his room to pack his scanty belongings. The ship sailed at noon that day, the 20th of July.

They made an easy trip, dropping anchor at the mouth of the Rangoon River twenty-five miles below Rangoon on the evening of August 2nd. When the pilot came aboard the next morning, Adoniram demanded news of the mission.

"There is no mission, O foreigner!" grunted the pilot. "Three weeks ago, all the people sailed for Calcutta. They were afraid of the cholera and the printer wouldn't do printing for the viceroy. If they had waited a little while, things might have been better. The old viceroy has been recalled to Amarapura."

"Who is the new viceroy?" asked Adoniram.

"I don't know him," replied the Burman, evasively.

There was nothing to be done but pace the deck until the Shwé Dagôn pagoda, the one permanent fact in a world of change, gleamed through the early twilight and the ship once more made anchor. As Adoniram stood in the customs-house, impatiently waiting for the Burmese inspector to finish preparations for a chew of betel and begin the examination of his handful of luggage, he suddenly observed in the flickering light of the earth-oil lamp, the horsehide trunk with which Ann and he had begun their honeymoon. It stood in a corner under a pile of boxes.

"That's Ma Judson's luggage!" he cried.

"Yes," said the Burman, "she returned two weeks ago from the boat."

"Returned?" shouted Adoniram.

The Burman started a voluble explanation but Adoniram would not pause to hear it. He left his carpet bag gaping in the official's brown hands and ran out of the customs-house, across the rotting wharf and into the familiar flooded streets.

Once more, the sad, silly town in the rain!

He ran across the empty bazaar and up the Pagoda Road, turned down his own lane and opened his own gate. There was a light in the house. He leaped from stepping stone to stepping stone and up to the veranda. There he paused for very excess of emotion. The light shone through the window, throwing Mr. Beg Pardon into silhouette and it shone through the door revealing the familiar table in the living-room, and it shone on Ann's face lifted startled from her book.

He was home to the heaven of Ann's arms.

CHAPTER X

THE ZAYAT

IT was midnight before they finished telling their stories. Ann's was as heart stirring as Adoniram's.

For a little while after his departure, all at the mission went smoothly. But about the time Ann began to look for his return, the old viceroy was called to a position in the king's council and the new viceroy did not arrive till March. During the interregnum, robbery and murder held high carnival in Rangoon and the Houghs became uneasy. Hough worried constantly about the womenfolks.

When the new viceroy arrived, one of his first acts was to order Hough to come to the palace and explain his business in Burma.

"The foreign animal," ran the viceroy's message, "is to come to me with truth on his tongue or I will write it with his heart's blood."

Thus encouraged, poor Hough found it doubly hard to be dependent on Ann as interpreter. He firmly believed the viceroy would attack her. As it turned out, under Ann's management, the investigation resolved itself into a business consultation in which it was agreed that beside a heavy tax of five ticals of flowered silver a month, the mission would pay the viceroy personally five sicca rupees. After this, for a short time, there was quiet at the mission. Then cholera broke out in Rangoon and day and night the air was filled with the beating of the gongs by which the Burmans endeavored to frighten off the death nats. Day and night, through the rain, the unceasing booming of many gongs. It was these, Ann thought, that finally broke the Houghs' morale.

THE ZAYAT

It was at this point in Ann's story that Adoniram himself became conscious of the deep, murmurous beating that swept in from the jungle.

"You have no fear, Nancy?" he asked.

"Oh, yes, 'Don, I was and am afraid. But—well, let me finish my story and you'll see just how much of a silly coward I am. Mr. Hough heard a month ago that there was going to be a war between England and Burma and when English ships began to leave the river, he urged me to go with him and Mrs. Hough to Serampore until things were better. He held out to me that we'd be able to discover your fate, once we got clear of this 'pestilential spot.' And I want you to believe I was more influenced by that, 'Don, than by fear of the cholera. But I held out against him until three weeks ago. Then we heard that no more English ships were to be allowed to enter Burma and so we were certain that if you were living, you'd not be permitted to return. Then I decided to leave and seek you.

"We sold everything here that we couldn't pack into trunks except Felix Carey's table and chair and put the place in Koo-chil's and Ma Baik's and her husband's hands. There was just one English ship left in the harbor and we went aboard her on July 5th. Yes, I deserted my post, Adoniram! There's no other way to describe it. I deserted the mission to Burma."

Adoniram kissed her. She shook her head and smoothed his dark hair with the old loved gesture, then went on:

"We were several days going down river. Something was queer about the vessel. Just before we crossed the bar into the gulf, the captain discovered that she was improperly loaded, so they cast anchor and prepared to put in a week or so redoing the job.

"Adoniram, the instant that anchor splashed into the red water, I knew why the ship had been stopped. I knew that God had spoken to Ann Judson.—I refused to hear another word from the Houghs but I made the captain send me up here in the long boat. Of course, I had to lose my passage money. I got back to Rangoon on the 20th. The customs officials wouldn't let my trunk through but they washed their hands of *me*. And here I waited—under God's orders—my dearest husband—"

And so, once more, the Judsons were alone in Burma. They were very poor. The little money realized from the sale of the furniture had gone for passage money. Hough had taken the printing press with him. The remittances from the American Baptists were a year overdue. But they had the garden and three servants so overjoyed to see Adoniram and Ann again settled at the mission that they volunteered to work for their food until better times came.

Adoniram's thought while at Madras had been that the attempt to reach Chittagong by sea having been so complete a failure, he would, if he found all well at Rangoon, attempt to accomplish his errand by a trip over land. But Ann could not be left behind now, nor could she undertake such a heavy journey. The visit to the king was thrust further into the future than ever, it seemed, for every reason.

The two missionaries had many long talks on an immediate program during the days that followed Adoniram's return. Ann was in favor of his leaving her and making the journey to Chittagong. Adoniram absolutely vetoed the idea and at last put forward a concrete plan on which he invited no discussion.

"Somehow," he said, "we've got to gather enough money together, after we've bought a few sticks of furniture, to buy the bit of land between the mission and the Pagoda Road. I'm going to build a zayat there and preach to the worshipers as they pass by. Viceroys or no viceroys, gaing-ôks or no gaing-ôks, kings or no kings, Buddhas or no Buddhas, I'm going to begin my appointed task."

"A zayat!" exclaimed Ann.

In the shadow of every pagoda was a rest house, or zayat, used by the Buddhists for meditation and prayer. It was

THE ZAYAT

in the zayat too that the monks sat to expound the principles of Buddha.

"A zayat!" Ann repeated. "But you *are* astute, Adoniram! Who but you who know Buddhism so well would have thought of using a stronghold of Gautama from which to expound Jesus Christ! We'll have to dig into what's left of our home gifts. There's about a hundred dollars remaining, I think."

Adoniram shook his head, ruefully. "I'm afraid the land and the zayat and furniture can't come out of that."

"We can go without furniture," declared Ann. "By the way, that sandalwood box could be sold for a great many ticals, though I hate to part with anything you give me. Is the old book of any value?"

"Yes!" said Adoniram. "When my eyes are well and we have leisure, I think we're going to find untold treasure in that book."

"That's interesting," was Ann's absent-minded comment. "I'm thinking, 'Don, you'd better go to your old friend the builder and see what you can do with him."

"I wish Maung Shway-gnong were here to advise me," said Adoniram. "No news at all of him, I suppose?"

"None! And if he were here, he'd certainly advise you not to build a zayat."

"Oh, I'd bring him around," replied Adoniram, picking up his umbrella, preparatory to setting off.

"Humph!" said Ann. Then she cried, turning very pale, "Adoniram, there are white people coming in our gate!"

Adoniram whirled to look. Two men and two women were moving hesitatingly into the mission yard. It was impossible to guess who they might be, but they were *white!* And Ann and Adoniram rushed down the steps to greet them.

The American Baptists, after all, were neither asleep nor negligent.

These were four American missionaries: Mr. and Mrs.

James Colman, Mr. and Mrs. Edward Wheelock. All of them were young and both the men were ordained ministers. They brought with them books, clothing, money and many loving messages and gifts from the Judsons' families and friends. The mission welcomed them as the direct answer to prayer ought to be welcomed.

There was but one fly in the ointment. Wheelock, a delicate boy with transparent skin and sunken blue eyes, was so ill that he had to be put to bed as soon as he arrived and Colman, also delicate but with more reserve strength in his gaunt frame than Wheelock had, was so exhausted that he fell asleep over a cup of tea.

Adoniram, after every one had retired for the night, shook his head sadly. "They're a godsend and they're as lovely persons as could have been sent us, but, Ann, both those boys are consumptive!"

"I'm afraid poor Brother Wheelock won't live a year!" sighed Ann as she brushed her brown curls.

"I shall write to America," said Adoniram, "and warn the Society against sending out any more missionaries whose zeal for the pagan must be inextricably mingled with zeal for a warm climate! Anyhow, Rangoon's a terrible place for consumptives. Colman isn't as far gone as Wheelock and he has a more sprightly nature so he'll fight longer. But they're both doomed men."

"Poor boys!" sighed Ann.

"Boys!" chuckled Adoniram. "They're each as old as you!"

Ann tried to examine herself in the only mirror remaining in the house, her husband's shaving glass, four inches square. "If the rest of my face is as leather-like as the section I can see, only the record in the old Bible at home would convince anybody of that fact.—'Don, my beauty is quite gone."

Adoniram lifted the lamp and by its fluttering glow scrutinized her smiling face deliberately. Then he said,

THE ZAYAT

slowly, "Ann, it's my studied and cold-blooded conviction that you have a face of the most extraordinary beauty. You are tinted like old ivory, I'll admit, but your features are perfect and nothing can mar them or their expression."

"Mercy! Stop! Stop! You overwhelm me!" protested Ann.

"It's the truth and you adore hearing it! Give me a kiss in pay, Mrs. Judson," demanded Adoniram.

Ann paid, with interest, and then as she resumed her hair brushing said, "I don't want to appear too worldly minded, but you don't know what a joy those new dresses are to me. Do you realize that this is the first new frock I've had since we were married?"

"I know! Poor Nancy! As a provider I'm a disgrace to my New England ancestors!"

They smiled at each other in complete understanding. Then Ann remarked, "And I know those white linen suits warm the very cockles of your heart. You do hate the black merino."

"I washed my white clothes on board the *Flying Squirrel* till both the soft water and I gave out," admitted Adoniram. "The crew must have made way with all of them. My sea chest was empty when they put me ashore.—Ann, is that vanity or old maidishness?"

"A good deal of both, I should say," answered Ann judicially.

"Thank you!" Adoniram joined her in laughter.

They completed their preparations for bed, and just as he was about to extinguish the light, Adoniram said:

"It's good to have them under our roof. We are singularly blessed, in all things, Ann!"

"Perhaps we are," she murmured.

And so the zayat came to be built. Wheelock remained ill, but Colman was soon well enough to lend a hand. The new building was placed cheek by jowl with monasteries, nat shrines, lesser pagodas and images and several Burmese zayats. It was a small house only eighteen feet by twenty-seven but carefully planned. It was raised from the ground four feet, Burmese fashion, and roofed with bamboo. The front third was a veranda, directly on the road. Behind the veranda was a small room to be used for public worship and at the rear an entry way leading into the mission yard.

As far as the missionaries knew, the authorities in Rangoon paid no attention to what they were doing. This might have been due to the monthly bribe of five rupees. Colman was troubled about this method of protecting the mission and for that matter it troubled Adoniram too. But he would not listen either to his associates' protests or to those of his own conscience. As he had declared to Ann, he was going to begin to preach without regard to any other fact on earth. He was utterly weary of shifting his plans in response to the brutal vagaries of the government of Rangoon.

There had been, of course, the usual delays incident to accomplishing any job in Burma, so that it was spring before the zayat was actually ready for use. They opened it on the 4th of April.

It was a Sabbath day, with a burning dawn and a jungle still as death. Immediately after their early breakfast, the mission household followed Adoniram to the zayat and held worship in the little meeting room. Then Adoniram went alone to the veranda and seated himself on a mat.

People were passing steadily to and from the Shwé Dagôn. The young clergyman sat in silence for several moments. His mouth was dry. His heart throbbed heavily.

An old woman walking by with a dak blossom glowing in her hair called him a ribald name. Adoniram's head came up with a jerk. He lifted his deep voice and in the Burmese vernacular uttered the noble invitation of Isaiah.

" 'Ho, every one that thirsteth, come ye to the waters, and he that hath no money, come ye, buy and eat! Come, buy wine and milk without money and without price.—Incline your ear and come unto me; hear and your soul shall

THE ZAYAT

live and I will make an everlasting covenant with you.—
Seek ye the Lord while He may be found, call ye upon Him
while He is near—'"

He paused.

The teeming stillness of the jungle. From the monastery
to the north, the voices of many little boys repeating the
words of the Buddha Gautama. A tiny knot of Burmans
gathered in the shade of the fig tree across the road and
spoke loudly of the obscenity of the foreign animal's clothing. A Burmese gentleman who was sheltered from the sun
by a pink-fringed umbrella with an eight-foot handle said
something to the servant who held it and quickened his
steps. But he had not passed out of hearing before Adoniram fed him another promise from Isaiah:

"'Let the wicked forsake his way and the unrighteous
man his thoughts and let him return unto the Lord and He
will have mercy upon him; and to our God, for He will
abundantly pardon.'"

Thus, all the morning.

In the afternoon when the palm trees cast long, sword-like
shadows along the zayat steps, the mission family joined
Adoniram on the veranda and he preached his first sermon
in the Burmese tongue. Young Wheelock had insisted on
leaving his bed for the occasion and he sat with beautiful,
fever bright eyes on Adoniram, moving his lips to repeat the
few words he understood and clasping his little wife's fingers
in his own. When the last hymn was being sung a smear of
red appeared on his pale lips and Mrs. Wheelock led him
back to the house.

The others followed quickly. The poor fellow had a
severe hemorrhage and it was dark before, by their united
efforts, they had stopped it. When all was quiet again,
Adoniram stole out to the front porch for a moment alone.

It had been a day of tremendous strain.

The Shwé Dagôn was glorious in the moonlight. Adoniram nodded to it and said softly, "Men can't live and die by

a philosophy, Prince Gautama! Hence the nats—the Mr. Beg Pardon in every home. If you don't give people God, my prince, they will make themselves demons!"

"But how do you know God?" asked a familiar voice.

Adoniram started. An emaciated, haggard face, old ivory in the moonlight, appeared beside Mr. Beg Pardon's house. It was Maung Shway-gnong. He came softly across the veranda and seated himself as casually as though he and Adoniram had parted only an hour before.

"But, my dear teacher, where have you been this time?" cried Adoniram. "You come and go like a nat!"

"I was in trouble," replied Maung Shway-gnong, lifting his unhappy eyes to Adoniram's. "I have been on a long journey, trading among the Shans."

"What was your trouble, O teacher?" asked Adoniram, gently.

"But you know my trouble, best of pupils. It came from too great an interest in you. The viceroy and the gaing-ôk incited the golden presence at Rangoon against me. His majesty has hunted me as the tiger stalks the sick buffalo. I have been north to the snow-topped hills of the Kachins and south to the coral beaches of Malay and east to the jungles of Cambodia. But I have come back."

"Then the king has given up his hunt?" asked Adoniram, eagerly.

"The golden feet," replied Maung Shway-gnong, carefully, "will, it is thought, shortly take a journey to seek amusement in the celestial regions."

"The old king is dying?" demanded the missionary.

The Burman's face was sardonic in the moonlight. "I taught you long ago, that the lord of life and air is immortal. We Burmans merely admit that he is going out of our earthly sight. But, my pupil, that news isn't what brought me back. I only learned that news this evening. I returned in the face of the hunt to ask you the question, Who

THE ZAYAT

is God? And I find you murmuring to the Buddha Gautama!"

Adoniram turned these last statements over in his mind. He doubted very much if the teacher had overcome his fears and started back for Rangoon before he heard that the king was dying. But Adoniram was unfeignedly glad to see his old friend although he no longer needed his services as a teacher. He resolved to ask no awkward questions.

"Would you like to hear about a long adventure that befell me, while you were away?" suggested Adoniram.

"Later," replied Maung Shway-gnong, "but I have come a long way and in the face of danger to ask you, Who is God."

The man was in earnest! Adoniram gathered his resources.

"Who is this God?" shouted the teacher. "You gave me a thought that won't let me rest—a being, you said, without beginning or end. That's impossible."

"If there's no eternal being," asked Adoniram, "how do you account for this world and all we see?"

"Fate," replied the Burman.

"Fate? But, my teacher, the cause must always be equal to the effect. I raise this mat. There is an ant crawling beneath it. Suppose I was invisible. Would a wise man say the ant had raised the mat? Now, fate isn't even an ant. Fate is a word; that's all. It's not an agent, not a thing. What is fate?"

"The fate of creatures is the influence their good or bad deeds have on their future existence," replied Maung Shway-gnong.

"Ah, but if influence be exerted, there must be an exerter. If there be a determination, there must be a determiner."

Maung Shway-gnong stared in concentration. "No, there is no determiner. There can be no eternal thing."

"Consider this point," urged Adoniram. "It's a main

point of true wisdom. Wherever there's an execution of purpose, there must be an agent."

"Ah, yes," agreed the teacher, "if you admit there is a purpose, you admit God. But I can't admit the purpose."

"Who is it sits in judgment, my teacher, stating which of your deeds is good or bad?"

"The precepts of Buddha Gautama decide that in this life," answered Maung Shway-gnong promptly. "My dear pupil, that's where our religion excels yours. There he stands," pointing to the Shwé Dagôn, "the gentle Lord of Compassion, where the simplest of us may commune with him." Both men turned toward the spire. Wind stirred the palm leaves and the casuarina tree sighed. "The Buddha is *there*," the Burman went on, softly. "How can one's soul commune with an *agent?* Could you, O friend, sit in your place of religious exercises and see your God? Nay, you could not. You were obliged to bring your God to earth in the shape of the Christ you call God's Son."

"But Buddha Gautama is not at yonder shrine, Maung Shway-gnong. There are eight of his hairs imbedded in the solid bricks of its walls. That's all. And isn't it a little grotesque to do reverence to eight hairs of a man's head?"

"Is it more grotesque than to think a being like your God would enter a woman's womb and be born as a human baby?" asked Maung Shway-gnong. Adoniram stirred in protest but the Burman raised a thin hand. "These comments aren't worthy of either of us," he protested.

"You are right," agreed Adoniram.

The teacher leaned toward him, brown eyes probing hazel eyes. "Let there be only truth between us, O pupil! Tell me. Does your soul commune with God?"

Adoniram drew a deep breath. He clenched his fingers on his knees while every force of his intellect concentrated on his friend's question. Within the house Ann spoke soothingly to some one. The nightingale sobbed in the garden. Remotely the harsh cry of the king crow on his night hunt rose and fell—

"Maung Shway-gnong," said Adoniram, "I believe absolutely in God. I believe without doubt or waver. But to me He is the Great Unknown. I cannot find Him." He ended with a dry sob.

"Amé!" ejaculated the teacher. Then a startlingly beautiful smile illuminated his saturnine face. "You are honest! Only a very great teacher is honest." And to Adoniram's astonishment, Maung Shway-gnong prostrated himself in the manner used by the Burmans only toward their most venerated monks.

He put out his hand in protest but Maung Shway-gnong ignored the gesture. "Lord," he went on, addressing him as he would address a monk, "Lord, you have removed my last doubt of the feasibility of believing in God. If *you* can believe, yet not understand, so also can I. But as to Jesus Christ and his teachings;—Lord, I cannot take him as God. He was a man like Gautama."

Adoniram could not speak at once. That, after six years of hope deferred, even this much conversion should come about so simply and with so fine a type of Burman was too much to bear with equanimity. But after a little time, during which the teacher arranged the inevitable betel cud, he said, softly:

"Yes, my teacher, the two had many things in common, purity and gentleness and great wisdom and compassion. But the Buddha had no such love for human beings as Christ. Jesus Christ died on the cross to save mankind."

"That could not be," declared the Burman flatly.

"Every man is full of sin," said Adoniram.

The teacher nodded heartily.

Adoniram went on, slowly, his voice moving because he himself was so much moved. "The man who sins does so because he is alienated from God. Christ came to earth to remove that alienation. He accomplished it by His infinite wisdom, His example of obedience to God's commands even to die on the cross. Ever since, those that become Christ's disciples are released from the punishment they deserve in the hereafter."

"No! That I never can believe," ejaculated Maung Shway-gnong. "My mind is very stiff on this point, that all existence involves in itself principles of misery and destruction. The whole universe is only reproduction and destruction."

"The whole universe is God," insisted Adoniram.

The Burman rubbed his chin and moved his head and shoulders uneasily. "Too large a thought— Let us talk no more at present, my mind is heavy with ideas. I shall come again, lord. But now if it please you, I go."

"Go then," returned Adoniram with a smile.

Maung Shway-gnong prostrated himself once more, then departed as he had come, around a corner of the house.

Adoniram rose and went to find Ann.

CHAPTER XI

JESUS CHRIST'S MAN

THE following day, Koo-chil brought word that the bazaar was full of rumors of the old king's illness. The Burmans were very fearful for the future. The succession of a king was invariably accomplished by one aspirant to the throne murdering all other aspirants, and the murder-contagion usually spread throughout the kingdom. Rangoon, the capital of one of the chief provinces of Burma was always in anarchy at such a time. But for the present, pending the death of the lord of life, the town was sullenly quiet, each householder keeping his spear within reach and his knife hanging round his neck.

The members of the mission family hoped that, in its preoccupation with political matters, Rangoon would forget to make trouble about the zayat. And for a little while their hopes were fulfilled and Adoniram continued on the course he had laid out. The Colmans worked industriously at the language with Ann as their teacher. But poor Wheelock did not improve and it was decided that a sea voyage might prolong his life. This could not be undertaken, however, until an English boat again ventured into the harbor.

To Adoniram, sitting in the zayat, hour after hour, and day after day, all these happenings were less real than the astounding fact that at last he was shouldering the almost intolerable burden of saving from hell the souls of eight million Burmans. It was his never-remitting consciousness of this burden that enabled him to chain his active mind and body to the zayat, week after week, calling his great news to the shadows of sambur and tiger moving stealthily through the jungle and to the unheeding brown pagans who pattered through the rains now falling daily.

Hour after hour of torrential downpour, and of no single inquiry if one except the probings of Maung Shway-gnong who came only after dark. And then, one June day, Ma Baik, the cross-eyed, who had done a good deal of sub-rosa muttering against the zayat, stopped at the veranda on her way home from the bazaar. She carried a Chinese umbrella from which the rain sprayed like a waterfall. She looked vixenish but cold, under her short black Shan coat, with tamein kilted to her knees and her legs covered with gooseflesh. She meant to be extremely offensive for she marched up the steps and stood before Adoniram without removing her sandals.

"Foreign teacher," said Ma Baik, deliberately, "we are going to move, me and my husband, Maung Nau, and my chickens and my water buffalo. We shall go back to the fishing boat."

"And why, O Ma Baik?" asked Adoniram.

"Because you insult Buddha Gautama with this zayat. There can be nothing but bad luck in this yard."

"Come! Come, Ma Baik, you have lived too long with us and have been too kind to us to make threats," said Adoniram. "Take off your sandals and sit on the mat with me and let us discuss the matter."

"Me, put a bare foot in this house of devils? You don't understand," her voice beginning to rise shrilly, "you don't see that a blight is descending on the yard! Why is yonder white animal bleeding to death at the mouth? Consider? Are we all to stay thus and no one try to drive you from this accursed house you've built to your God?"

Adoniram hesitated for a moment, seeking the right word. An old woman carrying a basket of green figs on her head, attracted by the prospect of a quarrel, paused before the steps. Adoniram replied to her inquiring look:

"Ma Baik is angry because I'm trying to do what my Lord has ordered done."

"Aye?" queried the old woman, peering into Adoniram's

face. "Aye? They've all told me you were a savage but you speak the tongue better than many a monk."

Ma Baik thrust furiously at the newcomer with her muddy sandal and shrieked, "Begone, Ma So!"

But Ma Baik had met her match. The grandam pinioned the younger woman's ankle and with lightning-like quickness ripped off her tamein. "Go home and cover your nakedness, Ma Baik?" she advised.

Ma So had committed a criminal offense in uncovering Ma Baik! Adoniram gasped and half rose. Ma Baik burst into tears and darted under the veranda. But the old woman smiled reassuringly at the missionary.

"If my son would use sense, he'd soon make a good tempered woman of my daughter-in-law," she said. Then, thrusting the tamein under the porch, she added, "Go, daughter, and report this to the viceroy!"

A low sob was the only answer.

"Will you come up out of the rain?" asked Adoniram politely.

Ma Baik's mother-in-law hesitated, put one muddy foot on the lowest step and then turned back. "One risks too much," she muttered. "Tell me as I stand here what your Lord has ordered you to do, O foreign teacher!"

"He has commanded me," replied Adoniram in a voice that would carry well beneath the veranda, "to tell the Burmans that there is a way by which all their sins may be wiped out and they may enter into eternal peace the instant they leave this life."

"Aye?" exclaimed Ma So.

All this while the basket of figs had remained neatly balanced on her grizzled head. Now without removing her eyes from Adoniram's she slid the basket to the veranda floor and leaning toward the missionary deliberately studied his features.

"It is a face of truth and tenderness," she muttered. "I am a woman of many sins. My karma is altogether bad.

Do you say these sins may be wiped out? How can that be, teacher, when the Law knows only unmovable justice?"

"That law is the law of Buddha Gautama," answered Adoniram. "The Law I obey is the law not of a man but of the Creator of the Universe Who sent His Son to the earth to tell men how to be eased of their sins."

The sobs under the veranda had ceased. For years, Adoniram had tried to enveigle Ma Baik into listening to him! Amusing as was this contretemps, he believed there must be a Providence in it and he went on clearly:

"That Son was Jesus Christ. Give heed, Ma So, while I tell you of Him."

The most moving, the most perfect story in human history; Adoniram's intense pale face above his white clothing; the gloom of rain and crowding bamboo and Madeira vine; the staring, fast breathing old woman in her drenched jacket and tamein; and the deep tender voice of the young preacher; Ann coming to the door of the meeting room, stared at this picture, then her eyes filled with tears and she drew back, unobserved.

It was an hour before Adoniram neared the end of the story. " 'And he went a little farther and fell on his face and prayed, saying, O my Father, if it be possible, let this cup pass from me! Nevertheless, not as I will but as Thou wilt—' "

Ma So's old face worked. She twisted her fingers.

" '—When Jesus therefore had received the vinegar, he said, "It is finished," and he bowed his head and gave up the ghost.—' "

Adoniram paused. The old woman wept for a moment, then she stooped and peered under the veranda. "My daughter, come out," she ordered in a subdued tone.

Ma Baik crept forth.

"You heard the foreign teacher expounding?" demanded Ma So.

"I heard," replied Ma Baik, meekly. "I never heard before."

"And you've lived all this time in the teacher's garden! Fool!" sniffed the mother-in-law. "Now, what is this about your calling the zayat a place of demons?"

Ma Baik threw out both her hands in appeal. "But I hadn't heard the story, O teacher! And what shall I do? The monk ordered me to speak so!"

"Tell the monk you obeyed him and tell him I said he must speak directly to me, that you are powerless," said Adoniram.

"And tell him I said I'd beat you if you moved from the teacher's yard," added Ma So.

Ma Baik's hard face twisted into an amused smile. "Beware of a man's relatives and of a bee's sting," she remarked. "Well, for once I will obey you, O Ma So!" and she unfurled the Chinese umbrella and disappeared into the garden.

Ma So grinned toothlessly and gathered up her basket of figs. Then she set it down to say, "I'm a very sinful old woman, teacher. Yet you say the Lord Jesus could remove the sins from my karma?"

"If you believe in Him," replied Adoniram.

She sighed and once more placed the basket on her head. This time she walked off with it into the dripping dusk. Adoniram rose to go, then paused as footsteps again approached the zayat and Ma So's old face once more peered up at him.

"Those words of the Lord Jesus," she said, "take hold on my very liver."

Before Adoniram could respond she again moved off, this time for good.

The next morning, when Adoniram entered the zayat, he found Ma So there with three or four men.

"We've come to hear about the Lord Jesus," said the old lady, "I and my husband and my two brothers. They will listen."

The men may have been brought under compulsion. But certainly they remained because of interest and delight.

They spent the entire day with Adoniram, plying him with questions and listening with eagerness to his replies.

Adoniram found it intoxicating. It seemed not too much to believe that after the lean years, a rush of spiritual plenty had suddenly appeared for the harvest. And when the next day and the next day the crowd grew, until a score of men and women were sitting around him, there could be no doubt that given opportunity, the Burmans would listen to teachings other than Buddha's.

There was one drawback. It was a shifting crowd. At first it seemed as if no single person ever appeared more than twice with the exception of Ma So and her son Maung Nau with Ma Baik. And as the days sped on the character of the inquirers changed. The earnest folk seemed to have passed on and there came in their stead a disorderly, impertinent string of idlers, glad to find an interesting place in which to pass the dragging hours of rain. Adoniram refused to converse with these men, sometimes walked out of the zayat and left them. Such groups as these were very exhausting.

In June, Ma So moved into the mission yard and, having discovered Ann, inveigled her into teaching her to read. Little by little she transferred her allegiance from Adoniram to his wife and her keen interest in Christianity faded when she found that its tenets were even stricter than the Buddha's. It was very trying, this casualness of the Burmese mind. In the weeks from April to June, Adoniram ran the gamut of feeling: from intoxicating faith in immediate success to a moderate surety that in the course of a year one convert beside Maung Shway-gnong might be made: for Maung Nau showed consistent interest.

They began to call Adoniram Jesus Christ's man in Rangoon, and it was a strange creature who coined the term. One of the viceroy's executioners came to Adoniram one morning, the first of the daily string of visitors, and after making a sheeko, said:

JESUS CHRIST'S MAN

"O lord teacher, I am an executioner."

"I know that from the brands on your face," replied Adoniram, trying not to show his horror.

"Will this Jesus you're telling about, remove these letters burned on my cheeks and forehead, if I bring him offerings?"

Adoniram hesitated.

"You're Jesus Christ's man, aren't you?" urged the man. "You know what he can do."

"If Christ were in Rangoon, to-day," said Adoniram, "and you went to Him, O executioner, and showed Him a heart of sorrow and repentance and a perfect faith in Him and His purity and power, He could remove your scars. If your faith and repentance were great enough now, though He is in heaven, He could do it. But how repentant are you? How sad are you? In whom do you believe, Jesus Christ or the Buddha Gautama?"

"I can't believe in what I can't see," said the Burman, sullenly, and he went away and although Adoniram tried to speak to him several times when he saw him skulking like the pariah dogs in the town, the executioner would have none of him. The man haunted Adoniram for he felt that his own faith had not risen to the occasion. And whenever passing children called "Jesus Christ's man," after him, he was depressed for hours after.

Maung Shway-gnong was a disappointment too. After his fine show of confidence and intellectual frankness, he had fallen back into his old habit of continuous questioning and spiritual bickering. He did not recede from his stand on the Deity but he rejected all else connected with Christianity. Yet Adoniram's reasoning powers appeared to fascinate him and when during an evening in the zayat, the teacher heard his old pupil down some popular Burman disputant, he would applaud and murmur, "I have knowledge, but here is pure wisdom."

One evening, the gardener, Maung Nau, and the teacher

were alone in the zayat with Adoniram. Maung Shway-gnong was particularly captious and for an hour tore the idea of the atonement to shreds. Adoniram sat for the most part, silent and discouraged. His attitude finally impressed the teacher and he too fell silent, his eyes uneasily on Adoniram's face.

It was then that Maung Nau spoke for the first time.

"My lord teacher," he said, "can you help me? I can't eat, I can't sleep for thinking of my many sins. Buddha can't take them from my karma. Out of the darkness and uncleanness of my whole life, I see no helper but Jesus Christ. I wish, O lord teacher, how much I wish to belong to Him!"

Maung Shway-gnong shuddered. "If one had no horror of persecution!"

Maung Nau's fat brown cheeks twitched and his eyes filled but his voice was steady. "I will certainly be tortured. But my mind is made up. If the lord teacher will show me how, I will belong to Christ."

"It's a terrible thought to me," said Adoniram sadly, "that through me you may be brought to suffering. Perhaps I may be able to save you from the worst, for if it comes to the point that you openly acknowledge God and Christ and are arrested, I will offer myself in your stead." His lips paled as he spoke but his hazel eyes were steady.

The two Burmans stared at him, slow to take in the idea. Then the teacher gave a short laugh. "It wouldn't be understood, I assure you. They'd merely crucify you both!"

"Why do you laugh, O tax collector and run-away?" demanded Maung Nau indignantly. "Is it humorous that the foreign lord so loves me that he'll give his body to suffer in my place, as Christ did? Do you cackle because he lives his religion as only one of the very highest of our monks does? And did you ever hear of one of them dying for one of his disciples?"

"Tut! Tut!" grunted Maung Shway-gnong. "The lord teacher hasn't died yet."

JESUS CHRIST'S MAN

"Nor shall he, for me," exclaimed the gardener. "I wouldn't permit it. But I won't forget that he offered."

"You make too much of it, friend," protested Adoniram. "As a matter of fact, I'm as filled with fear and horror as Maung Shway-gnong and it would take a gigantic effort on my part to keep my promise, though I'm sure God would enable me. But I'm not the stuff of which heroes are made, I assure you!"

Maung Nau gave him a deep look. "My mind is made up, lord teacher. If you'll show me how, I'll give myself to God."

"I will try to show you," replied Adoniram humbly and thankfully.

"How can one give oneself to the Unknowable?" cried Maung Shway-gnong, irritably.

"Jesus Christ has shown us how," answered Adoniram with renewed patience. The gardener had wiped all traces of discouragement from his mind.

The teacher mumbled crossly to himself.

Maung Nau grinned at him. "The tiger growls only when he's afraid," he observed.

Adoniram repressed a smile and addressed the gardener. "I must be very sure you're going to live according to Christ's teachings before I baptize you, friend. I'm going to put you on a month's trial. Suppose as a test of your understanding you go to Ma Judson and ask her to interpret while Maung Colman asks you questions."

Maung Nau leaped to his feet, only pausing to ask with a mischievous twinkle in his good brown eyes, "Won't it be a test, lord teacher, if I live in peace with Ma Baik, the best of wives, for a month?"

Adoniram laughed. "I'd almost say yes, O friend, were it not for the talk I've been hearing of your getting a second wife."

The gardener moved hurriedly out of the zayat.

CHAPTER XII

THE LOTUS LAKE

THE old king was a long time dying! But one day in mid-June, the viceroy announced that he'd been ordered to hurry up to Amarapura on state business and every one believed that the end had come. A hurried departure on the part of a Burman high official was a scene to cheer the saddest European heart. A great crowding on the beach; a rounding up of an enormous number of boats, half of which would prove unseaworthy before they were loaded and a quarter of which would founder after loading; an enormous bustle of messengers running back and forth between the wharf and the palace; hundreds of pariah dogs barking and fighting; elephants laden with members of the viceroy's household, the wives apparently carrying one garment at a time to be packed in the lacquered boxes on the decks of the canoes; water buffalo loaded with firewood and food supplies; and most prominent of all, the viceroy in a white robe roaring confused orders at every one from his howdah.

Only a few days after the viceroy's departure, word came to Rangoon that the king was gone and that his grandson Bagyi-daw had ascended the throne. There had been bloody work and nobody knew whether the carnage would extend to Rangoon or not. Most of the Burmans now dared hope that it would not. The viceroy would have been the center of any trouble and he was safely, or unsafely, out of reach on the Irrawaddy.

Within the mission, the chief interest lay in Maung Nau. The missionaries watched him unostentatiously but nonetheless carefully. But the Judsons long had known that he

THE LOTUS LAKE

was a man of great natural goodness and it did not take many weeks of observation to convince every one that his desire to embrace Christianity was sincere.

His wife, Ma Baik, and his mother, Ma So, were not at all enthusiastic over Maung Nau's aspirations. They thought that he was decidedly presumptuous to push ahead of them and no comments on their own dilatory attitude toward conversion served to lessen their scorn. Certainly as he had suggested Maung Nau's living with his wife, during this month of June, was a complete test of his Christian worth; to say nothing of his enduring his mother!

There were tremendous issues hanging on Maung Nau's baptism. It might mark the actual beginning of Christ's reign in Burma. It might, on the other hand, invite death and destruction into the mission. But, in spite of all advice to the contrary, Adoniram would consent to no skulking. He was determined to baptize the gardener where any one who wished to do so, could see it done.

There was a little lake up toward the great Pagoda, set sweetly among palm and acacia trees, with pink lotus jeweling its surface and with a fine, heroic statue of the Buddha on its edge. It was the only clean bit of water easily accessible outside of the water tanks.

Late in the afternoon of Sunday, June 27, 1819, the members of the mission family repaired to the lotus lake. The rain ceased as they neared the shore and the sun pierced through the dripping acacias and lighted the marble Gautama to warm beauty. The little sheet of water gleamed in a thousand opalescent tints. Curiously there was no sound of bird note or monastery gong. The high silver tinkle of the bells that crowned the Shwé Dagôn were the only music that attended Maung Nau's immersion. Adoniram's voice was too broken with emotion for the little group beside the Gautama to hear even his prayer.

The ceremony was over before passers-by could gather but as the minister and his convert came dripping up the bank, a monk appeared from among the palms and, calling out indignantly, rushed up to the mission group. It was the gaing-ôk.

"You think I don't know what this means, foreign animals?" he cried. "The Portuguese priest at Amarapura explained your ceremonies to me! You"—pointing a stout fore-finger at Maung Nau—"will answer severely for this. And you," giving Adoniram the benefit of the menacing digit, "have at last reached the point for which we've been waiting. I have a writing from the lord of life ordering you out of Burma."

Adoniram stepped before Maung Nau. Young Colman, sudden red in his thin cheeks, put his hand on Adoniram's arm, as if to hearten him. But, the dreaded moment having at last arrived, the older clergyman, to his own surprise, felt no fear.

"The writing, O gaing-ôk," he said quietly, "must have been from the old king, who has gone on to the celestial world. His writing now lacks authority. I have heard that the new lord of life is very fond of Europeans and so I would advise you to be careful how you move without the golden authority."

The old monk scowled thoughtfully, holding his yellow robes close that the wind might not blow them against Adoniram.

"Why not leave us in peace?" suggested the missionary, gently. "Surely one who has ascended so high needs no merit acquired from abusing a foreigner! You have attained to peace. Why make a Government 'eater' of yourself or a servant of the golden presence? Buddha never asked you to persecute non-believers. You remember what he said to the herdsman Dhaniya. *'I am the servant of none, said the Blessed One. I have no need to serve. Then rain if thou wilt, O sky!'*"

The old man's eyes softened. His lips parted, as if he would give the herdsman's reply, but he caught the words

THE LOTUS LAKE

back, firmly. "I have heard of your scholarship," he said coolly. "But I am not that buffalo Shway-gnong, to be moved by it."

He turned on his heel and made off through the trees, his robe still wrapped about him.

"He will go up to the new golden presence for a new writing!" gasped Maung Nau.

"I also shall go up to the golden presence," announced Adoniram, moving quickly off, Ann's hand in his.

"Do you really mean it, 'Don?" she asked.

"Yes. I do, Nancy. I'm sure the hour has struck," he replied.

"I'm afraid you're right," she sighed after a moment's thought. "What of Maung Nau?"

"He must stay in the mission house until we are ready to start, then he must come with us."

Colman spoke eagerly. "By we, I hope you mean to include me, sir?"

Adoniram nodded. "If we can make arrangements for our wives' protection, yes, Colman."

That evening which they had planned to spend in quiet rejoicing over the day's great event, was spent, instead, in anxious consultation over Adoniram's decision. All agreed that the petition to the new king was the next and essential move, but the difficulties that lay in the way of the trip seemed almost insurmountable.

There was poor Wheelock to be cared for and the three women. There was a boat for the journey to be bought, a passport procured as well as fitting gifts for the king and his officials. All this, with speed the chief element in the success of the trip, was coupled with the impossibility of accomplishing anything in Burma in a hurry.

Maung Nau, whose help as an old fisherman would have been invaluable in procuring a boat, they dared not let out of the house. But Maung Nau was of the opinion that his wife and mother would be as efficient as he on such an errand. Ann undertook to beguile the two women into action and was so successful that before noon on Monday, both Ma Baik and Ma So had set off on the search.

But with this accomplishment nothing else moved and July crawled by without even the purchase of a boat. Maung Shway-gnong, told of the emergency and urged to come to the rescue, was panic stricken and barricaded himself in his house where he remained for many weeks. Mercifully there was no more than the habitual disorder in Rangoon during the viceroy's absence so that both Adoniram and young Wheelock were able to leave the mission freely and after the purchase of the boat was made, early in August, they gave many hours a day to refitting the little craft.

Adoniram continued to give his mornings to the zayat. But the gaing-ôk had done his work well. Not a Burman came to his veranda after that memorable Sunday baptism. And in spite of the hopeful plans they were making, the missionary had his moments of depression, his days when even his work of translation could not crowd down entirely the lurking doubts of his own ability to do the task God had set him. It was the doubt that had been born on the *Flying Squirrel* and he told himself that it belonged to a sick and not to a well brain. Yet the doubt persisted, and beginning with this, by a natural progression of thinking, his memory brought him to the scene in the Madras mission when Madame Guyon was introduced to him. In the rush of events since his return to Rangoon he had all but forgotten the French woman. And one particularly dark and rainy morning in August, he took her autobiography to the zayat with him.

There could be no doubt but that it was a fascinating story, this account of a soul's struggle to solve the riddle of human yearning toward the eternal. She left nothing unsaid. Beginning with her little girlhood she took Adoniram on an agonizing adventure of the spirit. He saw her mother, a harsh woman, partial to Jeanne's brother, the father, peculiarly sympathetic to the little daughter and the daughter, little Jeanne Marie, learning in a convent to conform to the rigid formulæ of medieval Catholicism and blindly trying to find consolation in it for her mother's harshness and neglect. He followed her as a young girl, gay, vain and living the life of a courted beauty, as the girl wife of a man old enough to be her grandfather, and through the sufferings mental, moral and physical that came of that marriage until she at last burst the bonds that had imprisoned all the enormous mysticism that fought within her for expression.

Ann, coming to the zayat with a cup of tea for Adoniram, one morning, found him weeping over the book. She took it gravely from him and gave him the tea.

"I don't like that woman, 'Don," she said. "She was half insane. Yes," in response to his look of surprise. "I've read it. There are some wonderful thoughts in it. But she takes too little account of the legitimate happiness of this life. She's too fond of mortifying the flesh. She invited people to torment her, really."

"I don't think she was insane," protested Adoniram. "She was fanatical, perhaps. But, Ann, there's a great deal of food in that book for any one who seeks to touch God."

"Maybe—" Ann's tone was grudging. "But you don't need that sort of food, my dearest."

"Nancy, you know as well as I do that overconfidence in myself has always been one of my besetting sins!" He sighed. "Madame Guyon would tell me and she'd be right, that I was a poor worm."

"Nonsense!" Ann leaned forward and retied his neckscarf and smoothed back his hair. "Do you think this worm idea will give you any standing with the Burman king? You'll need all the pride of a Christian and an American to make any decent impression on him, I assure you. Worm! Really, Adoniram—" She eyed him half humorously, half belligerently.

"Well, Nancy! I'm hardly such a fool as to mean literally that I feel like an angle worm or—"

Ann suddenly interrupted with a chuckle. His hazel eyes caught the amusement in hers.

"*What* a conversation!" she exclaimed.

She bent toward him, still smiling, and suddenly they were locked in each other's arms, helpless with laughter.

But when she returned to the house a moment later with the teacup, Madame Guyon was tucked under her arm.

Early in September, things began to move. A French trader, the *Ile de France,* came into the harbor and passage was taken for the Wheelocks to Madras where they could get a ship for home. It was heartrending to carry the sick man aboard and leave him with his girl wife to the mercy of the sea. Had not the invalid himself been insistent, none of the others would have consented to his departure. Yet there was the fighting chance that his life would be prolonged by the trip. And so the pale, emaciated boy sailed away. . . . Three weeks later they learned that a week out from Rangoon Wheelock threw himself from the ship into the Bay of Bengal and was never seen again. . . .

The viceroy, reaffirmed in office, returned in October and M. Lanciego with him. The Spaniard was complacent and friendly. The new king had loaded him with favors and out of his plenty the collector spared the missionaries a kind word with the viceroy which, combined with a rich present of silks which Adoniram had purchased from a Shan caravan, produced the passport, late in November. And a gift to Lanciego of some fine books, brought out from America by the Colmans, resulted in Lanciego's undertaking to see that the mission was fully protected during the absence of the men. On the 21st of December, by which time it seemed probable that if the gaing-ôk were influential with the new ruler, the missionaries' trip must be fruitless, they were ready to begin the journey.

It is not in a true man not to take peculiar joy in owning

THE LOTUS LAKE

a boat and, curious as their craft was to American eyes, Adoniram and James Colman were very proud of it.

It was of the type used by the Burman of moderate circumstances in traveling. The hull was hollowed from a single teakwood log, was forty feet long and stretched to a middle beam of six feet. The prow and stern curved up from the water, the latter fully two yards and here the steersman perched.

The missionaries had had a deck laid throughout and on this the rowers sat. Two tiny cabins of bamboo occupied the after deck, with space behind for a cooking place.

The two travelers would not permit their wives to see them off, but good-bys were said at dawn, at the mission. The wharf was deserted, when they pushed off at last, but a moment later, Maung Shway-gnong appeared.

"There's little-man-much-afraid!" ejaculated Adoniram. "Will you come with us, my teacher?" he called.

"I cannot come!" replied Maung Shway-gnong.

"Poor fellow!" murmured James.

"Poor fellow, indeed!" sighed Adoniram and he watched the lean figure of his friend on the wharf until a turn in the river hid it from view. Then he turned to the young man sitting on the deck beside him, and said with a tired smile, "Well, we're off, Colman! Actually! We're about to make a formal offer of God to one of the most despotic monarchs on earth. It's a portentous trip this!"

"My mind won't compass it." Colman shook his head.

"Nor mine," echoed Adoniram.

As a matter of fact, they were both worn out with work and worry. Before they had progressed a mile upstream, James crept into his cabin for a sleep and Adoniram stretched himself in the shadow of the great sail and gave his mind over to vacuity. He was greatly in need of rest and the flat monotony of this delta country was graciously stupid. The bright blue of the sky, the red of the water, the gay green of the paddy fields, all were familiar. He closed his tired eyes and in five minutes was asleep.

It was not until three days later when they were entering the waters of the Irrawaddy that the two men roused themselves to take in new impressions. Here was a new kind of Burma. Thick forests of mangrove and teakwood pushed down to the water's edge and canals that were blue with sky and red with silt marked attempts at real cultivation of the soil. The mosquitoes were even more deadly here than in the delta.

There were more villages, too, with the house stilts actually in the water or straggling up the banks. Here was the beginning of pirate country and they tied up each night at some populous spot and paid the chief man of the village for protection. This gave the inhabitants an unprecedented opportunity for examining white men. They swarmed over the boat, men, women and children, asking endless questions and examining their belongings. The children were timid. A frown sent them over the side and swimming for shore like frightened minnows. The women were the most venturesome. At Prome, half way to Amarapura, a pretty brown girl of sixteen penetrated into the mysteries of Adoniram's trunk and came forth, shrieking with laughter and clad in a pair of his white muslin under drawers. He had great difficulty in rescuing these intimate articles of apparel.

Along the shores above Prome were heavenly fields of indigo. Great jars, in which the dyes were made, stood on the river's edge with fresh dyed cloth blowing in the sun. Hills were lifting now, every one pagoda crowned. The river moved in majesty between wooded promontories. There were green islands in the river from which at sundown little shaven-headed boys swam the buffalo to mainland. It was remarkable to see a child of ten now jumping from one red back to another, now swimming after a straggler, always forcing the great beasts to keep their heads

THE LOTUS LAKE 123

upstream and bringing them straitly through the fierce current to the home shore.

Twice they tied up at night at a Shan encampment and wandered among the black-coated merchants, watching their trade with the Burmans:—stick-lac and quicksilver and rhubarb, umbrellas, verdigris and live pheasants, onions and turmeric and sugar cake. Adoniram and James loved to repeat the mellifluent names.

It was a dream trip—pagodas, rice boats, the king's elephant herd drinking in a majestic gray line under a red bluff side, the king's war fleet of thirty gilded boats carrying a thousand rowers with turkey red twisted in their hair, singing and rowing in gorgeous unison, the king's peacocks, parading against the brown walls of a ruined pagoda.

A month after they left Rangoon, the river took an eastward turn and their boat—one morning—crept past the ancient town of Sagaing, on a wooded shore beneath noble hills crowned with white marble pagodas, and, in the afternoon, passed old Ava, opposite, half hidden by tamarinds and toddy palms. Six miles still further, they came to a long flat shore of sand and mud and made anchor. The white pagodas they could see glowing several miles inland belonged to Amarapura.

CHAPTER XIII

THE KING

AMARAPURA! The two missionaries looked eagerly about them. They were near a little suburb of huts and pagodas, set among mangoes and toddy palms. A small boy smoking an enormous cheroot stared at them from the back of a dripping buffalo. Women, pounding out their laundry in the shallows, lifted their heads and gaped. A crowd gathered quickly with the usual comments on the bleached ugliness of the foreign animals. Pariah dogs snarled.

Adoniram made inquiries. When it was found that the stranger spoke the tongue, every one talked at once. From the babel he gathered two or three pertinent bits. He could not rent a pony or a bullock cart for fear the owners would be in trouble with the authorities. The gates of Amarapura were four miles distant and the road easy to follow. The golden presence had been in Ava that day so all the ordinary folk had been obliged to leave the town which he was restoring. He would remove the capitol there shortly.

The head man of the village asked to go aboard the boat. He brought with him his wife and four children and a gift of pickled tea, drenched with sesamum oil. Further than this he would do nothing, not even sell them food. No one knew yet how the lord of life felt about them. It was a little depressing.

They slept in their cabins with the tinkle of pagoda bells lulling them and were wakened by the creaking of bullock carts, to a dawn all lavender and silver in the river mists. They dressed carefully in fresh linen suits, with glove-fitting pantaloons strapped under their feet, and with snowy collars

THE KING

and stock-ties. Maung Nau and a friend who was one of the crew, Maung Ing, followed them carrying gifts. Maung Nau was as thin and tall as Maung Ing was short and fat, and there were many facetious comments made on this fact as they followed the missionaries over the long road.

Passing elephants and carts kept the dust heavy. Women carrying bazaar purchases, garlic, greens, dried lizards, fish, fruits, made remarks about the immodesty of pantaloons. Strange smells were blown across their faces by the hot wind. The missionaries would have found the road picturesque had they not been so weighed down with concern for their errand.

It was mid-morning when they reached the east gate of the city. It was shaded by two magnificent tamarind trees. A guard in a red leather helmet, shaped like a pagoda, looked at the passport, grunted and opened the gate. They entered Amarapura.

It was after all only a larger and drier Rangoon, this golden city of great kings, with differences only in detail. Every house was shaded by a grape vine trellis. And there was an enormous weaving of silk. A hundred looms flashed rich and varied colors from as many poverty-stricken verandas as the missionaries passed. On the principal street, the houses were set behind high white palings. This was the street used by the king and no common man must be in sight when his majesty passed.

Their first call was to be made at the house of the former viceroy of Rangoon who was now one of the four members of the king's privy council. His house was just outside the palace gates and they were fortunate enough to come upon the official and his wife as they were about to enter a bullock cart at their gate.

The viceroy wore a gorgeous robe of pink-flowered silk above which his flat, scowling brown face seemed particularly coarse and savage. He gave no heed to Adoniram's bow but continued to crawl past the near bullock's red rump into the cart. But his wife paused to look at the two men with a pleasant smile. Maung Ing ran forward, dropped to his knees and held toward her a large fitted sewing basket. The lady's eyes sparkled.

"I have seen Ma Judson use just such a contrivance!" she cried, taking the basket eagerly, and beginning to examine it.

The viceroy having squatted himself under the jeweled canopy of the carriage stared blankly ahead, until Maung Nau, from his knees, offered a man's toilet case. The viceroy took the offering without enthusiasm but after looking over its contents, he smiled, showing his broken and betel-stained teeth.

"What do you want of me, O foreign animal?" he asked.

"An audience with his majesty, O great councilor," replied Adoniram.

"For what purpose?" demanded the Burman.

"To behold the golden face," replied Adoniram.

The viceroy grunted skeptically, then said, "Amé! The louse would bite the elephant!" Then he laughed. "Very well, drink the bitter water if you must. You know that it makes mad all who drink?"

"We're not afraid!"

Again the Burman laughed. "I'll arrange it. Go back and stay at your resting place until it's done. A man will come for you, to-morrow."

"We are going back, my lord." Adoniram bowed deeply.

"Go then,—poor louse," chuckled the Burman.

The driver squatting on the wagon tongue, smacked the bullocks smartly with a lacquered stick and accompanied by an enormous rumble of wheels and tinkling of little bells, the equipage moved off under the toddy palms that fringed the road.

Adoniram and Colman smiled cheerfully at each other and obediently started on the walk back to their boat. They paused only once. This was at a zayat under a glorious

THE KING

tamarind, beside a lake which lay east of the town. Colman was tired and they rested long here, disturbed only by the murmur of boys' voices in a near-by monastery and by the occasional boom of a pagoda gong, struck by a worshiper. Adoniram eyed his companion a little anxiously. There could be no doubt that the boy had small endurance. His face was drawn, his yellow hair was gray with sweat and dust. But he was incurably optimistic.

"I know precisely what you're thinking, sir," he grinned at Adoniram. "But it's not so! I'm quite well and the world is a good world."

"So it is!" agreed Adoniram. But he was not sure that he was speaking the truth!

When they reached home, Colman was induced to take an early supper and go to bed. Adoniram sat alone on deck watching the moon rise and listening to the rush of the waters. He could think of nothing but the impending interview and did not go to bed till midnight. Then he found young Colman awake and they talked and prayed until daylight.

The messenger from the viceroy arrived when they were eating their breakfast of rice and fish. They were to follow him at once to the palace. The messenger rode a pony and they followed the little animal as best they could along the road of yesterday. Maung Nau carried the king's gift, a four volume Bible which they had had specially bound in leaf gold. Adoniram had insisted that the present must be in proportion to their means and have a direct relation to their work. They reached the palace entrance at noon. There was a postern beside the main gate through which they were admitted to an open yard about which were scattered various buildings.

Their guide led them to one of the smaller houses and left them on the veranda. A wizened man, with an elaborately tattooed stomach above his paso and with the silk cords of high office hanging over his left shoulder now took them in charge.

"What, exactly, do you want of his majesty, O foreign animals?" he demanded.

"We have here a petition, asking the lord of earth and water to permit us to teach our religion in Burma," replied Adoniram, handing the carefully prepared paper to the official. He at once began to read it.

"He'll never let us in," said Colman in English. "You needn't, sir, have been so frank!"

"Hush! I was ashamed of my subterfuge yesterday." Adoniram watched the Burman.

After a long time he looked up into the missionaries' faces, with a scowl. "And who is God?" he demanded.

Both men began to speak but at that moment there was a shout. "The golden foot is about to advance!"

The official hastily threw a green silk robe over his shoulder, touched up his hair knot and said: "We must seize this opportunity!" But, before moving on, he said with a derisive glance, "How can you propagate religion in this empire?" Then without waiting for an answer. "Come along! This is the day his majesty celebrates his late victory over Cathay. It's not the most propitious moment, I assure you!"

The two missionaries hurried after this most unenthusiastic patron. He led them past a beautiful pool of water in an exquisite marble basin, past doorways with gilded pillars, past lattices of delicate alabaster fret-work and stairs with balustrades formed of dancing nats and dewas carved from teakwood, to a huge open hall. It was set on a stone platform eight feet above the ground and as they paused to remove their shoes, their patron ordered them to sheeko to the palace, which they did.

The hall was magnificent. The roof was supported by several scores of intricately carved pillars with crimson bases. The floor was of smooth white stone. The rest of

THE KING

the interior, pillars, roof beams and the throne canopy was a blaze of gold leaf. The two missionaries were placed in the middle of the room with perhaps half a dozen other suppliants. They had scarcely seated themselves and were gazing about them when all the Burmans leaned forward, faces on hands, knuckles touching the floor. The two Americans remained half kneeling, half sitting but they put their fingers before their faces.

The king was moving slowly across the hall.

He was about thirty-five years of age, a small man not much over five feet two and bow-legged to a remarkable degree. He had a cheerful face, not at all handsome and marred by a forehead that sloped so abruptly as to be almost a deformity. He wore a paso of white silk shot with crimson. His white silk jacket was almost concealed by gold chains and cords. He carried in one hand a gold-sheathed sword and in the other the tail of a white Thibetan cow.

His majesty moved superbly with a not-to-be-ignored dignity and pride. As he came opposite the two white men he halted.

"Who are these?" he demanded.

No one seemed to dare to answer so Adoniram spoke, his deep voice, deeper than ever, following the shrill tones of the king.

"We are the teachers, great king."

Bagyi-daw smiled and Adoniram thought he had a look of benevolence. "What, you speak Burmese? You are the monk I heard of last night?"

"We are the teachers, O lord king," repeated Adoniram.

"When did you arrive?"

"Just before sky closing time, two days ago, your majesty!"

"Are you teachers of religion?" was the next question, while the king looked from Colman's ethereal face to Adoniram's, sunburnt and strong.

"We are, great king."

"Then you are monks and unmarried?"

Adoniram explained that they were not monks and described their way of living at the mission. The king listened, brushing himself meantime with the cow's tail. Not a Burman had thus far lifted his face from the floor, but the missionaries crouched with what comfort they could on their heels, frankly staring.

"Why do you English wear those tight coverings for your legs and for your heads?" was the next query.

"It's our custom, sire. We are Americans, though, not English."

"You're all the same, you Europeans!" grunted the king. He suddenly picked up Adoniram's broad-brimmed straw from the floor, by the simple expedient of sticking it through with his sword. He examined it and then placed it on his own head. If any of the groveling courtiers were amused, not a shoulder quivered to incriminate him. Bagyi-daw tossed the hat to the floor after a moment and asked if the missionaries had children, if they drank rum and got drunk like other foreigners, if they had any theories contrary to the Burmese about the starry systems and if they killed animals for food.

When Adoniram had replied, to each question, Bagyi-daw smiled in a pleased way and strode on across the hall to his throne. He brushed the seat with the cow's tail and then sat down.

"I am now ready to hear the petition," he announced.

The missionaries' patron raised his head just high enough to focus his eyes on the paper on which his forehead had been resting and began to read:

"The American teachers present themselves to receive the favor of the excellent king, the sovereign of land and sea. Hearing that on account of the greatness of the royal power, the royal country was in a quiet and prosperous state, we arrived at the town of Rangoon, within the royal dominions, and having obtained leave of the governor of that

THE KING

town to come up and behold the golden face we have ascended and reached the bottom of the golden feet.

"In the great country of America we sustain the characters of teachers and explainers of the contents of the sacred Scriptures of our religion. And since it is contained in those Scriptures that, if we pass to other countries and teach and propagate religion, great good will result, and both those who teach and those who receive the religion will be freed from future punishment and enjoy without decay or death, the eternal felicity of heaven—

"That royal permission may be given; that we taking refuge in the royal power, may preach our religion in these domains and that those who are pleased with our preaching and wish to listen to and be guided by it, whether foreigners or Burmans, may be exempt from government molestation, they present themselves to receive the favor of the excellent king, the sovereign of land and sea."

The king listened, his eyes fastened intently the while on the missionaries. Then he stretched out his hand. Their patron crawled forward and handed up the petition. His majesty deliberately read it through. Adoniram, while the king was thus occupied, crept over to the official and gave him a copy of a tract which set forth in simplest form the tenets of the Christian faith. After the king had finished with the petition he gave it back to the official without a word and took the tract.

Adoniram moistened his dried lips— O God, have mercy on Burma, have mercy on her king!—

Bagyi-daw read the first lines which asserted that there is but one eternal God who is independent of the incidents of mortality and that other than He there is no God. Then he contemptuously dashed the tract to the floor.

The official picked it up and gave it to Adoniram.

The king was staring eagerly out through the pillars to the court whence came the faint stir of drums. The official undid the wrappings of one of the volumes of the Bible and held it up to his majesty. Bagyi-daw took no notice. Adoniram choked back a sob.

After a few moments' careful study of his liege lord's profile, their patron interpreted the royal will, thus:

"The golden king says, why do you ask for such permission? Have not the Portuguese, the English, the Mussulmans and people of all other religions liberty to worship according to their own customs? In regard to the objects of your petition, his majesty gives no order. In regard to your sacred books, his majesty has no use for them. Take them away."

He paused. The king made no sign.

"Tell the great king," said Adoniram desperately, "that Maung Colman, my associate, has skill in medicine."

Without glancing in the missionaries' direction, the king now said, "Let them proceed to the residence of my physician, the Portuguese priest. Let him examine whether they can be useful to me in that line and report accordingly."

He then descended abruptly from the throne and strode to the edge of the hall where he threw himself on a cushion and fastened his eyes on the procession which now began to move across the courtyard.

Their patron jumped to his feet. "Come along, in a hurry," he ordered brusquely.

They hurried. He moved rapidly down the steps at the side of the building. They caught a fleeting glimpse of a white elephant sheltered by several golden umbrellas, of a long line of officials in red velvet robes, of spearsmen in green, of dancing girls, of astrologers in white robes studded with gold stars, of musketeers in blue. Then the postern gate which, their patron told them with a grim smile, was used only to carry out the bodies of the dead was opened and the two were ordered to follow a servant to the house of the Portuguese priest.

The priest was an old man, with a grave, smooth-shaven face. They found him standing in the doorway of his church, two miles south of the palace. It was a small teakwood building set near the Irrawaddy in a yard filled with cocoanut trees.

The priest invited them to be seated on a bench in the church porch and listened without comment to the servant's report. Then he turned to Adoniram and James.

"Although I suppose you speak French as I do, sirs, it were wiser to speak in Burmese, so that my words may be understood. I shall ask you no questions not having to do with medicine. I shall give you no advice. I am in Burma solely to minister to the Catholic mixed-breed descendants of the French who were brought prisoners from Syriam here generations ago. My presence is tolerated here only because I touch nothing political nor any faith save my own nor any people save Catholic. The king has a great desire to discover a medicine that will secure him from all disease and enable him to live forever. If you have no knowledge of such a remedy, you will be useless to him."

The three white men looked gravely into one another's faces. The turtle doves cooed. A door swung and the sound of a chant floated under the trees. Colman smiled, gently.

"My dear Mr. Judson, why prolong the agony?"

Adoniram nodded. "My friend says that we need no longer trouble you."

"I am sorry," murmured the padre.

"Thank you," murmured Adoniram.

The three bowed and the missionaries with the Bibles in their arms began the long walk back to their boat.

Still they would not give up.

The king was a Burman, therefore he was venal. They could not give him adequate money gifts, but they could try other forms of temptation.

They learned from the head man of the village that their patron had been no less than the prime minister, the man next in authority to the king's self. After a night of thought they decided to push their acquaintance with the prime minister. They returned to the city the next day, with Maung Ing and Maung Nau loaded with gifts and went to the official's house. A paso silk-length and a box of China tea bought them immediate audience.

The minister was half reclining on a mat, a cheroot in his mouth. He looked as wizened as a baby monkey but intelligent.

"My lord," said Adoniram, "it is our understanding that the glorious king discourages trade between this and other countries because he fears that the wealth of Burma would be carried out of the land."

The Burman's sunken black eyes became speculative. "You are right as to that, foreign animal. Then what?"

"Would not your people, my lord, be more taxable, more pagodas be built, more alleged merit acquired, did you have more trade?"

"That too, is admitted," agreed the official. "Be seated, foreign teachers. How do you propose to bring about this state of bliss?"

Adoniram dared not look at Colman who he knew was straining to understand the conversation. He dared not let the boy see the hope he felt must be in his eyes. They sat down on mats and arranged their awkward legs so that their feet would not point toward the minister. This was no moment to add insult to petitioning!

"My lord, if it was known that the royal favor was extended to foreigners, if it was known that the golden king would permit Christianity to spread in his empire, many, many Christians would settle here and it's notorious that trade is always brisk where there are Christian communities."

The Burman puffed his cheroot for a time, then said, "If you care to remain awhile in Amarapura, I'll try to find a favorable moment to present this thought in the golden presence."

THE KING

"May we send you a writing, setting forth the idea more fully?" asked Adoniram.

"You may. Though I won't deceive you. The king was prejudiced against you before he saw you. You offended a monk high in the monasteries and his majesty's chief wife, who rules him, listened to the great monk's tale. Myself, I have very little use for any of the lot of bowl bearers. Even if you see the king again—well, you know there are three chances in a snake's stare but only one in a king's! Go now!"

"We are going, my lord," said Adoniram.

Once more they were moving through the sandy streets of the golden city with Maung Ing and Maung Nau trailing despondently behind. Only young Colman was able to say a cheerful word and he spoke with a twisted smile. "It's a good world after all,—for the Burmans!"

They sent the proposed writing to the prime minister that evening. The following day was Sunday and they rested. On Monday they waited all day on the prime minister's veranda for an audience. The moon was up when he came out to them and said, not unkindly:

"There's not the least possibility of your obtaining the object contained in this writing about trade, no matter how long you wait. And there is grave danger in your staying here. You must go about your own business."

He turned and went into his house.

The long-prayed-for expedition to Amarapura was a failure.

The two missionaries were too much stunned to speak. They dragged their heavy feet along the road under palm and tamarind, hand in hand, tears dripping down their cheeks. The miles were very long.

Talking that night, after Koo-chil's curried chicken had heartened them a bit, their chief concern was to discover what was God's purpose in blasting their hopes. Colman, who was as simple in his faith as Maung Nau, finally said that, of course, the result of the trip would seem wise to them if they had God's power to see the end, from the beginning, and when Adoniram's tragic eyes did not lighten, the younger man added:

"We must trust in Jesus Christ."

"I do trust in Him," exclaimed Adoniram. "He is here, in my heart. But where is God?" a great sob bursting from his aching throat.

Colman was frightened and said nothing. And after a while they both went to bed.

CHAPTER XIV

THE LITTLE CHURCH

ON February 6, the missionaries pushed off into the Irrawaddy.

The return trip, with current favoring them, would be made in half the time consumed in the journey up. They were glad of that. Travel on the Irrawaddy had lost its savor. Sightseeing was merely depressing and they did not leave the boat even when it tied up for the night at Prome, a week below Amarapura. Prome, with its magnificent pagodas, had no appeal to them now. They sent Koo-chil ashore to buy food and when he returned with a mysterious buffalo steak they did not question him.

The blackness of their depression was undoubtedly due to Adoniram. Young Colman had not given six years to preparation for the petition to the king! He tried for the first few days of the voyage to cheer Adoniram, but finally desisted. The older man's mood rose from depths the younger had not sounded.

When, therefore, as they sat at their supper of steak, that night at Prome and a familiar face appeared casually around the edge of the cabin, Colman gave an actual roar of welcome. It was Maung Shway-gnong! Perhaps this old friend could help the head of the mission.

Adoniram was indeed glad to see the teacher. He hugged him affectionately and insisted that he share the steak with them, and his eyes twinkled for the first time in many days as he served Maung Shway-gnong bountifully.

"I know you Burmans enjoy eating what we lost souls butcher," he said.

Maung Shway-gnong grinned and repeated a portion of

the Burmese funeral ceremony. " 'May the deceased and all present share the merit of the offering!' "

"Did you come to meet us, O friend?" asked Adoniram.

"No, lord teacher," replied the Burman. "My brother is ill here and I came up to see him. But I'd like to return with you to Rangoon if I may. Tell me what happened to you at the golden city, lord."

Adoniram sighed. He was extremely reluctant still to talk about his defeat but Maung Shway-gnong's advice might be valuable. So with an occasional word from Colman, who was now fairly proficient in the ordinary vernacular, he described their reception at the court.

"And thus," he ended the tale, "we must make up our minds, I suppose, to leave Burma and go to Chittagong."

"Did you hear talk of war with the English up yonder?" asked the teacher.

"Only the usual boasting of the Burman as to his prowess," replied Adoniram. "What has that to do with our situation?"

"My thought was, lord, that unless the golden presence actually was going to fight the English, he wouldn't dare to have an Englishman tortured."

Adoniram shook his head impatiently. "You know as well as I do, O teacher, that I'm an American. And our fears are not chiefly for ourselves. There's Maung Nau—a disciple, and Maung Ing who hopes to be baptized soon, and others about whom I'm hopeful."

"You needn't fear for me!" The Burman managed a defiant expression.

"Why should we?" asked Adoniram. "You have taken great pains, I was told before I left Rangoon, to be seen at the Shwé Dagôn, worshiping."

Maung Shway-gnong groaned in great agitation. "You wrong me, O lord. Since you left Rangoon, I've not lifted my folded hands before a pagoda. It's true, sometimes I follow the crowd, just to avoid suspicion. But I walk up one side of the pagoda and down the other. Now will you say I'm not a disciple? What lack I yet?"

"O teacher," replied Adoniram, "you are not a disciple if you keep Christ hidden in your heart and deny Him before men."

The Burman did not reply.

There was a pretty sound from the shore of girls singing over their rice husking.

After a time, young Colman said, "Will any one dare to come to the zayat, O Maung Shway-gnong, as soon as it's noised about that the king has denied us protection?"

The teacher did not reply directly. "I tell you what I'll do," he cried. "I'll go to the gaing-ôk, myself, and silence him. I know I can—for truth's on my side."

"Ah, my poor friend," murmured Adoniram, touched by this show of valor, "you may have a tongue with which to silence him but he has a pair of fetters and a maul with which to silence you. Remember that!"

"Am I likely to forget it?" demanded the Burman, passionately. "Isn't it remembrance that makes me less than a snake stealing the tiger's kill?"

Adoniram patted his arm softly. "Some day," he said, "God will enable."

Young Colman suddenly jumped to his feet. "See the evening star, how brightly and truly it rises! And hear the peaceful frogs! After all, it is a good world, O friends!"

"Youth! Youth!" sighed Maung Shway-gnong as he also rose. "I will go back to my brother's house but will return at dawn for the sailing."

"Go then, my teacher," Adoniram nodded and they watched him fade into the dusk.

"What a way he has of appearing and disappearing," remarked Colman. "I wonder that his fellow citizens don't accuse him of witchcraft."

"Ma So has a saying about him," smiled Adoniram, "'A jumping flea raises no dust.'"

Colman laughed. "Anyhow he lifted us out of our despondency, didn't he, sir?"

"I'm afraid I've given you a sad time of it, my poor boy!" exclaimed Adoniram contritely. "I'll try to do better." And during the remainder of the trip, he did make an enormous effort to throw off his sense of hopelessness. This was possible with Maung Shway-gnong aboard for the Burman insisted on Adoniram's carrying on their accustomed debate on religion. And it was not easy to give the mind to the crime the king had just perpetrated against his subjects when another Burman was demanding an explanation of each of Christ's miracles.

They reached Rangoon on the 18th of February.

All agreed in the conference that was held as soon as they reached the mission, that the only feasible move was to go to Chittagong. Adoniram voted with the rest. But he did so with a melancholy so profound that he became actually ill. After the conference was ended, he was obliged to go to bed. And there he turned his face to the wall and begged God to let him die.

Ann watched him sadly but dared not speak. He had descended, she too recognized, to depths she could not plumb. All night he wrestled with the despair that sought to paralyze him. A mental picture obsessed him. He saw Adoniram Judson, a pale distraught figure on the deck of a ship; a ship that sailed a sea of most sensuous beauty. Yet at its beauty he could not gaze because floundering in its golden waves were countless hosts of little drowning children, sobbing, frightened children pleading, *"Adoniram, lord teacher, save us! save us!"* and he saw Adoniram look fearsomely around him and mutter, *"I dare not! No, I dare not!"*

And he saw himself alone in all the world, damned to live beyond the life of humanity itself, beyond the very confines of time, forever seeking the God he did not know.

It was nearing dawn when he covered his face with his trembling hands and prayed. "Almighty Father, show me

THE LITTLE CHURCH 141

the way! For the sake of Your Son, writhing on the cross, for the sake of all that struggling, falling, failing procession of human beings who seek to find the path Your Son revealed, make me to know if this suffering of the Burmans is a part of your great plan. Must they die in order to live? Must they be tortured if they come to Thee? Jesus, must You put Your own bitter cup to their poor lips? Ought I to stay in Burma and put my disciples to the torture? Is that the way and the truth—?"

He paused and held his breath in that exquisitely concentrated sense of listening with his soul. But there was within him only a silence as of universal death. . . .

The next morning, young Colman went to the beach to look up a coasting vessel. Ann and Mrs. Colman began their packing. Adoniram paced the veranda, hands clasped behind his back, chin on his chest, struggling to bring himself back to the world of sunshine and singing birds and tinkling pagoda bells and it must be admitted, the not unhappy hum of the two women making their preparations to leave the sad, silly town. He had kept up the pacing for an hour when he was roused by a voice at the veranda edge.

"Lord teacher!"

He lifted his heavy head. A group of Burmans was standing at the steps; Ma Baik, the cross-eyed, and her mother-in-law, Ma So, Maung Nau and Maung Ing, his friend, and four others, men and women whom Adoniram did not know.

"Lord teacher," repeated Maung Nau, "we have brought a petition."

"Come up with it, O friends," said Adoniram, wonderingly.

The group slipped off sandals, sheekoed and squatted on the mats. Adoniram seated himself before them. Maung Nau opened his lips to speak but Ma So forestalled him.

"Lord teacher, we wish you not to go away!"

"But it's useless to remain, my friends." Adoniram

smiled sadly at them. "We can't open the zayat. We can't have public worship. No Burman will dare to examine this religion."

"Lord teacher!" exclaimed Maung Nau, his thin face screwed up as if he were about to weep, "my mind's so distressed since you made known your going that I can't eat or sleep. I've been round among the neighbors and I've found all those who even now are examining the new religion. Here are my brother-in-law and his wife and her cousins."

The new-comers nodded vigorously. Maung Ing, who was an older man than his friend, leaned forward and said in his pleasant voice, "Stay with us just a few more months, lord teacher! Stay till there are ten disciples. Then appoint one the teacher of the rest and we needn't worry. From what I have already observed of the new religion, even should you leave the country, after thus propagating it, it will spread of itself. The golden presence, even, couldn't stop its growth."

Ma Baik, her lean face suffused with tears, gasped, "Amé! why have I put off my baptism? What'll become of my karma now? Lowest hell gapes for me!"

With quickening heart, Adoniram looked from the little group of petitioners to Ann and Mrs. Colman who had come to the door to listen. Before he could tell them how sweet their words sounded in his ears, one of the newcomers, a woman, said:

"Lord teacher, I've attended many of the zayat meetings. I thought you'd always be here and there was no hurry. Is it right to forsake us? Haven't you preached again and again that this work of conversion wasn't yours, but God's and that He wouldn't recognize its dangers?"

A third neighbor raised his hand and called in a loud voice, "As for me, I'll pray! Let us all pray!"

"As for me," said another neighbor, "I have built a pagoda to acquire merit, to obtain the last release from rebirth. I taxed much money from the people when I was an

THE LITTLE CHURCH

official and I built a beautiful pagoda up the river for my sins. But it gave me no satisfaction. I found no resting place for my soul, until last rainy season when I heard you preach the religion of Jesus Christ. If Maung Nau didn't selfishly keep the copy of the gospel you loaned to him, I would undoubtedly be ready for baptism now."

Adoniram repressed a smile. Maung Shway-ba having delivered his broadside, the little company became silent, waiting. After a moment, the missionary lifted his face in prayer.

"I have received your reply, O Eternal God, and now I promise you never to leave Burma until the cross is planted here forever. Help us, Father, help us, your little church in Rangoon! If torture comes and in its dread hold we recant, be patient with us, God, for it will be only our frail bodies failing you. Our souls are forever thine! Amen."

When he opened his eyes it was to look first at Ann. She smiled at him through tears.

As soon as Colman returned from his visit to the beach, there was another conference among the four missionaries. After much discussion it was decided that the Colmans would go on to Chittagong and there establish a mission as already planned. Then, in case the Rangoon mission were wiped out, Chittagong would form the reserve from which a new attack could be made. The Colmans would have preferred to remain in Rangoon, but, after all, Adoniram was head of the mission and his orders must be law. There was no dearth of native coasting vessels in the harbor and passage was taken for the two young people that very day.

As it was Burma, the ship did not sail for two weeks after the day set and Colman helped Adoniram to put the zayat in order and tested his vocabulary by trying to answer some of the questions put by the tiny group that gathered behind the closed doors each evening. He did not make much headway but won the Burmans' hearts by laughing as heartily as they over his failures. He was a born missionary and it cost the Judsons a bitter pang to send him and his girl wife away from them. They sailed, in March.

After their departure, Adoniram settled to a new routine. He worked all day on the translation of the Bible and spent his evenings in the secret meetings in the zayat. The secrecy hurt him but it seemed the only way.

At first, they expected each day to be attacked either by agents of the king or of the gaing-ôk, and suffered all the nerve tension of the besieged. But March merged into burning April, and they were not molested. Why, they could not be sure. But there was always to be considered the childishness of the Burmans and especially of the king, which prevented them from acting except on impulse. Perhaps the impulse to torment the Americans had petered out. The gaing-ôk they heard had been kept in Amarapura to instruct certain of the royal children. Perhaps the missionaries were forgotten and would remain forgotten as long as the zayat appeared to be inactive.

Also was to be considered the fact that affairs of great importance were pressing on Burmese officialdom. The great king, the lord of white elephants, the golden presence, was carrying on a war in Assam and was openly planning to take over the whole of the Indian territory lying south of the Himalayas and as far west as Calcutta. To his majesty, British possessions in India meant nothing. He or no other Burman knew anything of geography.

The center of the Burman world was a mountain, five million miles high. Round about this mountain were four great islands. On the southernmost island dwelt the race of man, occupied by the Burmans and other Buddhists and by the Indian heretics. On the five hundred islets surrounding the southernmost island dwelt the English and all other nations.

Such being the state of the Universe, it was utterly absurd for the English to venture upon the southern island as they were doing and it was incumbent on Bagyi-daw, king of

THE LITTLE CHURCH

great and exalted virtues, the arbitrator of existence, to bring them under the royal feet which closely resembled the golden lily.

Therefore, the king's nets were spread to the borders of his kingdom and men were caught therein for his army. It behooved every householder to walk softly and to let his paddy fields perish rather than be seen and caught by the king's men. One now had perhaps something to do beside playing spy on the foreign mission.

And therefore predatory expeditions of appalling viciousness and of unrivaled ineffectiveness, so far as annexing territory was concerned, were sent into sections of Assam which were under the British protectorate. It was only a question of time when the British would have to give up written protests for something more drastic.

The Burmans interested in the zayat meetings escaped the dragnet until early summer. Then, Maung Shwaygnong was caught and hustled off to the armies encamped on the Brahmaputra River, far to the north. His wife and daughter accepted Adoniram's invitation to build a hut in the mission yard. Maung Ing was baptized and also the neighbor who had built a pagoda. And then, early in May, Ann was smitten with her old liver trouble in a highly aggravated form and for a time Adoniram forgot all else on earth save the fight for her life.

She did not respond to mercury and calomel. Adoniram wrote a letter to the doctor at Serampore asking for advice.

He was down with a bout of jungle fever when the doctor's reply came. He and Ann lay side by side with Ma Baik doing what she could for them. When Maung Nau brought Adoniram the letter, he read it at once, then laid it down with a groan.

"What does he say, 'Don?" asked Ann, weakly.

"He says I must have my right arm amputated and my right eye extracted for a period of two years," replied Adoniram

Ann tried to raise her head to look at him, but had no strength, "Please, dearest! What do you mean?"

"What I say, darling Nancy! He says he can bolster you up for a few weeks but the only chance for saving your life longer than that is for you to leave the Orient for two years. I suppose that means America."

"It means nothing of the sort," said Ann in a faint imitation of her old decisiveness. "I shall not put a foot outside Burma."

Adoniram closed his eyes and groaned again. He knew that when his fever left him, he would have to send Ann away, but now he could not, he dare not let himself think of it.

Ann, responding to the Serampore doctor's remedies, was on her feet before Adoniram. But the first day he could crawl out to the veranda, he said to her with a crooked smile:

"Well, my dear wife, I'm ready to sign my own death warrant."

Ann, standing beside his chair, caught his thin hand in her delicate fingers.

"I can't leave you, Adoniram! I can't. I'd far rather stay here and die." She bent over to look into his face. She was like a figure in a strange painting. Even her eyeballs were yellow. The luster had left her hair. Adoniram returning her gaze, set his teeth.

"I'm willing to pay every price to save the Burmans except some catastrophe to you which I can avert," said Adoniram, desperately earnest. "You will have to go, Ann, heart of my heart!"

She fled into the house and he heard her weeping. But he dared not risk his own resolution by going to her.

In the end, of course, she gave in, and made her preparations for the journey as sadly as though she were preparing to die. The Houghs had settled down at Serampore and Adoniram wrote, telling George Hough to see Ann aboard a

THE LITTLE CHURCH

ship bound for America or for England if America was impossible. Maung Nau and Ma Baik would accompany her on a Portuguese boat as far as Calcutta.

Ann was her usual practical self during the last few days of preparation but when they had at last helped her aboard the ship and Adoniram had established her in the little cabin she looked up from the berth where she was resting and said:

"How can you think I will thrive in America with you in Burma? I don't see how you can be so cruel, Adoniram! It's not too late. Take me back with you to the dear old mission. If I must die, let me die in your arms. Or don't you—"

Adoniram placed trembling fingers gently on her mouth. "Ann! Ann! Don't break my heart! What would I be if you were to die? This awful separation is only for the one purpose—that you may live. That knowledge is all which makes it possible for me to let you go."

She lifted his hand aside. "How can I rest, wondering how it is with you? Who will poultice your poor eyes when the pain returns, or see that you don't forget your meals?"

Adoniram set his jaw. "Those things any servant will do. What no one can do except you is to uphold my hands when God seems too far away. You'll pray for me, always, Ann?" He dropped to his knees beside the bed and clasped her to his heart.

They did not weep and they did not speak again. When his moral strength was sufficient to lay Ann back on her pillow, he did so and with a great sigh walked out of the cabin.

CHAPTER XV

THE WITCH WOMAN

IT was very, very lonely. Only God could know how lonely Adoniram was in his tiny corner of Burma. The long wet days of summer merged into the brilliant days that followed the rains. The fig trees were filled again with little green pigeons and the nightingale made his invisible nest in the casuarina tree. And this was Adoniram's world. Wars and rumors of wars did not touch him. Even the fear of molestation left him and he baptized his converts openly in the lotus lake until the little church numbered ten souls. He never saw a white man. He forgot that all faces, including his own, were not yellow. But even so, he was filled with a loneliness that after a long while he recognized as cosmic and not personal.

He tried to find the answer. Perhaps he was not appreciating to the full the privilege and the responsibility of preparing the Bible for the Burmans. God's words! He, Adoniram Judson, of all the living and dead world chosen for this. He touched each word delicately, tenderly. Every one was God's!

Nay, after long contemplation, he told himself, here was not the cause for his emptiness of soul. Why not be honest? Why not admit that it was his perpetual consciousness of the unknowableness of God that would not permit him to rest content with his conversions and his translations? Why not look for help where he was certain it could be found?

It was midnight when he rose from his bed, lighted the earth-oil lamp and sought the sandalwood box. He never had opened the box since the day Ann had taken the autobiography from him, but he knew that it was there. Ann

THE WITCH WOMAN

never was high-handed in her discipline! He found the box at the top of the teakwood closet where white ants did not travel. He lifted out the book and settled himself to read.

"When the good father opened his mouth to preach," said Madame Guyon, "I was so strongly absorbed in God, that I could neither open my eyes nor hear anything he said. I found that thy word, O my God, made its own impression on my heart and there had its effect, without the mediation of words or any attention to them. So deeply was I settled in the inward spirit of prayer that I could scarce any more pronounce the vocal prayers. I stayed above five hours in the church. I was penetrated with so lively a dart of pure love that I could not resolve to abridge by indulgences the pains due to my sins. 'O my Love,' I cried, 'I am willing to suffer for thee. I find no other pleasure but in suffering for thee!' I now quitted all company, bade farewell forever to all plays and diversions, unprofitable walks and parties of pleasure. My only pleasure now was to steal some moments to be alone with thee, O thou who art my only love!"

Adoniram read until daylight, then rose to take his morning walk. It was easier to think dispassionately when walking than at night, motionless in one's bed.—She had sought, this French woman, for God even as he was seeking. She had found Him by sloughing off every earthly hold save those that were in the nature of discipline.

But did God wish one to be supine, to be useless, to be a mere pipe through which wafted heavenly influences? His active mind rejected the thought, utterly. Perhaps Ann was right about Madame Guyon. And yet—he could not leave the book alone. He read it that night and the next, seeking now, not so much the author's method of cultivating her soul as her achievement. The result was disappointing. She wasted her life in hysterical futilities.

When he reached this conclusion, one rosy dawn, he closed the book, placed it again in the sandalwood box and said aloud: "There, my very dear Nancy, I know you feel better!" Then he went for his walk.

That day, he baptized Ma Baik. And that evening, in the solitary shadows of his study, he drew up some rules of living for himself.

1. Be diligent in secret prayer, every morning and every evening. 2. Never spend a moment in mere idleness. 3. Restrain natural appetites within the bounds of temperance and purity. *"Keep thyself pure."* 4. Suppress every emotion of anger and ill will. 5. Undertake nothing from motives of ambition or love of fame. (Note. Do not write down a translation of the "Blessed One and the herdsman Dhaniya" for Blackwood's.) 6. Never do that which at the moment appears displeasing to God (Meditate for this). 7. Endeavor to rejoice in every loss and suffering incurred for Christ's sake and the gospel's, remembering that though like death, they are not to be willfully incurred, yet, like death, they are great gain. 8. Rise with the sun. 9. Suppress every unclean *thought* and *look*.

He read these through critically when they were done. He thought that Ann would say that there was something of Buddha in them and of Madame Guyon. But he would answer her in Buddha's own words, "A man is the result of all that he has thought." At any rate, here was a tangible, a concrete program with which to fight his unrest.

Ann had been gone six months, when Maung Shwaygnong came home. He had seen no fighting, but had been kept in Prome as a recruiting officer, had had a long bout with small pox and was on the Burmese equivalent for a furlough, in which to gather strength for going into Assam.

His first request to Adoniram, after he had told the story of his adventures, was that he be baptized.

"I have done away with all my doubts, lord teacher. I am willing to tell the lord of white elephants himself, that I am a Christian."

"That is good hearing, my friend," said Adoniram,

THE WITCH WOMAN

gravely. "Are you willing to undergo the test I apply to all my suppliants: are you willing to live for one month as you know Christ would wish you to live; live it here in the yard, where every act will be known?"

The teacher smiled whimsically. "Jesus doesn't sit at ease in a Burmese house, O lord teacher!"

"He's at home anywhere He's made welcome," replied Adoniram.

"I will take the month's test, my teacher," sighed Maung Shway-gnong.

By some subtle twist of mind, the month's probation seemed to rob the teacher of such shreds of self-confidence and courage as he possessed. He seemed afraid to move lest he offend the Almighty and clung to Adoniram like a little child. It was good for the lonely missionary to have at this moment some one of whom he was fond thus dependent upon him. So Maung Shway-gnong shared Adoniram's morning and evening walk, and sat every night in his study.

The probation period had lasted about two weeks when, one evening, the two strolling along the edge of the lotus lake came upon a strange scene, strange at least to the American. The afterglow still was brilliant and as it turned the marble Gautama to gold it lighted also the face of a woman staring up at the calm features of the Buddha. She was sobbing pitifully and as the two drew nearer, it was to be seen that her hands and feet were manacled. A monk and several soldiers, with an official in a white robe, stood just back of the woman.

"What are they doing?" exclaimed Adoniram.

"Ordeal by water," replied the teacher. "If she sinks, she's guilty."

"But, of course, she's helpless and will certainly sink!" Adoniram took a hasty step toward the group.

"Wait! Don't move!" exclaimed the Burman. "You

mustn't interfere with her karma. It's a true test. I've seen it used many times."

"What's the monk doing?" asked Adoniram.

"He reads the sacred formula," mumbled the teacher, looking uneasily at Adoniram. Then he burst forth, angrily, "Jesus never told us to interfere in the working of the law!"

Adoniram's heart was beating heavily with the fear of the thing he knew he had to do. He buttoned his linen coat and took a long stride toward the woman whom the soldiers were now edging toward the water. Maung Shway-gnong gave an agonized groan.

"My lord teacher, they'll kill you!"

"What would Christ do?" Adoniram jerked back over his shoulder.

Maung Shway-gnong did not answer. Adoniram as he ran forward was thinking hard. He must not touch the monk for his person was sacred. He must not touch a Burmese woman. Still, the soldiers were manhandling her so it would be permissible for him to seize her round the waist and— Maung Shway-gnong passed him on the run, muttering, "Jesus! Jesus! Jesus!" His long hair, his cherry-colored paso rippled behind him.

Adoniram leaped after the teacher. The two men were not five feet from the woman when she was flung screaming among the lotus pads. Maung Shway-gnong sprang into the water. It took but a moment to hale her out. Adoniram waded after him and helped to carry her ashore, where she lay, moaning.

The monk and the official as well as the soldiers stood as if petrified. But when Adoniram stooped and cut the thongs that bound the woman's feet, the official shouted:

"Put the two of them in prison!"

For just a moment, Maung Shway-gnong had the look of a lion. "Not the foreign teacher, O judge! It was I, alone. He only helped me."

"Not true," contradicted the missionary. "I was first

THE WITCH WOMAN

to start to the rescue. My religion doesn't permit me to see a test like this carried out, O judge."

"Nor will mine." Maung Shway-gnong spoke very loudly.

The monk spoke for the first time. He was little more than a boy and Adoniram thought he looked frightened. "We were told that the golden presence had refused his protection to the foreign animal and that he had ceased to propagate his religion. But here is a convert he's made!"

"It shall all be investigated," promised the judge. "Take them," to the four soldiers.

"What shall you do with the woman?" asked Adoniram as the soldiers closed in.

"What business have you with a confessed murderer?" demanded the judge, thrusting his chin into the missionary's face.

"I don't believe she confessed," cried Adoniram, belligerently. "At any rate, I'll give you ten rupees for her life."

"It's not worth it," grunted the judge, "though I might look into the offer, but that won't save *you*. You go to jail!"

It was dark when they reached the main street of the town so that their ignominy was not observed by many. Still, it was a relief to reach the shelter of the empty courtroom.

A soldier lighted a lamp on a tripod near the dais and the judge took his place. He was a small, gray-bearded man with a piercing eye. Adoniram, squatting unwillingly on his haunches, said again:

"Let all the punishment be mine, O judge!"

"Wherefore?" inquired the judge.

"Because I'm the propagator of the religion that made my friend do what he did."

"You mean that you will take the maul instead of Maung Shway-gnong?" asked the judge.

Adoniram felt the hair rise on the back of his neck but

he managed to answer, steadily, "I mean just that! It is according to the religion of Christ. I have no strength of my own."

Maung Shway-gnong moaned and writhed, his forehead on the floor.

The judge leaned forward and stared into the missionary's face. It was a more attractive face than ever before. Burma had etched some fine lines upon it.

"Ah," said the judge, "I've heard you called Jesus Christ's man. What does your Christ say about enduring the maul?"

"He said nothing about the maul. He knew only the crucifix. But he did say, Greater love hath no man than this, that a man lay down his life for his friend."

Adoniram smiled at the judge who continued to stare, heavily. The night wind rushed across the palm trees without and through the courtroom bearing the evil odors of Rangoon. The soldier at the door stretched toward them, listening.

"Did Christ *do* that beside saying it?" asked the judge, finally.

"Yes, He let Himself be crucified for his friends."

"And you would let yourself go to the maul for a poor jackal like the tax collector yonder?" jerking his firm brown chin at the groveling teacher.

"The jackal did a very brave thing, to-night, O judge, braver than I for he went against his life training and I only followed mine!"

The judge stared contemptuously at poor Maung Shwaygnong, then grinned. "It must be a strong faith that made a fighting bull out of that poor worm, even for a betel's chew.—What's that saying you quoted?"

Adoniram repeated the matchless words and the judge's lips moved with the missionary's.

Mosquitoes settled in a cloud on Adoniram's hands and neck. The judge pulled at his lower lip. "A faith that

THE WITCH WOMAN

made a fighting bull of yonder poor jackal!" He smiled grimly. "The lord of white elephants had better feed it to his army!—Soldier," loudly to the guard at the door, "go quickly and bring me word where the witch woman has been put!"

"I go, O judge!" There was a quick thud of bare feet on the veranda.

Bats fluttered about the judge's head and their wings beat away the mist of mosquitoes from the flickering lamp. Pigs grunted in uneasy sleep beneath the floor. A tiger roared remotely. The judge deliberately prepared himself a chew of betel, then rose and, without a word, moved out of a door behind his dais.

Five long minutes passed and he did not return. Maung Shway-gnong raised his head, then his shoulders. Ten minutes passed. Maung Shway-gnong sat back on his haunches. Adoniram watched him silently. At the end of twenty minutes, the teacher rose and adjusted his turban.

"We may return to the work of translating in the study," he remarked in his old assured manner.

Adoniram got stiffly to his feet. "What does it mean, O friend?"

"It means that Jesus Christ's man gave the judge food for thought. We are free." The Burman gazed intently at Adoniram, then for the second time in their strange friendship, he prostrated himself before the missionary.

"Don't, brother!" protested Adoniram. "I don't deserve it, you don't know my sins."

"You have deep wisdom. It's a marvelous religion that not only gets a man into trouble but also gets him out of it! Come, lord teacher!"

He took Adoniram's arm and like two children speechlessly grateful that the rod had been spared, they went out into the night.

Just as they crossed the bazaar, they bumped into the soldier, who instantly recognized Adoniram's white clothing.

"How'd you get out?" he panted. "What does this mean, Jesus Christ's man?"

"The judge allowed us to depart, O soldier! Tell me of the witch woman," demanded Adoniram.

"While we were concerned with you, at the lake side, she crept to the jungle edge. The monk, who pursued her, says a tiger got her. Does one go to your zayat freely now, lord teacher?"

"Come some time and observe for yourself," replied Adoniram, moving onward through the night, and pondering heavily on the inscrutability of God's ways.

CHAPTER XVI

JONATHAN DAVID PRICE

ADONIRAM felt, after sleeping on the problem, that Maung Shway-gnong deserved a fitting reward for his behavior on the lake shore and told him so. The teacher lifted his tragic eyes from the translation of the Psalms he had been reading and said:

"Then let me be baptized now, O my friend!"

"Most willingly and gladly!" exclaimed Adoniram.

And so that evening he went into the water with Maung Shway-gnong and brought him out, a new man for God in Burma.

The conversion of Maung Shway-gnong was an immense stimulation to the tiny church. He was a distinguished figure in Rangoon in spite of his weakness and his many enemies. Others now took heart and came forward and by the end of the next rainy season, the number of those baptized had increased to eighteen.

Adoniram's complete segregation from the outer world was broken in upon by a letter from the secretary of the Baptist Foreign Missionary Board telling him that again they were sending him reënforcements, one Jonathan David Price, a medical missionary and his wife and that they had urged Mr. and Mrs. Hough to leave the safe haven of Serampore and return to the firing line at Rangoon.

Adoniram experienced a curious sensation both of gladness and uneasiness on receipt of this news. Thus far, with the exception of James Colman, the recruits from America had not been an unmixed blessing and Colman's ill health was a distinct handicap in spite of his cleverness and pluck. He was doing good work at Chittagong, but his strength was failing him steadily. In his latest letters to Adoniram, the poor fellow acknowledged that the hand of death was on him. Adoniram could not help wondering what handicap Dr. Price might possess. He wondered if Ann had seen him? It was frightful to think of the many months that had passed without any knowledge whatever of his wife. Since she had left Calcutta the year before, no line from her had reached him. It was barely possible that she had seen Price and approved of him. If she had, all was well.

The Prices followed hard on Dr. Bolles' letter, reaching Rangoon early in December, 1821.

Dr. Price was a tall, gaunt, rawboned, sandy-complexioned man with stiff, light hair standing erect all over his head, a retroussé nose and pale blue eyes. Certainly he was not handsome but there was a kindliness of expression in his ugly face that overcame somewhat the shock Adoniram felt at his first sight of him. Price was all Yankee and his New England accent gave Adoniram such a homesick pang as he had not experienced for many months.

Mrs. Price was of the delicate, worn New England type, nervous and intelligent, so familiar to Adoniram's youth. She was more intelligent, he thought, than her husband and her presence cheered him.

He turned the mission house over to them and moved into the zayat. Maung Shway-gnong, after a seemingly casual glance at the doctor, refused to undertake teaching them the language but found an instructor for them, a man who, he remarked ambiguously, had no scholarship to offend.

For the first few weeks, the families in the mission yard and the Christian congregation refused to take the doctor seriously in any capacity. But Price was entirely unoffended and assured Adoniram that "these folks would sing a different tune, presently. Wait till I perform an operation on one of them!"

"I hope the victim won't sing his tune in heaven,"

remarked Adoniram, half facetiously, half in warning.

Price had had hospital experience and was clever with his fingers as his contrivances for making his wife comfortable in the bare mission house showed. But Adoniram could find little of the physician in him.

The Houghs returned in January with the much-traveled press, but by some inexplicable mischance had forgotten to bring the type! Adoniram established them in the house with the Prices and was grateful for the zayat! Little chance now for meditation, but a vast opportunity to test the usefulness of the rules of living so prayerfully drawn up!

One day, after the Prices had been three months in Rangoon, the doctor sought out Adoniram, writing in the zayat.

"Brother Judson!" he cried. "Ma Baik's new baby isn't blind. Its eyelids are held together by a bit of skin. I can give him eyesight in ten minutes if you'll persuade her to let me slit that skin."

Adoniram said, warningly, "Do you know what Ma Baik will do to you if you hurt her baby? She's prayed for that baby's coming for years."

"She'll tear me limb from limb, I cal'late," grinned the doctor.

"No joke! She'll really try," insisted Adoniram.

"That's why I've come to you," said Price, coolly. "She'll take anything you say."

"But what can I say, doctor? I know nothing of your skill. And that little fellow's eyes—"

"They're no good to him. Never will be unless I open the lids. Look here, Brother Judson, how am I going to begin my work of salvation unless I *begin?*" Price ran his fingers through his bristling hair.

"That's true," admitted Adoniram, rising. "Well, I'll go talk to Ma Baik."

She was sitting on her veranda nursing her baby. Adoniram squatted beside her and told her the precise truth as to the doctor's offer and his own feelings with regard to him. To his surprise, Ma Baik did not at once refuse to listen.

"What would you do, O lord teacher, if this were your baby Roger?" she asked.

"I don't know," he replied. "Let me think a little. Put him in my arms."

He paced up and down the veranda, looking into the pretty little brown face and now and again touching the eyes, with gentle fingers. The eyeballs felt full and firm behind the closed lids. At last he laid his cheek on the downy head. "What would you have us do, Ma Baik's little son?" he asked. Then he and the mother smiled at each other.

"I think if it were little Roger I'd run the risk, Ma Baik," he said. "After all, the baby can be no blinder than he is."

"Send me the foreign doctor while my heart is still firm," exclaimed the mother.

A few moments later, the doctor and his wife were at work on the little boy and shortly a shriek of joy came from Ma Baik. Her son's brown eyes had opened full upon her.

From that day, Dr. Price was a made man among the Burmans of Rangoon. He removed cataract from the eyes of the viceroy's father and a wen from the neck of the most vicious of the tax collectors. He had a passion for cutting and slicing. It seemed to Adoniram that the doctor's skill was entirely mechanical and that he had little exact knowledge of the territory that lay beneath human skin and that he therefore concentrated on external malformations and growths. But Adoniram was devoutly thankful for whatever prestige the mission gained as a result of the doctor's work. He could only pray that he would not lose a patient, under the knife.

It seemed now as if the ill fortune that had pursued each group of recruits had run its course. Adoniram remarked on this one day to George Hough.

"Don't boast yet," warned the printer, tugging at his chin beard. "Mrs. Price has been fighting off ague for a week. I guess the doctor's knife can't help there."

Adoniram hurried to the house to bring to bear his superior knowledge of Oriental sicknesses. One glance at delicate little Mrs. Price was enough to alarm him. He sent her to bed and insisted to her skeptical husband that ague was the least of Mrs. Price's troubles. She was ill also of one of those dread diseases bred in Rangoon, called by the Judsons by the generic term, jungle sickness.

He succeeded at last in frightening Price and the doctor turned to with a will to nurse the suffering woman. But there was no staying the fever. She died on the night of May 2.

They laid her beside little Roger, under the casuarina tree.

The missionaries were deeply depressed by this untimely withdrawal. Death made a terrible vacancy when it visited so tiny and so isolated a group of exiles. Adoniram liked Price better for the way he took his loss. He wept bitterly for a day and then plunged harder than ever into the study of the language and his cure of the Burmans' bodies.

In spite of this tragedy, the outlook for the mission began to be distinctly optimistic. No one bothered them and the zayat had many visitors. If only Adoniram could have heard from Ann, he would have been completely cheerful. But May slipped into June and June into July and no letter came. Then, early in August, came a break in the serene routine of the missionaries.

The viceroy, passing on his elephant, paused before the zayat and gave Adoniram an order, couched in flowery terms, but none the less imperative.

"Foreign teacher, the golden presence, the lord of white elephants, having removed his palace and his court to Ava now finds time to consider the good of his subjects. He therefore directs me to send to him the foreign doctor, and you, as interpreter."

Adoniram bowed but was utterly unable to reply in words. However, the viceroy was quite content with merely issuing the mandate and ambled off without further remark. Adoniram gazed after him, then sank down on the zayat steps weak with a confusion of violent feelings.

What a people! After all the agony of the king's refusal, after the skulking, the fears, the hopes, the despairs, to be *invited* to visit the court! And as if that travesty on the character of the mission's aims were not sufficient, to be invited on the strength of the prowess of Jonathan Price with the scalpel!

Adoniram's first reaction was that he would not go. He would not leave the church in its first moment of prosperity, would not leave the all-important translating—he was now at work on Romans—to travel that weary way up the Irrawaddy to meet at Ava, what? The chances were large that they would meet a rebuff or worse from the unstable personage who occupied the golden throne.

However it was hardly fair to make the decision without hearing from Price so, having reached this point in his own conclusion, he went to the main house to tell his news.

None of the other three could understand his reluctance to obey the king's commands.

"You've worked for such an opportunity to establish the mission on an open, permanent basis ever since you came to Burma," exclaimed George Hough. "It won't pay to refuse, not from any point of view."

"I've about come to the conclusion," said Adoniram whimsically, "that there's nothing permanent in Burma but the jungle." Then he added seriously, "Don't build false hope, my brethren, we're sent for to remove wens, not to plant the cross."

"But—but—but—" spluttered Price who had been walking the floor with excitement, "but we can't refuse! It's a king who orders us,—a king!"

"A king!" grunted Adoniram. "Price, he's a feckless, irresponsible, undeveloped pagan, in the complete control of a woman more wicked than Jezebel and Salome combined. You speak from a boundless ignorance."

But the others would not have it so. And in his heart, Adoniram knew that they were right; that no matter what the outcome, it was his duty to use this opportunity to do what he could for the cause. Finally he admitted that he was "fanciful and too much wedded to the mission yard"— Mrs. Hough's single contribution to the debate,—and he said with a comical groan:

"The very smilax vines are growing over me! Very well, doctor, your interpreter is ready, whenever you are!"

Dr. Price gave a cheer and the Houghs clapped their hands. Adoniram looked from one face to another, seeing not these, but his own and James Colman's that moonlit night on the prime minister's porch in Amarapura. Still it had its amusing side, this second embassy in comparison with the first, when one considered all that had gone between, and suddenly to the utter bewilderment of the other three, he burst into gigantic laughter.

CHAPTER XVII

SURGEON TO THE KING

ON the 28th day of August, 1822, they embarked on one of the king's dispatch canoes and just a month later anchored under the wooded shores of Ava.

The lord of white elephants was in process of removing the court from Amarapura to the reconstructed town of Ava. No one save his majesty was enjoying the removal. Rich and poor alike found it a hardship to leave their homes in the tamarind- and palm-grown older city and without any financial compensation find place in the newly planted and starkly modern capital. It had required a generation to grow the roses and the grape-vines of Amarapura. On their way from the boat to the immediate audience ordered by the king, the petty official who conducted Adoniram and the doctor complained bitterly of the new conditions. Dr. Price, who with Adoniram's help got the substance of the Burman's remarks, said that he was astonished at the man's disrespect for the king's plans. Adoniram smiled, but made no reply.

The new palace was not yet completed and the golden feet were stayed in a barn-like structure on stilts at one side of the new palace enclosure. The two Americans docilely put off their shoes at the main gate and followed their guide across the sandy courtyard.

"There's the king, the lord of air and water and so forth, my dear doctor," said Adoniram as they skirted a new-built water pool.

"Where?" demanded Price, staring eagerly in every direction.

"Yonder! The personage riding pig-a-back." Adoniram smiled grimly.

The doctor's jaw dropped. A fat and perspiring Burman with a strip of muslin between his teeth for reins, was being driven past the pool by a gentleman, mercifully of slight proportions, who perched comfortably on his back, legs locked neatly under the other's well-padded chin.

"Well—I—I *swan!*" ejaculated Price, in so crestfallen a voice that Adoniram was sorry for him.

"Never mind, doctor! There'll be plenty of times when you'll be glad to recall his majesty in this guise!"—laughing as he took his friend's arm and hurried him on toward the palace.

Their guide left them in a small bare room adjacent to the main audience-hall. They waited here alone and in silence for some time before the king entered with his retinue. He was no longer playing the buffoon but walked toward them with great dignity on his own legs. He wore a paso of red checked silk and a white muslin jacket and carried a little sword. The Americans sheekoed and then, as all the members of the retinue were standing, they also rose. His majesty walked directly up to the two visitors and asked which one was the doctor. He gave no sign of recognizing Adoniram.

"This is the American doctor, O gracious king," said Adoniram, putting his hand on Price's shoulder.

The king stared up into the doctor's ugly face. Perhaps it was not ugly to Burmese eyes, for he smiled in a pleasant way and asked eagerly:

"Can you give a medicine that will produce endless life?"

"Tell his majesty I cal'late to prolong life as much as any doctor on earth," replied the doctor, "and that my galvanic battery is a long step in that direction."

The king's eyes widened as Adoniram described this, the most interesting article in Dr. Price's equipment, and he demanded to see it. Maung Ing was called and staggered in, bearing several cases of medicine and surgical instruments, beside the little black box containing what Adoniram had named to the lord of white elephants as the lightning shocker. His majesty seated himself cross-legged on a gilded chair and the remainder of the company squatted on the floor while Price set up his exhibition.

For an hour, the battery fascinated the Burmans. Then the king asked to see the medicines and surgical instruments. Followed a long discussion of diseases and cures, with special emphasis laid by Bagyi-daw on the treatment of sore eyes, wens and broken bones.

Adoniram, interpreting with the greatest care, watched the king's face with growing confidence that all would go well; the galvanic battery was not to be accorded the treatment that had been allotted to the Bible, two years before! Nor was his confidence misplaced. After he had exhausted the resources of the American's surgical case, the king sent for his own. It proved to be one of ancient Portuguese derivation and when the doctor exclaimed in wonder over its contents, his majesty told him to take the instruments with him and use them.

Price's sunbrowned cheeks burned with gratification and he said to Adoniram, "I consider that equivalent to fixing me here for life."

"Perhaps," murmured Adoniram. "Let's hope his majesty won't forget we need proper housing for these instruments!"

The king did not forget. He spoke to a tall official, in a bright green paso.

"See that a house is found near the palace walls for the foreign doctor, and look up all the diseased people here and in Amarapura, that we may hear his decision about them. Lanciego was truthful. This man undoubtedly has wisdom."

With this, Bagyi-daw jumped from his seat and rushed from the room so rapidly that his attendants bearing spittoons, peacock-feather fans and cheroots, were obliged to break into a run. The rest of the retinue followed quickly, only the tall official named by the king remaining. He strode up to the two Americans and, pausing before them, remarked with a little smile that it was a fine day. And he spoke in purest English!

They gazed at him, astounded. To the casual eyes he was a Burman about sixty years of age. His iron-gray topknot was bound with a strip of white muslin. His beard was plucked, Burmese fashion, leaving only a long tuft hanging from the center of his chin. All this at the first glance. With the second, they saw that the eyes beneath the shaggy brows were blue!

"My name is Rodgers, gentlemen," said the official.

"Are you a half-breed, sir?" demanded Price.

"Certainly not!" drawing himself up. "I am an Englishman, formerly second officer of a ship of the East India Company."

"Then why on earth dress like a native?" insisted the doctor.

"Perhaps Mr. Rodgers prefers to dress like a native," suggested Adoniram dryly. Price's curiosity always annoyed him. "I think you were collector of the port of Rangoon at one time, sir?"

"And shall be again, if Lanciego ever gets his fill at the trough," said Rodgers. "I've been serving the king for forty years and I must admit that his rewards come with discouraging infrequency."

"Forty years!" exclaimed Price. "Well, I don't know as I blame you for sticking to him, not if the previous king was as kind and pleasant as this one. I'd serve Bagyi-daw that long with pleasure!"

"Humph!" grunted the Englishman. He glanced from the doctor to Adoniram and said, raising his enormous eyebrows, "Court fever already?"

"We'll have to admit his majesty was extraordinarily affable to the doctor," smiled Adoniram.

"That affable surface can be lashed to fury by very trifling cause, my friend," was Rodgers' return. "It's well, I assure you, that we all crouch in the king's presence! He frequently gives way to gusts of passion during which he's like a raving madman, and will thrust his spear through any one. But we must get on with his orders. The finding of a plot of ground for you isn't going to be easy!"

Nor was it. The two missionaries were obliged to live on their boat for several days while the search for an abiding-place went on. They did not find one until Prince Mengmyat-bo, the king's brother, opened his heart and his dooryard and offered space in his palace enclosure for the missionaries to erect a hut. They moved into this early in October.

In the meantime, Rodgers was faithfully executing the remainder of his majesty's order, and the boat, then the hut, were besieged by the maimed, the halt and the blind. Pitiful folk dogged Dr. Price's footsteps, crowded the yard, the veranda, the very house, until they were obliged to bar the doors in order to obtain time and space for sleep.

The good doctor was in his element. He and Adoniram repaired to the king's presence every morning immediately after breakfast and remained there for as long as his majesty found interest in the subject of disease. Then they returned to the hut and Price physicked and sliced until even he was sated. But the pressure on the doctor was so great that Adoniram suggested that two promising Burmans be taken on as surgical apprentices and this was done, to the vast approval of his majesty.

Adoniram served faithfully as interpreter, although deeply impatient to be about the Master's business, as he wrote Ann. . . . Ann, of whose whereabouts he had now been ignorant for a year! He tried to persuade old Mr. Rodgers to take his place with Price, but the Englishman would have none of it. Lanciego was in town and Rodgers was engineering a political intrigue against him that gave the old man no time for lesser matters. And, he admitted to Adoniram, he had no use for missionaries, anyhow.

So for several weeks, when he was not down with fever and ague, Adoniram translated the ailments of Ava into the American vernacular and was glad that Price at least waxed great in the king's favor. And the doctor, attending the king, the queen and the royal offspring, developed the enthusiasm for court life and noble names possible only to the most independent of Yankees! His calling-list read like a court-register.

Among the handful of Europeans in Ava, in fact, Price had for the moment no rival save in the person of a young Englishman, Henry Gouger, who had reached Amarapura in September with a canoeload of goods for trade. He was little more than a boy. Adoniram caught sight of him frequently at the palace, where Gouger was a great favorite, the waspish chief queen having taken him up: a tall, blond youth who, when he was not attending very cleverly to business, was riding a hard-bitten little pony about with a group of young palace bloods.

But Adoniram's turn was to come. One morning late in October, after a long discussion of smallpox cures, the lord of life turned suddenly to the interpreter and for the first time recognized him as a human being.

"And you in black, what are you? A medical man too?"

"Not a medical man, O lord of white elephants, but a teacher of religion," replied Adoniram, with quickening pulse.

"Has any one embraced your religion, foreign teacher?" His majesty scowled thoughtfully.

"Some, your majesty; not here, but in Rangoon."

There was complete silence in the room. A peacock walked deliberately across the audience-hall and, stepping within the door of the little reception-room, spread its tail and stared from one face to another. An old gentleman in a white silk robe gently shooed the creature out. Adoniram took a quick breath. He recognized the old personage as the man who once had put his nephew to the iron maul for embracing Catholicism!

The king spoke again. "What do you know about astronomy, O foreign teacher?"

"I know the Copernican system, your majesty."

"Explain further."

Adoniram was no scientist but he gathered his wits together and gave so lucid and so picturesque a lecture on the starry ways that the king obviously was charmed. When he had finished, Bagyi-daw smiled. "You have a delightful voice, O teacher, deep yet soft. I shall be glad to hear more of it."

Then with his customary abruptness, he rushed away. Adoniram stood for a moment trying to assimilate the tremendous fact that the ruler of Burma had distinctly understood that several of his subjects had embraced Christianity, yet he had not been moved to wrath. Thanks be to God for His infinite mercy!

From this moment Adoniram took his proper place at court. There were keen minds in Ava, eager for new ideas, and they welcomed the opportunity the king's tacit approval of the teacher had given to inquire into this new religion about which much had been rumored. Prince Meng-myat-bo, who was a cripple, sent for Adoniram the following day and, after asking him to explain the Copernican system, commanded him to describe Jesus Christ, of whom the prince had heard through a Portuguese padre. The king's older sister, a very intelligent woman, next called for Adoniram. He gave her a copy of the little Burmese catechism Ann had completed before her departure and embraced the opportunity to tell the Princess of Ann's dream that all Burman girls could be taught to read, as were the boys.

"It seems such a pity about Burmese women," Adoniram

said to her, as they sat together on the veranda, eating pickled tea and watching the king's peacocks parade on the garden paths. "It seems such an unfair law of Buddhism that no one can attain the great peace, the nigban, who doesn't undergo Buddhist baptism and that that baptism can be got only by going for a period into the monasteries, where females are not permitted to set foot."

The princess turned a keen black eye on him and said, as she accepted a lighted cheroot from an attendant, "There are no women in nigban. If a woman behaves herself in this life, she's a man in the next and thus has her chance."

"But Buddha Gautama never taught any such thing," protested Adoniram. "He had women as well as men disciples . . . At any rate, my wife taught several women in Rangoon to read, and if they can't have access to your sacred law, they can to ours."

"You mean Ma Judson has taught Burmese women to read English?" cried the Princess.

"No, your highness,—Burmese. Thus, they read my translations of the Word of God, and are put in the way of salvation. Christianity doesn't recognize sex."

"I'm not sure that's a happy fact." The princess' round cheeks, liberally yellowed with sandalwood powder, suddenly dimpled, and she arched a carefully plucked and blackened eyebrow at the missionary. The look of youth was still strong in Adoniram's wistful and burning gray eyes. Then —for she was keen—she sobered quickly, and said, "But I would like much to read, myself. Bring your wife to Ava, O foreign teacher, and let her teach me and my friends to read your sacred scriptures."

Adoniram jumped to his feet and strode up and down the veranda. He looked out over the glowing colors of the palace yard and above the walls to the hills of Sagaing, thick-studded with pagodas. Quick tears blurred his vision. He sat down again, quickly, and said with a voice deepened by emotion:

"When my wife returns, O princess, she will come and, with great joy, teach you."

"I will be her patron," said her highness, complacently. "You must build a monastery and live in it. What a monastery that will be, admitting women!"

"Can you sell me land, O golden princess?" asked Adoniram, who was not unlettered in the whimsicality of the royal breed and would strike while the iron was hot.

"Alas, lord teacher, I own nothing here. The lands that support me are far down the Irrawaddy. Go to Prince Meng-myat-bo. He has property here and at Sagaing. Go now, O teacher. I thirst for knowledge."

She seemed in earnest. Adoniram needed no urging. He hurried off to the surgery, where Dr. Price was struggling to teach his two assistants the rudiments of surgical cleanliness and urged the doctor to accompany him on an embassy to the prince. The doctor was delighted.

"Haven't I told you a thousand times, Brother Judson, that it was through healing bodies that Jesus Christ reached folks' souls? That's why this visit to Ava is striking roots and sprouting at the same time!"

"Perhaps you're right, Brother Price," returned Adoniram, meekly.

The doctor, moreover, declared that his standing with the king was now so secure that he'd not bother with the prince, but go at once to headquarters! Easier to work down than up, said he.

Nothing loath, Adoniram followed him to the palace, to which the doctor now had perpetual access. They found the lord of white elephants in the audience-room, playing at leapfrog with several of his courtiers. News had come of the success of the Burmese general, Bandula, against the British in Assam, and his majesty was expressing his delight. It was a good moment. Bagyi-daw paused long enough to slap Dr. Price on the back and pull off his neck-scarf, then he addressed Adoniram courteously:

SURGEON TO THE KING

"Tell some one to sell you ground, provided there be some not in use."

They dared not urge a more definite order and so went to the prince, after all. He was affable, even enthusiastic, over the suggested monastery and told them to search for what they needed. He would try to force the owner to sell.

The search naturally devolved on Adoniram. The doctor had to get on with his practice. Land in Ava was as scarce as it now was plentiful in Amarapura. But after a week, Adoniram located a desirable plot on the bank of the river, where once a Burmese monastery had stood. This could be purchased but only with the sanction of the king, although it belonged to Prince Meng-myat-bo.

Adoniram sought the king. But the golden feet had chosen to spend a few days in the old water palace at Amarapura. Prince Meng-myat-bo also was out of town. Court etiquette required all court officials to leave Ava when his majesty left. Adoniram dared not delay the purchasing of the plot, lest some one change the king's mind for him. So he hired a bullock-cart and, with the creak of the solid wooden wheels competing with the tinkling of the bells round the bullocks' necks, trotted gayly over the long road to the deserted capital. It was the same palm-set road along which he and Colman had plodded so many times with hope and despair in their hearts. Colman was much in his mind these days. After all, the boy had been right: it *was* a good world!

He passed the zayat beside the lake and he passed the monastery where some one had told him the gaing-ôk was detained, teaching the royal children. There were monks sweeping the yard under the acacia and tamarind trees. He went creaking and tinkling through Amarapura, his squatting driver carrying on an affectionate conversation with the fat bullocks as they went. But the lord of life and air was not to be found at the gilded summer-house on the river's edge. He had gone to pay a visit to his co-sovereign, the white elephant. This was no moment to approach the golden presence. To-morrow one could place one's head beneath the golden feet! Thus spoke the keeper of the gate.

Adoniram sighed with impatience and turned back.

As they neared the zayat by the lake, a monk stepped from the shelter of the fig-tree beside it and deliberately placed himself in their path. The driver, with a cry of consternation, halted the bullocks just before they nosed the untouchable yellow robe. It was the gaing-ôk!

Adoniram jumped from the cart and faced the monk. The Burman stared at him with interest. They were an astounding pair!

"You must have been waiting for me, O my lord," said Adoniram with a smile. "That was most courteous of you."

"Come into the zayat, O foreign animal," ordered the monk, abruptly. "We must talk, and the sun is hot."

Astonished, Adoniram laid off his shoes and followed into the well-remembered shelter. They seated themselves on the windswept floor, facing each other.

The Burman laid aside his palm-leaf fan and said in a troubled voice, "I am willing to admit that you have some of the properties of a sacred character. They have been written in your face since first you came to Burma. I will not admit that you have a karma, but I will say that if you were a Buddhist in the same degree that you are a Jesus Christ man, you would have great merit."

Adoniram's hazel eyes opened very wide. The old monk had made an admission that must have been torture to him.

"Your religion, O lord"—Adoniram bowed—"is very beautiful, but it is not meant for me."

"And your religion is not for me," returned the gaing-ôk. "At Prome, not long since, I examined Maung Shwaygnong thoroughly on the subject. I will admit that a faith which makes a man of my old disciple is not to be despised. I will admit that his reading to me of your sacred writings moved me. But it is a sad tale: a tale with a moral too unhappy for a simple people like us Burmans. Having said this much, I have said all that I can. And I ask you, by the kindness inherent in your teachings, O foreign teacher, to go back to your own country and leave us alone." The old man's face was strained, his eyes were passionately pleading.

"But, my lord," exclaimed Adoniram, "since you are thus moved, why not investigate further? Why not let me explain to you—"

The gaing-ôk suddenly put his fan before his face. "No!" he thundered. "I will not hear! Go back to your own land!"

"You are not so liberal a people as you boast of being, O gaing-ôk." Adoniram leaned earnestly forward. "If you came to my country you could propagate your religion anywhere, so long as you didn't break the laws of the government. You see, my country was founded by people who crossed the unknown seas to find a land where no king, no law, could force them to worship save as they thought best."

"You say so?"—dropping the fan. "Which of the five hundred islands did they leave?"

"The world isn't like that!" Adoniram was purposely scornful. "Look, O gaing-ôk, I will draw you a map of those portions of the world I myself have seen."

He had in his pocket the bit of crayon he used in describing the Copernican system to various inquirers. With this he drew a sweeping line on the floor at the old monk's knees, —the eastern coast of America. Here was Boston and here Plymouth, where he had played as a boy, and here the broad Atlantic and England and the coast of France.

The Burman stooped forward, his near-sighted eyes fixed unwaveringly on the chalk in the sunburned fingers. When he had finished the outline of Africa and India, Adoniram returned to America and slowly, carefully, told the story of the Pilgrims. The sun crossed the zenith. The bullocks drowsed in their yokes. The driver crept on his knees to a spot just back of the monk and listened, breathing hard with wonder and skepticism. The shadow of the zayat crept eastward and was lost among the undulating lotus pads. A man on an elephant shuffling along the dusty road stared at the trio with dropped jaw.

But nothing disturbed the deep murmur of Adoniram's voice until an eagle shot like a falling meteor into the lake just beyond the zayat and rose with two yards of snake dripping and writhing from his talons. The little group of three started.

"It's a beautiful story," sighed the monk.

"It's a true story," insisted Adoniram.

"I believe you, O teacher!" returned the gaing-ôk, with a direct glance. He dropped his head and studied the map for a long time. When he lifted his eyes there was in them a new quality: a mingling of respect and of pleading. "And I will speak full truth to you, also, Jesus Christ's man. The head monk of all monks in Burma holds me responsible for your removal. If you do not leave, I may be set down, no man can say how far. So I ask you, will you not return to your own most free and happy land?"

"I cannot!" cried Adoniram, touched and unhappy. "O gaing-ôk, I speak truth when I tell you my God will not permit me to return."

"Then we both are lost, you and I," exclaimed the old man, desperately. He rose slowly and the bullock-driver slid backward rapidly to the road.

Adoniram came to his feet, more unhappy than he'd been for many days. "No! No! that must not be! Let me explain!"

"I have lost half a lifetime of merit already to-day, listening to your explanations," groaned the gaing-ôk. He gathered his yellow robes about him and rushed out into the road.

Adoniram drove dejectedly back to Ava.

He reached home to find letters which the Houghs had forwarded from Rangoon. One was from Ann, the first since she had left Madras Roads. She was near the equator at the moment of writing, nearly a year before. She was entirely recovered from her liver trouble and deeply regretted that she was committed to the long exile from him. Early in the spring of 1823 she was sure she would be in Rangoon again. Early spring! March! And it already was December! Adoniram's dejected spirits soared. Less than three months more of loneliness! His first impulse was to call on Price to rejoice with him, but second thought deterred him. Price was still mourning his wife, lying under the casuarina tree in Rangoon.

The other letter was only a note from Mrs. Colman. James had died early in the previous summer. An attack of intermittent fever, superimposed on consumption of the lungs, had been too much for the brave fellow. He was twenty-four years old.

Adoniram stood motionless, a letter in either hand. So much of joy and sorrow, so much of success and failure, had been packed into the last fortnight that he was bewildered, and the doctor did not lessen his feeling of confusion by choosing this particular moment to make what Adoniram considered an outrageous announcement.

He came into the little room off the surgery, which was used as both bed- and dining-room, and running his great fingers through his bristling hair, said with peculiar vehemence:

"Brother Judson, you've got a chore to do for me."

Adoniram, with Mrs. Colman's letter still in his hand, asked soberly, "What is it, doctor?"

"Well, you know that homely little Burmese woman I took cataracts off of a month ago—the one that's part Siamese?"

"Yes," replied Adoniram; "her ugliness makes her unforgettable although she seems amiable enough, poor soul."

"She's totally blind. I cal'late I failed on that job." Price watched his fellow-missionary closely, as he straightened his round shoulders. "I'm going to marry her, Brother Judson."

"What!" shouted Adoniram, dropping the letters. "Are you entirely mad, Dr. Price?"

"Not one iota mad, my friend," returned the doctor, calmly. "I'm very fond of that little woman and I'm going to marry her. Burma's no place for a white woman. No one should know that better than you, sir. And I'm a man. I don't cal'late to do otherwise than marry."

"But what can be so fine as celibacy for men in your position, Price?" demanded Adoniram. "Look here, are you being mistakenly altruistic and trying to make up for the failure of your surgery?"

"Nothing of the kind. She's a nice woman and she says she'll turn Christian. There's no need and there's no use of your protesting, Judson. It's my affair."

Adoniram stared at him, wondering how he could put into words what he felt without seeming narrow and bitter.

"Doctor," he began slowly, "I've been in the Orient nine years to your one, and I've yet to see a white man who has married a Burman who hasn't always had to choose between turning Burman himself or deserting his wife."

"I know that, Judson, but I cal'late to stay here in Ava the rest of my days. Where else on earth could I go to enjoy the position I have here, the personal friend of a king and his nobles? And where could I be as useful? You yourself don't desire the conversion of these people more strongly than I do. I say, Christ Jesus, come as quickly as possible. I pray for them as frequently and as passionately as you do, sir. I shall settle down here and not a day shall pass that I don't do my utmost to enlarge His Kingdom in Ava."

"Do you forget that you are an American so easily?" Adoniram spoke bitterly. "Man, don't you know that as the years go on, every ship you see sail westward will bear a portion of your heart?"

The doctor did not reply at once. Adoniram followed his gaze. Twilight was falling on the Irrawaddy. The last of the afterglow touched the white spires of the pagodas at

Sagaing. A line of elephants came slowly up from watering. A paddy boat, lateen sails full, drifted swiftly by with the current. A nightingale mourned from the prince's garden.

"And your unborn children, Price?" said Adoniram, gently.

"I guess God can take care of any little souls He has waiting for their turn on earth," declared the doctor, stoutly. "I plan to have you marry us, to-morrow, Brother Judson."

"I can't do it, doctor!" cried Adoniram. "Such marriages are wrong. What will our brethren in America say?—and your wife's people? Price, she's not cold in her grave, down there in Rangoon."

"You can't speak like that to me, Judson,"—bringing a fist against the door-frame.

"I must speak like that, dear Price. I'm your spiritual adviser, unworthy though I am. And I cannot consent to this miscegenation."

Dr. Price's gaunt cheeks reddened. "Brother Judson, the law of America and of nature provides for such cases when a minister is not to be found!"

Adoniram threw up his hands, figuratively as well as actually. "God help you, Price! The Orient has bitten you and only He can help."

"Will you perform that ceremony?" insisted the doctor.

"You have made it impossible for me to continue to refuse," replied Adoniram grimly. "But the woman will have to be a Christian first."

"I told you she wanted to be!" The doctor's tone was triumphant. "I've been instructing her ever since the operation, as fully as my language limits would let me. You'd better examine her to-morrow and baptize her."

Adoniram picked up Ann's and Mrs. Colman's letters. "She'll not be baptized until she's fit for the privilege, Price," and he sat down to write to James Colman's widow.

But it was difficult to concentrate. . . . The gaing-ôk's

tragic eyes came between him and the paper. The threat for Adoniram in the old man's last words meant nothing to him. He'd ceased to fear the gaing-ôk's power. But his curious and persistent liking for the monk made his obvious unhappiness an added burden for Adoniram to carry. Perhaps God meant this as a suggestion that eventually the gaing-ôk would follow in Maung Shway-gnong's footsteps. . . . It was a good, a hopeful world. . . . Ah, poor young Colman . . . that beautiful, happy, fervent boy. . . . Once more he picked up his pen.

CHAPTER XVIII

THE INWARD SILENCE

THE golden presence returned to Ava the next day and most graciously gave his permission for the purchase of the ancient monastery ground and thus automatically set the seal of his approval on the establishment of a "foreign religion-propagating" institution in his capital.

The Cross was planted in Ava.

That evening, as Adoniram sat in his little room, working on his diary, the doctor led the Burmese woman of his choice through the doorway. "This is Ma Noo, sir," he said quietly.

She moved with outspread hands and head thrown back in the too poignant attitude of the newly blind; a human being smitten with deep disaster at middle-age. Adoniram's heart reproached him. He sprang to his feet and led her tenderly to a mat beside the lamp tripod—as though the light she could not see might comfort her!

"Sit here, O friend of my friend," he said, "and let us talk together."

Price, staring a little sullenly from the doorway, gave a sudden sob and went out.

Ma Noo and Adoniram talked for a long time. She was a good soul, timid, simple, but adoring Price and, through him, the Christ that had brought Price to Burma. She was only too glad to obey Adoniram's command to come daily to the hut for religious instruction.

When she had gone, with a little shaved-headed child leading her, the doctor and Adoniram had a quiet talk. Prince Meng-myat-bo had given Price permission to build a house on land he owned across the river in Sagaing. The location was far too isolated for mission purposes. On the other hand, it was on high ground, and, the doctor was certain, was more healthful for white people than the newly purchased plot at Ava. He urged Adoniram to build the mission there. But Adoniram was not going to give up the hard-won victory in Ava for any mere considerations of health. He planned to have a house erected on his Ava plot and ready for Ann on her arrival.

"Well, perhaps, all things considered," said Price, "that's a wise decision. I'm equally set on living in Sagaing—for health's sake. My lungs are bothering me. And it's just as well for us to have separate households, Judson."

"Perhaps," agreed Adoniram, quietly. "I shall go down the river as soon as my house is finished, to meet Mrs. Judson," his heart leaping as he spoke.

The doctor eyed him seriously: the delicate face, with blue veins showing at the temples, the thick chestnut hair, damp with sweat though the night was too cool for comfort, the fine lips fever-cracked, and the hazel eyes contracted with pain.

"If you'll take my advice, Judson," he said bluntly, "you'll come over to Sagaing and get rid of that ague before we have to bury you in Ava. I tell you frankly, no man can live and work and suffer as you do. You ought never to enter Rangoon again."

"And I tell you, doctor," retorted Adoniram, "that only death itself can prevent my meeting my dear wife in Rangoon two months from now."

Dr. Price grunted and, opening his notebook, began to draw a plan for his proposed house in Sagaing.

But his warning to Adoniram proved to be not without grounds. Two weeks later, with the help of Maung Ing, the doctor carried Adoniram, raving in fever, across the Irrawaddy to the barely completed house on a Sagaing bluffside. Adoniram's marvelous vitality actually survived two weeks here of bleeding, Peruvian bark and calomel and by the middle of January he was negotiating through Maung Ing for passage in a small boat down the river. Early in the last week of January he paid farewell visits to his numerous friends among court officials, ending with the king.

Adoniram met Lanciego in the anteroom where his majesty was receiving informally. The Spaniard was very affable and the king, observing the two in conversation, asked curiously:

"What are you talking about, my two foreigners?"

"He is speaking of his return to Rangoon, your majesty," replied Lanciego.

"Why does he return?" exclaimed Bagyi-daw. "Let him not return. Let both the doctor and the teacher stay together. If one goes away the other must remain alone and will be unhappy."

"He wishes to go for a short time only, O lord of life," Lanciego answered, "to bring his wife, the female teacher, and his goods, not having brought anything with him this time and he will return soon."

The king looked sharply at Adoniram. "Will you then come again?"

"I shall come, O gracious king!" Adoniram spoke as ardently as he felt.

"When you come again, is it your intention to remain permanently, or to go back and forth as foreigners like Gouger commonly do?"

"When I come again, your majesty," replied Adoniram, "it is my intention to remain permanently."

"That is well!" Bagyi-daw nodded and left them.

That evening, Adoniram baptized Ma Noo in the shallows of the Irrawaddy and a little later united her to Dr. Price in marriage. Afterward he asked God to forgive him if he had done wrong.

On the morning of January 22, he embarked in a small boat for Rangoon. It was heavy-laden, for he was carrying all his food and fuel supplies with him. The king's eyes were on Assam and not on the Irrawaddy, and as a consequence, the river-banks were infested with robbers. The local authorities did what they could. The bodies of two robbers lay on the shore near Adoniram's place of embarkation, decapitated, the heads reversed and stakes driven through the mouths. There were undoubtedly many mute object-lessons such as these all the way to Rangoon. Nevertheless, Adoniram planned to keep to the middle of the stream and trust to speed at night rather than to the protection of the little towns.

As a consequence, he made a safe and rapid journey, reaching Rangoon at one o'clock on the morning of February 2.

He found a discouraging state of affairs at the mission. The new viceroy was taxing the people almost into active insurrection. He had been especially hard on the mission converts, and every one of them, excepting those living in the mission yard, had fled the town. Maung Shway-gnong, as Adoniram had gathered from the gaing-ôk, had been recalled to the army. The Houghs had done their best to keep the church going, but it had to be admitted that George was a better printer than he was preacher, even discounting the fact that he had no such knowledge of the language as had Adoniram. The missing type was still missing. It was not precisely a cheerful homecoming. Still, with Ann only a month away, Adoniram could not be much depressed.

But even this promised joy was to be denied him. The day after his arrival, a letter came from Ann in England. She was leaving for America and could not reach Burma before the summer of 1823.

Adoniram went into his bedroom and wept.

When he had recovered his poise and had excoriated himself for his weakness, he looked the situation over calmly. His first impulse was to return to Ava. He might not only make progress with the mission work there but might also prevail on the king to protect the Rangoon church. The

THE INWARD SILENCE

viceroy, hearing of his return without Dr. Price, had sent word that if a single meeting were held by the teacher, soldiers would be turned into the mission yard to burn and destroy. But the second thought on this was prompted by the memory of Prince Meng-myat-bo's remark that the king's most recent policy was to allow each provincial ruler to manage all affairs of his province independently, so long as he made proper remittances of money and soldiers to Ava. There was no use in appealing, then, to the lord of white elephants and, also, it was evident that the Rangoon mission depended on Adoniram's presence to preserve its very existence.

His final determination was that he would settle down to work on his translation of the Bible and await the turn of events with what patience he could muster. He recalled, with a twisted smile, a saying of his mother. He had been a very restless child, impulsive, tormented if he was obliged to wait on any one's slowness or deliberation. His wise mother would shake her head. "Some day, dear son, you'll learn that though patience is a tired nag, yet will she jog!"

He told quiet little Mrs. Hough his mother's words. She nodded. "I guess any one that has the nervous energy you have, Brother Judson, must feel like he had the itch when it's bottled up for a time. Why don't you get rid of some of your surplus by putting Maung Nau in training for the ministry?"

It was the longest statement Adoniram had ever heard from Mrs. Hough.

"Has Maung Nau talked to you about the ministry?" he asked, with interest.

She nodded. "He's afraid you men-folks would think him presumptuous. But he's a good little man, Maung Nau, and you ought to hear him preach. It's as pretty as a poem. He's better at it than Mr. Hough, I can tell you! You'll have to lecture him about his superstitions, though." She began to laugh.

"It's like removing their teeth, you know, Sister Hough," said Adoniram, ruefully. "At what are you laughing?"

Mrs. Hough had been drying tea-cups. She now began to wash out the towel, for Ma So and Ma Baik couldn't launder to suit her New England eyes. "Well, sir, one day not long after you left for Ava, I was pestered by an especially bad smell on the front piazza and I finally located it in Mr. Beg Pardon's house. So I took him down and undertook to empty out the trash through that little hole at the top.

"Of course, some one saw me. Never was such a nosey place. This time it was Maung Nau. He snatched the cocoanut-shell out of my hands and rushed it back to its peg. Then he raved. Told me I'd brought destruction on the house and I don't know what-all. Anyhow, he kept it up for an hour and was so frightened himself that he frightened me and when he finally said there was a way to placate Mr. Beg Pardon, I was only too glad to tell him I'd do anything within reason. And what do you think it was? Well, sir, I had to put a sicca rupee into the house and then I had to stand in front of it with Ma Baik's harp on my arm and strike a certain chord for a quarter of an hour. And I did it, like a fool! And I'll admit with shame that I was just as much in earnest as Maung Nau was! And we have been good friends ever since!"

Adoniram's hazel eyes twinkled. "Dear Mrs. Hough, is this by way of confession?"

"Well," she admitted, "for all I've laughed over it, I've been ashamed of myself and I've been planning to—well, confess to you . . ." a little anxiously.

He looked at her careworn, gentle face. "I'm sure the blessed Nazarene had a sense of humor and would have found nothing to forgive in the absurdity, Sister Hough . . . What a picture you must have made!"

They both burst into delighted laughter and Adoniram was still laughing when he went off to find Maung Nau. He felt better. He had missed nothing more than Ann's unfailing sense of humor.

THE INWARD SILENCE

What with Maung Nau and the translation of the Bible, spring passed and summer came—June, July. But there was no Ann. With the beginning of August, Adoniram extended his morning and evening walks always to include the wharf. Lanciego's men developed a kindly interest in his quest and each day gathered news for him. Adoniram knew more about the movements of ships than the collector himself—but he learned nothing of Ann's movements.

Early in September, when his drooping spirits could no longer rouse to the blundering attentions of George Hough and when Mrs. Hough's sympathy began to irritate him, he brought out Madame Guyon. She alone had power to take his mind from its brooding anxiety.

The French woman's insistence on her espousal with God seemed less offensive to him now than it had on first reading. After all, during her whole life, she had starved for human love, so it was natural for her to turn all the affections of her passionate heart to the source of all love: natural and right. Love, after all, said Jeanne Marie Guyon, is the only good. What then can be as right as a union with God by giving Him entire love, expressed in absolute surrender to His will?

One achieved this surrender, she said, through prayer. "Prayer is the intercourse of the soul with God. One must learn a species of prayer that can be exercised at all times. It cannot, therefore, be a prayer of the head but of the heart: a prayer that actually is a supreme inward silence: inward silence, wherein the soul is abstracted from all outward things in holy stillness and humble faith, and waits to receive the Divine Presence. One must quiet all reasonings. Deeply was it said, The Lord is in His holy temple, let all the earth keep silence before Him.

> "The love of thee flows just as much
> As that of ebbing self subsides.
> Our hearts—their scantiness is such—
> Bear not the conflicts of two rival tides."

The translation of the verses in the biography had been done perfectly by William Cowper, that most mystic of poets, who had found in Madame Guyon a kindred spirit.

> "My spouse, in whose presence I live,
> Sole object of all my desires,
> Who knowst what a flame I conceive
> And canst easily double its fires! . . .
> O glory in which I am lost
> Too deep for the plummet of thought,
> On an ocean of deity tossed,
> I am swallowed, I sink into nought!"

Adoniram, who so loved beauty—Ann's beauty, the beauty of the world of Burma—whose artistic sense yearned over the loveliness of Buddhistic learning and whose chosen vocation constantly urged him to deny this love—found something curiously attractive in the thought of discovering the perfection of beauty in God.

Was this Buddhism? "I have lost desire," said The Blessed One. "I sit as an empty chalice on the verge of nigban waiting to be filled with perfection, with peace."

He repeated the words softly, then shook his head. The essential element of Buddhism was inaction. Jeanne Marie was all fire, all action, save in her attitude toward prayer. But it was in her prayers that she touched God and for prayer she counseled inaction. Would he, too, be practicing what Gautama preached if he sought that inward silence? In his desperation he refused to answer his own query and made plans to test Jeanne Marie's method.

To be free from interruption and from Mrs. Hough's anxious eye, he moved into the zayat. . . .

It rained. The jungle for many months had been creeping upon the little building and now it was embowered in heliotrope and smilax. Fern and bamboo crowded against the eaves and snakes and lizards made free of the veranda. Against the zayat fence the viceroy had crucified and disemboweled a robber for his sins. Adoniram dared not have the body removed. Worshipers passing could not have imagined that a white man sat within the zayat, dreaming such thoughts and seeking such answers as their Buddha Gautama had sought.

And yet, although he fasted, although his efforts were great to the point of exhaustion, never for a moment did Adoniram create a state of mind from which the ache in his heart was excluded. Where was God? Yes—yes, but, dear God, where was Ann? Flesh of his flesh, most precious possession of his life or of heaven after life was done, where, oh, where was Ann?

September rains ceased. Lovely October burst upon the world, and with it the enchanting festival that ended the Burmese Lent. When Adoniram passed through the streets of the sad, silly town, it was all alight with Chinese lanterns and tripod lamps. Men were giving plays to acquire merit and inviting their neighbors to look on and to eat. When he reached the wharf at dusk, little lines of doll-size rafts, each bearing a lighted candle, were dancing out with the tide, pretty benefits for many karmas. It was a world, after all, of yearning souls! Adoniram was not the only seeker.

November, with brilliant swiftness, brought on the pineapples and the jack-fruit. . . . Maung Nau's wife divorced him for his Christianity and turned him out of the house. But his aspirations were unshaken and Adoniram, for all his abstraction, did not for a day relax his teaching and disciplining of the embryo clergyman.

George Hough, late in the month, told his wife that if the suspense didn't end pretty soon for Brother Judson, there'd be a third grave under the casuarina tree.

On the morning of December 5, Adoniram, standing wanly on the wharf, saw a boat put off from a native ship that had anchored overnight. He watched it idly until it was near enough for him to distinguish the figures behind the oarsmen—a man and two women in European dress . . .

white people . . . nearer—one of the women was Ann!

After a long time, a radiantly lovely person, clear of eye and skin, flung herself into his arms; and all else in the world ceased to exist. Still later, he was conscious that he had been introduced to a Deborah and Jonathan Wade. He clung to Ann's hand—that delicate hand of his dreams—while Rangoon, the sky, the new missionaries, danced like motes in the gay sunshine of his swooning happiness.

Somehow later—he had no cognizance of details—he found himself at home and alone with Ann, helping her to unpack. At least, he offered to help. As a matter of fact, he sat on the edge of the bed, staring at her, for the most part, unsmilingly. She was not real.

"But, surely," she insisted, "you received *some* of my letters? I wrote every day and sent off at least a dozen packets of the letters to Calcutta."

"I received only two letters, the last thirteen months ago," he said. "Last night, I finally steeled myself to face your death."

Ann ran to him and pressed his head against her bosom. "My dear, my dear! I told you I shouldn't have gone! I would have turned back from England had I not had a letter from the Baptists in America that a visit there would make the Baptist Foreign Mission Union safe for life. And I was delayed in America, as I wrote you, by writing a history of our work here for an English publisher. The money is to be used for the Rangoon mission."

"I know, darling Nancy," he smiled at her, uncertainly. "I have no thought of blame or censure. You must give me time to get used to my happiness."

She eyed him anxiously as she returned to her work, but she kept up the flow of happy talk. A little later she commented to Mrs. Hough on Adoniram's quick relapse from the ecstasy he had shown at the wharf.

"I suppose," said Ann, "that the long expectation and disappointment have given him an habitual sadness and dejection of spirit. It'll require all my exertions to make him Mr. Judson again."

"That's his chief trouble," agreed Mrs. Hough. "And he hasn't helped himself any by his perpetual reading of a book some French woman wrote—all about her own religious insides. Drat her!"

"Madame Guyon!" exclaimed Ann. "Humph! My poor darling! Well, I'm here, Mrs. Hough."

"Yes, you are, thank our Heavenly Father, in more ways than one," said the other.

They nodded understandingly at each other. Both were of New England!

CHAPTER XIX

HONEYMOON

ADONIRAM liked the Wades and approved of them, without a single mental reservation. Ann had known that he would, for she knew what Burma needed. They were young, both in their twenties, and they were in perfect health, and, what was extraordinarily important, their zeal for saving Burma was in no slightest degree colored by the hope of conserving their own bodily health.

The day after their arrival, when the three families were gathered round the supper-table, George Hough said to Adoniram, in his deliberate way, "Brother Judson, you may start for Ava to-morrow, if you wish. We four can hold the fort here now as long as any one could hold it. That's my honest conviction."

"Mine also!" Adoniram smiled contentedly.

"There's only one fly in the ointment, so far as I can see," said Jonathan Wade, rubbing a very firm young chin and looking at Adoniram out of thoughtful blue eyes. "The British may be forced to send a punitive expedition up the Irrawaddy. Dr. Carey told me that the Burmese king was determined to have war with them. It seems that Bagyi-daw has caused a letter to be sent to the British governor-general, warning him that he was about to take Calcutta, then march on to England and establish his son on the English throne. No amount of explanation on the part of the governor-general makes Bagyi-daw see sense. In September, the Burmans massacred the British outpost at Shapuri Island and garrisoned it themselves. The governor-general wrote to the king, asking him to reflect on what the result of this kind of thing must be, and offering him the loophole of disavowal. The British don't want a war here. Its cost would be far beyond any possible gain. They have their hands full with India. But so far as Dr. Carey was able to learn before we left, there had been no disavowal."

Adoniram thought of the gay, bowlegged figure at leap-frog in the gilded audience-room, and shuddered. Then he said, "We've lived in the midst of alarums and excursions ever since we reached Rangoon. As a matter of fact, nothing has happened. The only thing to do is to carry on the work as we can. You must learn the language, you and Mrs. Wade, and that is a long, long task. While you are doing so, keep the gate barred to any save such of the old disciples as may dare to creep out of the jungle."

"Then," said Ann, briskly, "there's no reason why we shouldn't leave for Ava, immediately. Frankly, Mr. Judson, the sooner you get rid of Rangoon, the better."

"I'd like to see you up there where Dr. Price can keep an eye on you," was Mrs. Hough's contribution. "What do you think of his marriage, Sister Judson?"

Ann shook her dark curls. "I never saw him, you know."

"We all wondered if you had," said George Hough. "He's a good fellow, but he lost his head when he heard the king wanted him, and although we haven't been able to pry much out of your husband, we judge he never got it back again!"

"He has a heart as big as all Burma," Adoniram remarked.

"But no head," repeated Hough.

The renewed activity acted like a tonic on Adoniram. He set about preparations for the trip the next morning with his old zest and for once Burma did not frustrate him. Eight days after Ann's return they were ready to start.

They had planned to leave all the people in the mission yard with the white family. But Koo-chil, when he found that the Judsons were to live in Ava, coolly announced that he was their servant and would work permanently for no other whites in Burma. Ann was eager to continue her efforts to convert Koo-chil and so they gladly consented to his going. Maung Ing appeared the day before they were due to sail. He announced that his wife was divorcing him because of his conversion to Christianity and that he was going to Ava to help establish the church in the golden shadow. As Maung Nau would be a pillar of strength to the Rangoon church, Adoniram yielded to George Hough's advice and welcomed Maung Ing. There was, of course, an enormous advantage in having a native convert help to initiate the work in Ava.

All was so propitious that a third uninvited addition to the party, discovered as they were about to embark, did not bother them as it might otherwise have done. Ann, standing on the beach with Adoniram, waiting for the tide to serve, pointed to the stern of the boat. A huge python was coiled just under the steersman's high perch!

The presence of the creature did not surprise the Judsons. Snake-worship was common among the Burmans. But they were none the less perturbed. Adoniram called the captain to him—the same capable Burman who had taken him and Colman up the river—and asked him in a low voice if it were possible to dispense with the python.

The captain stared at him. "The lord snake, O foreign teacher? But that's impossible. He belongs to the boat, which I bought from my brother. The lord snake is a power on the river, I assure you. No robber will touch us. He's as well known as the Shwé Dagôn. I suppose he's taken the trip to Ava as many times as one has lice."

"But how do you know he won't attack some of us?" asked Ann. "I'm afraid of him, O captain of the beautiful boat."

"Never,"—the Burman smiled at Ann, reassuringly,—"as long as he's full fed on rice, will he stir from meditation. Trust him to me, O wife of the teacher. Moreover, I tell you frankly that the boat will not sail without the lord python."

Ann saw that Adoniram was about to issue an ultimatum.

She laid her hand on his arm. "Never mind, dear! I'm sorry I protested. Think of me developing nerves in Burma!"

"From what I've seen of pythons up and down the river," said Adoniram, "I'd say there was no danger from them. The alligators are far more to be feared."

Ann suppressed a shudder as she forced herself to look at the grim, motionless coils. "I may end by liking him, as I have most living things in Burma," she murmured. "When may we go aboard? Koo-chil is there."

The Bengalese was starting his fire behind the little bamboo cabin amidships and Maung Ing was solemnly at work fastening a small object to one of the bamboo supports of the shelter.

"Look!" gasped Adoniram. "He's brought Mr. Beg Pardon!"

Ann stared, and they both burst into laughter.

"Ann, my darling," Adoniram said, "for over a year, I've counted the days until you and I could sail off on a second honeymoon without a soul aboard that knew us—"

"I know!" Ann slipped her hand into his. "I wonder if any one or anything else will appear before the tide does?"

The answer to her query was immediate. An old lady suddenly rushed out of the stockade gate, carrying a great bundle on her head tied up in pink silk, a cheroot dangling from a corner of her mouth.

"Wait!" she shrieked. "I, Ma So, am coming!" She panted up. "I only heard at dawn when I got back from Little Bridge!" she said, reproachfully. "What's to become of my karma unless Maung Judson tends it? Here, Maung Ing, take my clothes."

The prow of the boat was still high on the sand. Maung Ing walked slowly forward until he could look directly down at the little old lady. But he did not offer to take her bundle.

"Only the baptized," he declared, seriously, "may go on this trip with Jesus Christ's man."

"Is Koo-chil baptized, thou misbegotten twin to a baboon?" demanded Ma So shrilly. "Don't excite me, fool, or I'll lose merit."

"Hush! hush, Ma So!" exclaimed Adoniram. "Take her bundle, Maung Ing, and avoid a scene."

"But, lord teacher—" began Maung Ing in his slow voice.

Ma So interrupted. She jerked off her sandal and aimed it at the Burman's head. A touch on the head from a sandal is a deadly insult. The crew, which had been watching the embarkation of the foreign animals with breathless interest, uttered a unanimous cry of warning. Maung Ing jumped as the sandal flew, and as it whizzed past his ear, he meekly stooped and took Ma So's bundle.

"I hope our party is now complete," sighed Adoniram. "At any rate, Ann, the next wave will wet our feet, so let's get aboard."

Neither Ann nor Adoniram was to forget this voyage up the Irrawaddy, for it covered the most perfect six weeks of their lives. It turned out to be, in spite of minor handicaps, an affair of heart and mind far richer than a honeymoon.

Here were a man and woman, nearing the middle thirties, who had lived together in an intimacy and an interdependence rare even in that closest of all human relationships. They had been separated for more than two years; an acid test of their love for each other. For if that love had not been rooted in the essential fibers of their beings, the long separation would have alienated them. But they had come together to find their passionate devotion doubled. And for six weeks, nothing really mattered but themselves.

The hot weather had not yet begun and the air was perfect. Their progress was unprecedentedly slow, for an unburdened craft, due to the fact that the crew soldiered shamelessly though sympathetically on these white foreigners, who were as much in love as any boy and girl courting in the jungle.

The python's sleepy presence proved beneficent, for the

boat's snail-like progress was halted only once by any obstacle more serious than a sand-bar. In the neighborhood of Prome they came upon a huge fleet of golden war-boats and one of these was rowed rapidly out to intercept the Judsons. A Burmese officer, in a green paso and jacket, boarded them and asked a single question.

"Are you English?"

"Who inquires?" returned Adoniram.

"The great support of the golden throne, Lord General Bandula," answered the officer.

Adoniram took out their passports, saying as he showed them, "We are Americans, not English, going to Ava in obedience to the order of the lord of white elephants."

The officer examined the passports, smiled and returned them. "You may go," he said. He sheekoed to the python and leaped back into his war canoe.

A little later, close to the west bank, they caught a glimpse of Bandula's army, on its way, the captain thought, to Chittagong. The Judsons wondered if poor Maung Shwaygnong were one of that marching horde—for it was hardly more than a rabble, except at its head. Here an imposing officer rode an elephant, under a golden umbrella. Behind him squatted two servants, one holding the betel box and spittoon, the other the fan. Twenty or more elephants followed the first, bearing nobles with their umbrellas signifying their rank. After the elephants, perhaps five hundred horsemen, riding without stirrups. They wore bright green, red or blue coats and hats and were armed with reed spears. Next, a long, straggling line of foot-soldiers with long knives hanging round their necks on cords. Buffalo-carts, then, the creaking of their wheels rising in diabolical dissonance above the haphazard beating of gongs and the songs of men-dancers weaving in and out of the throng. Finally came camp-followers of every type and degree; Shan traders in their decent black coats, Chinamen in dull blue, naked Karens from the jungle and Chins from the mountains, Siamese and

Arakanese slaves in chains as exhibits, and mingled with these what looked like the male and female offscourings of every jail in Burma.

"Do you think there'll be fighting in Burma proper, 'Don?" asked Ann, as they watched the brilliant passing of boats and army.

"Certainly, if the British feel obliged to send a punitive expedition," was Adoniram's reply. "However, we won't anticipate trouble."

But Bandula was only a passing shadow. They forgot him as white pagodas flashed from little hills and the sunset gave them the Arakan Mountains in fiery splendor. Protected by the lord python, they tied up at night and slept close to homely, cheerful village sounds. And sometimes Adoniram would distribute tracts or seat himself in a group of curious villagers and tell them about his mission in Burma. But for the most part, they slipped the leash of duty and were gay and nonsensical and very, very happy.

A few hours before they reached Ava, Dr. Price met them. He advised them to come to his house at Sagaing rather than to go direct to Ava.

"It'll be better for your health," he said, "and—well, I'm out of favor at court, and I suppose you'll be, too."

"What's the trouble?" cried Adoniram in consternation.

"I don't know," answered Price. "The king hasn't exactly refused to see me, but he never sends for me any more and I have next to no patients."

"Have your patients been dying?" asked Adoniram, quickly.

"Well, one or two, but nothing above the average, and none of 'em royalty. I think it's due to the growing interest in war and the Burmans' disability to tell an American from an Englishman."

It was hard news. Two months before, it would have prostrated Adoniram, but now he was conscious of a rising tide of anger and determination. He would not be thwarted

HONEYMOON

by Jonathan Price's muddling nor by any vagaries of the Burmans that could be explained away or boldly thrust aside.

The doctor did not wait for the Judsons to speak. "When the queen meets you, Mrs. Judson," he went on, "all will be well. The women-folks among the royalty and nobility have been on edge to see you—none of them can imagine what a white lady is like. And when the queen is won, the king is settled. She rules him, absolutely."

Ann looked up, doubtfully. "I wonder— Is my old friend, the former viceroy's wife, still in good standing?"

Price shook his head. "She's no use now; her husband's dead. That young trader, Henry Gouger, has been friendly to me, lately. I had hopes that he would help us at court. But it seems the queen has turned against him, too. He doesn't know why."

"Well," said Adoniram, philosophically, "we'll take one day at a time and leave to-morrow to our Heavenly Father. It's certain that to-day is very beautiful."

The others agreed with him and they disembarked cheerfully at Sagaing.

The doctor's house was of brick and only half finished. To little Mrs. Price, moving about with astonishing agility for one newly blind, it was a palace but Ann found it very crude and damp. She took a chill the first night and was flat with fever and ague the next day. Price said the illness was due to the new bricks and regretfully advised Adoniram to throw up a bamboo house on the mission grounds in Ava. Adoniram was only too glad to do so and he and Maung Ing pressed the workmen to such prodigies of effort that in two weeks' time Ann was moved into a little house, set among wild plums and tamarinds on the bank of the river. And she felt better immediately.

Adoniram did not neglect during this fortnight, however, to visit the palace. As soon as the workmen had begun the house, he provided himself with the necessary gift—a pair of opera-glasses in this instance—and repaired to the gilded audience-hall at the hour of public hearing. But there was scarcely a familiar face to be seen. His old friends and advocates before the king were missing. Very few recognized the missionary and it was not until the audience was nearly over that his majesty greeted him and accepted the gift. But he would not converse and Adoniram was forced to leave without having advanced a step.

He went at once to call on Prince Meng-myat-bo, who received him cordially but told him bluntly that he must not speak of religious matters to him, as the chief queen was looking for a chance to have any of the king's relatives tied in the red plush bag and thrown in the Irrawaddy. He expressed a great desire to meet the lord teacher's wife, however.

Adoniram had been too long seasoned in Burma to be discouraged over his reception in Ava. It was disappointing. But actually nothing evil had ever come to the mission. The threats were all sound and fury, signifying nothing. And, gradually, one advanced the Cause.

As soon as Ann was fit, he took her to call on the prince and princess. They were naïvely delighted with her and called in others of the royal family to observe her. No one could excel Ann in ability to take advantage of such ingenuous interest. Shortly, all the royalties, save the king and queen, were inviting Ann to their homes and she was teaching a dozen of the princes and princesses how to make tatting.

Adoniram was content to let their social activities rest here. He devoted himself to getting in touch with such lesser Burmans as Maung Ing and Ma So induced to make religious inquiries and in preaching in Burmese every Sunday at the doctor's house where a few of the plebeian patients dared to gather.

A brick house was a necessity when the intense heat came on, so Adoniram procured bricks and set the masons at work, early in March. Ann took into their home two little

HONEYMOON

Burmese girls, whom Maung Ing produced, saying that their father gave them to the white teacher, for their mother was insane. She named them Abby and Mary Hasseltine and at once began their education.

They were scarcely moved into the bamboo house before Henry Gouger called on them. He was a charming English boy, about twenty-three years of age, who had been having a gorgeous adventure for two years, selling cloth, dishes, and what-not to the Burmans. He had had an absolutely virgin field and had made an astounding amount of money—some twenty thousand pounds. But, having made it, he was at his wit's end as to how to get it out of the country. Exports of goods or of money or of precious metals were absolutely forbidden. He was uneasy about the impending war and would have left earlier for Bengal, had not this financial problem held him. But in April he began to urge the Judsons to leave.

"You can't imagine how wild the talk is among the Burmese officials and the young bloods of the royalty, Mr. Judson," he insisted. "They are keen for war. They're going to equip themselves with white slaves! They're going to annex Bengal! You see, they know nothing but tribal warfare; they've never been whipped, and they think the long patience of my countrymen is due to cowardice. Do take Mrs. Judson to safety!"

It was Ann who answered him. "But we're not traders, Mr. Gouger. We're missionaries, here for better or for worse. And we're Americans. They won't bother us. They're all bluster, as you'll learn with a few more years here. We'll just keep away from the royal palace for a while."

Gouger ran his fingers through his blonde hair and eyed Ann half uneasily, half admiringly. Then he laughed, boyishly.

"Our friend, Jonathan David Price, isn't so diplomatic as you, Mrs. Judson. Yesterday at the bull elephant taming, he edged into the royal group and addressed his majesty. Even when the king ignored him and turned his head away, Price stood about, gazing hungrily at every one. Looking for more boils to conquer, I suppose."

"He really is a good fellow, Gouger!" protested Adoniram. "I don't like to hear him made sport of." He did not add that he had urged Price not to attend the elephant-taming, as an unbecoming spectacle for a missionary to patronize.

The young Englishman was not to be sat upon. "Of course he's a good fellow, but merely to look at him is a joke. He doesn't mind my laughing at him. I do it to his face. He and old Rodgers are really a glorious pair!"

"What is Mr. Rodgers doing in this crisis?" asked Ann.

"Ignoring all foreigners. He doesn't recognize me by the most distant nod. And old Lanciego has asked me to keep away from his house. I'm a political leper!" The young man shook his head ruefully, but at the same time his blue eyes danced with zest for the adventure.

Adoniram hadn't the heart to tell him that his constant visits at their house were a menace to the safety of the mission. But April passed quietly and the major part of May. In spite of the shadow of war, Ann and Adoniram were happy, and the outlook for the work in Ava was cheering. The king made no gesture when one by one inquirers came to the mission and these increased until there were sometimes eighteen or twenty Burmans gathered in the little bamboo house.

The Sunday morning services at the doctor's house were less well attended, probably because Price was known to be under disfavor. On the morning of Sunday, May 23rd, only the two mission families attended and Henry Gouger. But Adoniram preached as usual and had just completed the sermon when one of Maung Ing's friends came running in with news that would not wait till the services were over.

Rangoon had been taken by the English!

There was a startled silence. Adoniram's first feeling was

CHAPTER XX

HAND, SHRINK NOT!

FOR a week or so no further news came from the south, but there was enormous activity in Ava, where the king was raising a great army. Early in June, he sent ten thousand men off under the newly appointed viceroy of Rangoon. The military canoes flashed by the mission-house hour after hour, until Adoniram reckoned that a thousand had passed, each loaded with fighting men.

As soon as the army had been dispatched, the government bestirred itself to discover the spies who had invited the English to come to Burma. Henry Gouger was examined and a Scotsman named Laird, who arrived in Ava at this time. Laird had been the captain of a trading-vessel but recently had entered the employ of Prince Meng-myat-bo, representing him in the teak trade in Rangoon. Laird had brought with him to Ava a Calcutta newspaper which announced the impending departure of the Rangoon expedition. He had shown this newspaper to Henry Gouger.

In the examination, Gouger was asked why, if he had known of the impending move, he had not warned his majesty. He was accused of making maps and sending them to the enemy, of supporting the missionaries, of living in such pomp as only an official could afford, and finally, it was stated that he was brother-in-law to the East India Company,—that the East India Company had married Gouger's sister!

The danger in some of the accusations was that in spite of their absurdity they were partially true. Gouger had drawn many pictures of the temples, monasteries and scenery near Ava, much to the interest and amusement of his one of joy. One could preach Christ now in Rangoon! His next, was of fear. What reaction would this have on the whites in Ava? Young Gouger hurried off at once to protect his property, for it was probable that the first sensation of the Burmans would be that of rage. The missionaries talked for a short time, and then the Judsons also returned home. Gouger brought them word that evening that he had seen Prince Meng-myat-bo, who had assured him that the few foreigners living in Ava had nothing to do with the war and would not be molested. Ann felt reassured by this and so did Gouger but Adoniram carried always in his mind a picture of the lord of life playing at leap-frog. Children are changeable and cruel.

HAND, SHRINK NOT!

Burmese friends. And he had sent them to an English friend in Bengal. Also, he had given money to the Judsons when he had cashed drafts for them against the Baptist Board of Foreign Missions. But no explanations satisfied the examiners. Gouger was remanded to the custody of the king's guards and shut up in their barracks.

John Laird, a bluff, hardy sailorman with a face frightfully disfigured by smallpox, was accused of inviting the English to Rangoon and of having been false to the prince in not having shared his knowledge of British affairs with his master. Laird was also put under guard, but separately from Gouger.

Maung Ing attended the examinations, which were conducted with exemplary calmness and reported them to the missionaries. But the missions were not molested and when, after a few days, Adoniram and Jonathan David, as young Gouger insisted on calling the doctor, were summoned for examination, they were treated with respect. The only questions they were not able to answer satisfactorily concerned the cash received from Gouger. The Burmans could not understand the cashing of notes or checks. But they were sent back to their homes.

Ava settled to quiet. The women took up their endless weaving. The boys and girls with fathers at war planted the fields. The monks went out at dawn with their beggingbowls and offerings were heaped up at the pagodas. The brick walls of the mission rose apace. Ann supervised the planting of the new garden and the king announced his annual spring plowing, that ceremony so essential if showers were to be abundant in upper Burma during the crop season.

His majesty set forth to do his duty by the farmers one morning in the first week of June. The populace of the city was properly crouched behind high whitewashed palings when the lord of life, in a jeweled robe, passed along the streets of Ava on the back of the lord white elephant. He was followed by all the princes and the ministers of state in robes of crimson velvet, who, after the king had done his double furrow, must plow as long as his majesty enjoyed the spectacle.

The mission family, concealed behind their fence, watched the going with admiration and the return with amusement. For the white elephant came back minus his royal burden. The pachyderm was exhausted doubtless by his unwonted efforts, for as he shuffled through the street he was fanned and shaded by his sweating attendants, while he grunted like the gouty old royalty that he was. And Bagyi-daw returned in a gayly-painted European carriage drawn by sixteen noblemen. He appeared to be in high good humor and commented loudly as he passed on the charming appearance of the mission orchard and gardens.

But an hour later, as Ann and Adoniram were washing their hands before dinner, a Burmese official burst unceremoniously into the bedroom.

"Where's the foreign teacher?" he demanded.

"Here!" answer Adoniram, thrusting himself in front of Ann.

"You're called by the king. Come here, Spotted-face!"

An executioner, with the circular brands on his face which announced his profession, thrust his unkempt head into the room. He was followed by a dozen rag-tag Burmans.

"Take the teacher," ordered the official.

Spotted-face leaped quick as a tiger and bore Adoniram to the floor. Then, while the others held him, the executioner fastened the torture cord around Adoniram's neck, and bound his hands. Ann screamed and caught the executioner's arm.

"I'll give you money!" she gasped.

"Take her, too! She's a foreigner," ordered the official.

"No!" roared Adoniram. "I'll pay you with flowered silver if you'll leave my wife alone."

The official glanced at Ann's fragile body and said, with a sneer, "She's not worth silver, but if you're fool enough to think she is, I'm willing."

HAND, SHRINK NOT!

Adoniram said quickly, "Loose my hands that I may write the order."

The official laughed, glanced again at Ann and said, "I'll be back later, my lotus. Remove the prisoner, Spotted-face!"

Adoniram had a confused view of the two little Burmese pupils sobbing and clinging to Ann's skirt, of Ann's agonized face and of the bricklayers on the new house dropping their tools and running away. Then Spotted-face pulled the cord round his neck and he knew no more until he was revived by a slap on the cheek. He found himself in the court-house among a crowd of officials. One of them read the king's order to place the foreign religion-propagating teacher in the death prison.

Spotted-face fastened chains on his wrists and ankles and hustled him across the burning street to the prison designated. This was known to the Burmans by the phrase supposedly addressed to the chief jailer, "Hand, shrink not!" —from the revolting cruelties he was employed to carry on within its walls. It was a stockaded enclosure about a hundred yards square, from which, as one hurried by, rose weird cries and unspeakable stenches.

Adoniram was not to hurry by now! The gate swung open and he was delivered into the welcoming hands of the chief jailer, who with six or eight other reprieved murderers ruled over the prison. He was a lean old man, with broken black teeth, which he displayed in a grin as he dragged Adoniram to a huge granite block in the center of the yard. Here he stripped the missionary of all his clothing save his white linen pantaloons and knocked him down. An expert with the maul then riveted three pairs of fetters on Adoniram's ankles and the same number on his wrists. He was next ordered to walk to the prison-house, several yards away. As the shortness of the chains permitted Adoniram to advance the heel of one foot only to the toes of the other, the five yards might have been a quarter of a mile by the rate of progress possible. But he finally made his way up the ladder through the little bamboo door which a breech-clouted guard jerked open.

He found himself in a room about thirty by forty feet, without windows or ventilation other than could be obtained through chinks in the teakwood walls or through a tile that had fallen off the roof. The air was fetid and of a dusky blue, with trembling fingers of light through the wall chinks revealing the fact that forty or fifty human beings were huddled in the room. Adoniram discerned stocks along the sides all occupied by drooping figures. In the farthest corner a long bamboo hung parallel to the floor. Toward this a jailer urged Adoniram. As he reached the corner, a man spoke.

"Ah, I'm sorry they've got you, Mr. Judson!" It was said in Burmese, but Adoniram recognized Henry Gouger's voice. The young Englishman was chained to the floor. Beyond him lay Captain Laird and old Mr. Rodgers.

"It's not precisely a bed of roses, is it?" exclaimed Adoniram in English.

The jailer struck him in the mouth. "Speak Burmese only, if you don't wish to be brained. Those are the orders of the father of the jail." As he spoke he forced Adoniram to his length on the unspeakable filth of the floor, fastened his ankle-fetters to a ring beside Gouger, gave him a kick and departed.

For a moment, madness seized Adoniram. Only his pride kept him from screaming and tearing at his chains. He raised himself on one elbow. "Christ on the Cross . . . help us!" he gasped. "Christ—!"

The three Englishmen made no sound, and in a moment it was over. Adoniram managed to smile, although he remained rigid on his elbow.

"Poor Laird can't speak Burmese and Mr. Rodgers is so furious he won't," Henry said cheerfully. "You're a solace to my loneliness, sir. And you'll have to come to lying down,

HAND, SHRINK NOT! 209

sooner or later, so let me scrape a place for you. My stomach is stronger than yours."

"Thank you!" Adoniram felt humiliated, but his physical loathing was beyond control.

Henry scraped busily with a bit of bamboo, his golden head gleaming in the dusk. After a time, he said, "Your bed is prepared, my lord!"

"You are a good and a brave fellow!" exclaimed Adoniram.

"Not much of the first, and as for the second—well, my lifelong special horror has been a violent death," said the boy, helping Adoniram to ease himself to a recumbent position.

"And nastiness has been mine." Adoniram was getting back his poise. "Serves me right for my fussy old-maid ways. When did they put you here?"

"This morning, sir. Laird came next and then Rodgers. Come, Mr. Rodgers, we're not responsible for your trouble, I assure you,"—turning a sturdy, sun-tanned face toward the old man.

"Be silent, monkey," snarled Rodgers.

"Tut! tut!" Henry shook his head, with a grin.

"What can I do about my wife?" Adoniram burst forth.

"I doubt if they'll do her bodily harm so long as they can extort money from her," said Gouger. "They stripped me. Were you able to bring any cash here?"

"None," replied Adoniram. "And you know we must pay for all food in the death-house. . . . Perhaps Koo-chil and Maung Ing will help Mrs. Judson to go down the river to the English. Perhaps they won't imprison Dr. Price. She is so delicate, Gouger! . . . O Father of mercies, protect her, hide her in the shadow of Thy wings,—my darling, darling Ann!" he gasped.

"Amen!" whispered Gouger.

Both men fell silent, and after a little while Adoniram's brain steadied, and he began to study his situation calmly.

Since they were in the death-house, they would be tortured and executed, unless the king could be bought off. There was about a thousand dollars' worth of flowered silver, in the mission-house. If Ann could secrete this she could buy her own freedom and somehow he must get word to her to use the money in this manner. His own life or death she must leave in God's hands.

At this point in his thinking, a familiar voice rose above the general murmur. It belonged to Dr. Price, standing in bewilderment in the middle of the room. He could not see his fellow-white men, but was addressing the world in general.

"If anybody had told me the king would do a dirty trick like this to a man who cal'lated to be his best friend, I'd have given him the lie. Of all the pigsty holes, of all the stinking, lousy—"

The jailer shut him off abruptly and a moment later Price had joined the group below the bamboo.

"Have you heard of my wife, doctor?" was Adoniram's greeting.

"Not a word, Judson. Golly, what pollution! They dragged me from Sagaing this afternoon. I wish they'd left me my shirt."

"You're better off without one, doctor," grunted Henry Gouger. "Here comes the chief jailer. And, by Jove, he's got my Bengalese interpreter and clerk with him. Poor fellows!"

The two Bengalese were thrust to the floor. "Now, children," grinned the jailer, "I am your little father, and, dutifully, I am about to put you all to bed."

He gave an order, and the man who accompanied him helped him to pass the bamboo between the legs of each of the seven individuals now lying beneath it. When all were threaded upon it, the ropes were shortened so that the bamboo was raised to a height which allowed the men's shoul-

HAND, SHRINK NOT!

ders to rest on the ground, while their feet hung by the fetters from the pole. This delicate job of adjustment finished, the "little father" bade them an affectionate good night.

Adoniram looked at the row of tortured feet above them, and said with a dreary chuckle, "Dr. Price, apropos of this neat arrangement, do you recall that Mrs. Judson gave me a gentle reprimand the other day saying that my love of neatness, uniformity and order amounted to folly?"

"I remember!" answered the doctor, with a hard laugh that ended in something like a sob.

There was but one mitigating aspect to the horrors of that night: their sufferings of body made thought impossible! They expected to be executed in the morning, yet that fear was less terrible than their bodily pains.

With dawn, the jailers came and lowered the bamboo. The prisoners were led out in squads of ten and given five minutes for physical relief, then returned to the house, not to be taken out for another twenty-four hours. Gouger was an exception. He was again led into the yard, toward noon, and permitted to watch a judge try to torture a confession of robbery from a prisoner. After this object lesson the Englishman was required to give a list of all persons who owed him money, that the government might collect for him! He was then returned to his place beside Adoniram.

During the afternoon two more prisoners were added to the group: a Greek named Constantine and an Armenian named Arakeel. The two Bengalese were released. A servant of Gouger's bribed his way in about two o'clock with a little packet of food for his master, which the young man shared with the others. At three, a Burman was taken out to be executed. At dusk, the bamboo was raised once more. At dawn, again they lowered it to within a foot of the floor.

On the third afternoon, a jailer suddenly appeared, freed Adoniram's feet from the bamboo, and led him to the door. He expected to be killed at once and the revulsion of feeling unmanned him when he beheld Ann on the doorstep, beside the guard, with hands outstretched. Several moments passed before he recovered himself and gasped:

"Don't touch me—unclean! Ann, you must get a boat and get down the river at once."

She appeared not to hear him as she stared at the terrible condition of his body and clothing. Then she covered her face with her hands. Adoniram swallowed painfully but repeated his command in a stern voice. "Do you hear me, Ann?"

She dropped her hands. "I've no time to discuss nonsense, my darling. For two days I couldn't get out of our yard, but this morning I bribed my way to the governor of the north gate, whose wife I've taught to tat. He's let me come to see your condition for myself, and I've brought food." She thrust a heaped-up basket into his manacled hands, and with a deep sob went on speaking rapidly. "I'll do what I may, for all of you."

"Get out of Ava, Ann!" implored Adoniram.

She shook her beautiful head. But before she could speak again, the guard said, "Your time's up, Ma Judson!"

"But my orders—" protested Ann.

"Get out now or I'll drag you out!" The guard lifted a threatening hand.

"Don't touch her, you hound!" shouted Adoniram. "Go quickly, Ann!"

She clambered obediently down the steps, talking as she went. "Maung Ing shall come with food and I shall work ceaselessly—"

The bamboo door slammed.

Ann's miracle began an hour later. Maung Ing appeared before the "bamboo" prisoners, and told them that Ma Judson had arranged that by the payment of two hundred ticals ($100), two pieces of fine cloth and two pieces of handkerchiefs by each, they would be removed from the death-house and placed in a shed in the yard. Maung Ing was supplied

HAND, SHRINK NOT! 213

with writing materials. Would each write the order needed to give Ma Judson access to their property?

"God bless her forever!" Rodgers spoke for the first time in two days, as he grasped the pen.

That evening, the seven men, though still in fetters, slept in an open shed, in pure air, though uncovered and on the ground.

CHAPTER XXI

ORDEAL

THE prison-yard, though a vast improvement, was not altogether a gala spot. The governor's deputy used it as a court in which to try cases by torture, and the European prisoners were forced, on the following morning, to witness the efficacy of the maul in wooing confession from a man accused of theft.

Rodgers, who during forty years had come to look on Burmese brutality with indifference, was not affected by the dreadful scene until it suddenly occurred to him that this undoubtedly would be his lot. Then the old man went to pieces. Henry Gouger and Adoniram got through the ordeal by turning their backs and stopping their ears. Dr. Price took what Gouger said was a professional interest, and missed not a blow. Adoniram felt a sudden flare of anger toward his associate.

"Have you *no* sensibilities, Price?" he exploded, when, the prisoner having been carried back into the jail building, the Europeans gathered around the tray of rice and fish brought in by Gouger's servant and Maung Ing.

"I've got a scientific man's cool blood, Brother Judson," returned the doctor, amiably.

"Scientific!" Adoniram's nerves were on edge. "You disgrace the spirit of a missionary!"

"Ah, but he is scientific in his yearnings, at least, dear Mr. Judson," grinned Gouger, rubbing the tawny stubble on his young chin. "You remember when you tried to cure me of headaches, Jonathan David?"

"Well, but I did cure you," said Price, conveying a great handful of rice and curried fish to his mouth.

"You did!" Henry smiled at Adoniram. "I'll cheer you with a joke, proving our friend's scientific turn, sir. He gave me an opium pill. When I was under the influence, he shaved my head and applied leeches to it. And when I came to my senses, twenty-four hours later, he had his instruments spread and was about to trepan me! He said he had been shaking me for an hour and had concluded I was 'sleeping the sleep of death,' so took the opportunity to investigate the human brain!"

"I'd forgotten how big an opium pill I'd given you," said Dr. Price, apologetically. Then he added, "My idea is that our friend Constantine has leprosy, though I'm not conversant with the early stages of that disease."

"Of course he has leprosy, fool!" grunted poor old Rodgers, who had dried his tears and now joined the group round the rice.

The Greek had neither Burmese nor English, but he understood their stares of consternation, and sullenly drew aloof.

Adoniram laughed grimly. "There's a subject for your scientific scrutiny, doctor. Poor Constantine's condition ought to save the rest of us a good deal."

John Laird spoke for the first time. "You're all too hard on the doctor. He's made less fuss than anybody over our conditions here, and I call him a good fellow."

Adoniram was conscience-stricken. "I'm sorry, Price!" he exclaimed.

"Don't worry, Brother Judson. If my nerves were strung like yours, I'd be gnawing at my fetters with my teeth! You are doing fine, when you only bite me!"

Everybody laughed, and the atmosphere cleared.

The reprieve from the inner prison was not to be long. That night they were returned to it, but, happily, were not fastened up to the bamboo. Maung Ing said that the cause for the shift lay in the governor's not sharing his bribe with the head jailer. As Ann was not permitted to come to the prison for several days, the sufferers were obliged to endure the renewal of their troubles as best they could.

It was two weeks, as a matter of fact, before Ann came again. And Adoniram, shuffling to the door to meet her, for a moment did not recognize her. She was in rich Burmese costume: a white silk jacket over a saffron vest and a crimson silk tamein. Her dark curls were caught back from her forehead and coiled smoothly with a white cocoa-blossom drooping from the knot.

Adoniram, in his filth and wretchedness, stood speechless before her beauty. Then he gathered himself together and sheekoed. "You are very lovely, O lady of Burma! But why?"

"This is a gift from the wife of the governor, 'Don. She has taken me under her wing and advised me to dress thus to conciliate the people. You'd be surprised at the difference it makes. People have ceased to molest me, or even to look at me."

"Tell me everything," urged Adoniram.

To his great pleasure, the jailer allowed them to stand on the veranda for the fifteen minutes of conversation that followed.

Ann had visited the king's palace and the governor's house regularly on alternate days, bombarding the queen and the governor with petitions. The queen finally had sent word that the teacher would not die, but must stay where he was. The governor was very friendly, though Ann had not yet prevailed on him to put the prisoners back in the yard. He feared the queen, who now dominated the entire government. But he had ostentatiously taken Ann under his protection.

"Thank God for that!" breathed Adoniram. "If only you are safe, I can face things. A man can't know how he loves a woman till an experience like this comes."

"I don't think either of us needed this test," said Ann, quaintly.

Adoniram smiled into her dark eyes. Then he asked her the next question that had been tormenting him. "Ann, where are my translations of the Bible?"

"The manuscripts are wrapped in oil silk and buried under the house with our other treasures," replied Ann. "I'm afraid to think of what condition they'll be in, what with damp and vermin, but I can't think of anything else to do with them now."

"I have a scheme, so insane that it might succeed," said Adoniram. "Henry Gouger's servant brought him a little hard pillow and thus far he's been allowed to keep it. The next time Maung Ing comes, Nancy, have him bring me a pillow covered with matting; a very hard pillow, made of manuscript; so hard, even a jailer will scorn it. Then I'll have a portion of my appointed task with me, though I can't perform it."

Ann blinked and said soberly, "You poor darling!"

He was dirty, unshaven and unshorn. But his eyes were peculiarly clear and wistful and Ann suddenly pulled his face down to hers and kissed his tired eyelids.

Then the jailer called to her, and she went away.

The next day Maung Ing brought the pillow. The possession of it was an infinite comfort to Adoniram.

The prisoners now settled to a grotesque sort of routine. As their jailers found them docile, they lifted the ban on English speech, which was a relief to all, but especially to Laird. Adoniram held prayers for them, night and morning, and although the captain at first expressed contempt for the "Baptist chapel parson," he gradually changed his attitude and became ingenuously dependent on the missionary for spiritual food. Constantine and Arakeel for the most part sat despondent and made no attempt to learn either English or Burmese. Mr. Rodgers, during the first weeks of terror, tried to get his wife to send him poison, but she refused to accommodate him, and gradually the old man recovered his calm. He made friends with the Burmese prisoners, among whom he was far more at home than among his own kind, and spent his time smoking and exchanging histories with them.

Dr. Price was more nearly content with his situation than any of the others. He didn't mind the dirt much himself, but good-humoredly undertook to keep Gouger's and Adoniram's heads clipped and beards shaved, since they were really in torture from the body-lice. He paid one of the jailers to bring him some bamboos and lumps of clay, with which he prepared to make a clock. But after a week of failure he cast his materials aside and devoted himself to the ailments of the native prisoners—a rich field.

Adoniram seized on the materials discarded by Jonathan David and suggested to Henry that they make a set of chessmen. The younger man rose to the idea with avidity, and the two turned out a set of sorts—quite satisfactory to themselves, at least. For a board they utilized a piece of bullock hide, unearthed from the prison rubbish, marking the squares with lamp-black. The Burmans are very fond of chess. Except when in especially vindictive mood, the jailers made no protest and the two men spent many hours over the game.

None of them actually suffered as did Adoniram, because none of them was intellectually his equal nor afflicted with his physical sensitiveness. His mental and spiritual unease exceeded theirs in just the degree that his aims and ideals were greater. On the other hand, because his intellectual resources were infinitely greater than the others', he was able to give more largely to the sustaining of their combined *morale*. He recited poetry to them by the hour, English and Burmese and offhand translation from Greek and Latin. He dug deep into his memories of English literature and he even told them the story of Madame Guyon's life.

Henry Gouger and he shared equally a keen sense of the ridiculous and often Henry's rollicking humor or Adoniram's more biting wit saved the strangely assorted seven from quarrels that might have been serious.

ORDEAL

They were not, as the weeks went by, entirely without news of the war. In order that not a moment should be lost in conveying intelligence of battles lost or won to his majesty, it had been ordered that the war-boat bringing dispatches should fire one gun if a battle had been lost, two, if successful, three if the English had been driven into the sea. Twice during June, the single shot was heard by the prisoners, but it was not until July that they learned more than this of the progress of events.

At that time, an Irish soldier was brought to the yard of the death-prison and old Rodgers was taken out to act as interpreter. When he came back Rodgers, with the others, was fastened to the bamboo and strictly forbidden to speak. But the old man for once proved obliging, and the information gleaned from the Irishman was passed in a low whisper, a sentence at a time, from one to another.

There were 3,000 British soldiers and 8,000 sepoys, under General Sir Archibald Campbell, moving above Rangoon. They had a steamboat as well as small gunboats under sail. In the latest engagement, the Burmese commander-in-chief had been killed. This had been all the news to be drawn from the Irishman and the Burmese in exasperation had hustled him away. Whither, Rodgers did not know.

Followed a night not only of extreme physical but of mental discomfort. How would the Burmans retaliate on their prisoners for the British successes? They expected the worst. But although they were kept chained to the bamboo for several days, and starved, nothing else was done, and at last Ann got Maung Ing through to them, and they were released from the dreadful posture.

It was Dr. Price who won them their next interlude in the prison yard. One of their jailers was afflicted with a large swelling on the upper eyelid. Jonathan David's fingers and penknife itched for it, and he began to urge the man to allow him to remove the "wen." The others did their best to persuade the doctor not to attempt the operation.

"We're at the mercy of these spotted faces," Henry put it bluntly, "and if your work should be as disastrous on him as it was on your wife, you can't offer him the solace you did her!"

But Jonathan David was persistent, and one hot July afternoon, he actually operated. A week later, when he removed the rags from the patient's eye, the wound was cleanly healed, but—the eyelid was paralyzed, hanging helpless over the ball!

Spotted Face was inarticulate with rage, but the doctor was quite philosophical. "The eye will keep all the better," he assured the jailer. "When you need it, all you have to do is to lift the lid with a finger. When you have done with it, drop it. It will always be at hand, you know!"

The others held their breaths. But before Spotted Face could spring on the doctor, the chief jailer came in, and Price appealed to his sense of justice.

The Burman sense of humor is keen and sometimes expresses itself in an astonishing perversity. The little father gazed from his disabled henchman to the doctor and burst into roars of laughter.

"How shall I mark your great merit, O foreigner with the blunt knife?" he asked, when he could speak.

"Send us all into the yard for a little holiday," replied Jonathan David, promptly.

The little father rocked again with mirth, then he opened the bamboo door. "Out with you!" he shouted. And the seven stumbled, blinking and dumbfounded, into their old places under the shed.

Thus, with alarums and excursions, the summer crawled away and the cool season began, with the mercury at night dropping to forty-five degrees from its daily average of sixty-five degrees. Still they were kept in the yard. Price suffered severely from this and took a heavy cold which gave him a cough he could not throw off. But the cool weather put an end to the fever and ague that periodically affected

ORDEAL

Adoniram and to Gouger's dysentery. Both the missionary and the young trader were badly depleted and were suffering from fetter-sores, such as did not afflict the older men.

Ann brought them news in October that General Bandula had returned from Arakan and was raising an enormous army with which to destroy the invaders. Adoniram at once prepared a petition for her to present to the general. Ann was, as usual, successful in gaining access to the great man, and he treated her with courtesy. But all that he would promise to do was to give the matter attention after he had driven the English into the sea!

It was in October also that Ann reluctantly told her husband a secret which she dared no longer keep from him. A baby would be coming to them some time in January. After all the years of waiting, to have their prayers answered at such a time! It was hard to be grateful. Adoniram's anxiety now was doubled whenever Ann did not appear regularly at the prison yard. Her impending agony became the central fact of all his thoughts. His own increasing feebleness was of quite secondary importance. Early in December she was obliged to give up her visits, but Maung Ing came faithfully, or at times Koo-chil.

So long as he knew that she was safe, Adoniram was relieved that his wife did not appear at the prison during these weeks. A number of sepoys had been brought in and eight of the officers were chained next to the bamboo group. They had no friends, and although the Europeans did what they could to relieve the Mohammedans, all save one of them starved to death during the month. It was an orgy of misery and Adoniram was grateful for Ann's absence.

From these poor creatures the Europeans learned that the British had taken most of the Arakan coast and were occupying Martaban to the south. This was not an unmixed blessing, as it allowed the Burmans to concentrate all their energies on the operations on the banks of the Irrawaddy.

The slow days and the slower nights dragged on, and

January crept in. On the 24th of the month neither Maung Ing nor Koo-chil appeared, and Adoniram knew that Ann's hour had come. . . . On the morning of the 25th, Koo-chil, weary-eyed but jubilant, arrived with a great basket of plantains. Little Maria Judson had made her appearance in Burma and her mother was safe and very well content. Ma So said it was a fine baby. Koo-chil wished it had been a boy, but was willing to admit that girls had their uses. . . . Peace and thankfulness laid their soothing balm on Adoniram's troubled heart.

Twenty weary days later he was called to the bamboo door. Ann was there with a little bundle on her breast which she laid in Adoniram's manacled arms. Thus, with his chains dangling, he looked into the delicate face of his only child. . . . Nothing had so brought home the horrors of his position as this. He hid his feelings from Ann but when she had gone, dark waters swept over him.

For many days following, Madame Guyon, the touch of his priceless pillow, old faith, old resources, all failed him. That tiny face, Ann's ravished eyes, had uprooted the very vitals of his inward existence. Could it be that God was a conscious Being and cognizant of the sufferings of humanity? If so, was He not inconceivably cruel, and, if cruel, could He still be God?

Crouching, hour after hour beside Henry, who was suffering from an attack of neuralgia, Adoniram recited foolish tarradiddles from Burmese folk-lore to take his friend's mind from his pain. But his own inner brain wrestled ceaselessly with this frightful query.

Walking up and down in the impossible double-shuffle permitted by their gyves, with John Laird, who was afflicted with a desire to have Hell proved to him—a matter in which Adoniram certainly felt at this moment of his torment no special interest—his mind never ceased to center on that shattering doubt: Does God care?

His companions would have been filled with consternation

had they had inkling of the spiritual wrestlings of this man on whom they leaned. Adoniram was only thirty-six. They thought of him as immensely older than themselves, and yet only Henry was younger than he! He felt himself to be a monument of deception. But he must not share his questionings with mortal beings. As long as he lived he would never forget nor forgive himself for rousing the look of abject fear in James Colman's face that night on the Irrawaddy, when he asked the boy, Where is God? Nay, it was his punishment for his doubts, to suffer alone. . . . And there was always Christ—Christ the visible, the tangible, the *fact*. And, as on the *Flying Squirrel,* the firm, unshaking hold of those piercèd palms saved his soul alive, while these questions, too stupendous for mortal minds to compass, rocked the foundations of his reason. And after a time, steadied by that exquisite support, his thoughts returned to normal and he could gaze on little Maria with pensive delight.

CHAPTER XXII

BANDULA

THE white prisoners lived for the month of February in comparative freedom from extra attentions paid by the jailers. But after dark on the evening of March first they were suddenly seized upon by the spotted faces and rushed into the yard. Here, by torchlight, three extra sets of fetters were hammered upon their arms and legs. The Burmans worked in furious haste and in utter silence. The job done, the now practically helpless white men were dragged back into the inner prison and thrust into what was known as the death corner. The jailers then withdrew to sharpen their knives in the light of the tripod lamp. A Burman whispered that they were to be assassinated as soon as further word came.

For a long time the prisoners did not speak. Each man lay engrossed by his own fears. Constantine and Rodgers wept and moaned. Adoniram stared at the bats circling in the dark shadows of the roof and wished that he might have said farewell to Ann and the baby. But gradually he saw the selfishness of this desire. When Ann had left him that day, she had felt comparative ease of mind. She would sleep in peace to-night. To-morrow she would come and find all his troubles ended. It would be a supreme shock, but a harrowing farewell scene would have been avoided. She would rally for the baby's sake and take the step he'd never ceased urging upon her. Go down the river to the English as soon as possible. She had won the love and respect of the Burmans. Without him she'd be better off.

Before another year was past, she would be in America.— He would like to have seen Boston harbor once more and the beach at Plymouth. . . . He crowded this back with aching throat. . . . Poor failure, Adoniram— Well, it was worth it. Though the war had caused his death, militarism would plant Christianity where he had failed. He wondered if, by any chance, the pillow would fall into Ann's hands and he kept himself entertained for a while with a picture of the manuscript being brought to light after many years. Who would find it? What would be done with it? "Poor Judson! Well, he knew his Greek and his Burmese, anyway!—But we don't raise monuments to scholars nor to missionaries—"

Gouger turned a set young face toward him. "Will you pray, sir? It may calm some of us."

Adoniram lifted his deep, sweet voice. "O Lord, I have heard Thy speech and was afraid. O Lord, review Thy work, in the midst of the years, make known, in wrath remember mercy! Art Thou not from everlasting to everlasting, O Lord my God, mine Holy One? We shall not die! O Lord, Thou hast ordained them for judgment and, O mighty God, Thou hast established them for correction! *Thou art of purer eyes than to behold evil and canst not look on iniquity.* . . . The mountains saw Thee and they trembled. The overflowing of the waters passed by. The deep uttered his voice. Thou wentest forth for the salvation of Thy people—I will joy in the God of my salvation—"

After a moment, he repeated the words in Greek and tragic Constantine ceased to weep. He went on softly:

". . . Peace I leave with you, my peace I give unto you: not as the world giveth, give I unto you. Let not your heart be troubled, neither let it be afraid. . . ."

There was a music in his voice that was like balm.

After a long, long time, some one said, "Is it moonlight coming through the hole in the roof?"

"There's no moon"—Captain Laird's gruff tones—"that's sunrise!"

The door jerked open and long rays of glorious light penetrated the blue haze of the stinking room. The jailers began the daily task of leading the squads into the yard for their five minutes' relief. The Europeans were ignored. They were not to be taken into the yard until night, and then one at a time and surreptitiously. The day and a second night passed in misery and apprehension, but they now realized that death was not to be immediate. On the third dreadful day, Adoniram found a note from Ann in his rice.

She said that her friend the governor had received an order from the chief queen's brother to have the Europeans assassinated immediately and secretly. But the governor had had misgivings. This was not the king's order and its furtive aspect made him fear trouble for himself if the king found he'd carried it out. Moreover there had been more failures for the Burmans on the Irrawaddy and Ann had made some impression on him by her tales of what the British would do when they reached Ava if the prisoners were killed. The old governor therefore had ordered the extra fetters of the doomed for them and had put them, as it were, in hiding, pending further light. Ann bade them to be hopeful. She was at work on the king's older sister with gifts.

For a week they lived in an extreme of misery that made previous experiences as nothing. But on the tenth day they were put back under the bamboo, and actually welcomed the change! Adoniram dared ask for his pillow but could get no trace of it.

Hot weather came on and the vile effluvia of the room boiled anew. A day or so after their return to their city residence, as Adoniram called the bamboo, the "king's horse," that fat official on whose great shoulders it was his majesty's joy to ride, was thrust into the stocks near by. He was a friendly soul and talked freely. The British had taken the town on the Irrawaddy taxed for his support, and the king blamed him for the disaster: this, although the king's horse never strayed from Ava. He added the information that Bandula had retreated to Danubyu, sixty miles north of Rangoon. The fat man's stay with them was short. The king missed his horse and sent for him within twenty-four hours.

In mid-March, another distinguished prisoner was placed in the stocks. He was one of the king's ministers, known to the vulgar as the Tiger. He was an intimate of the chief queen's brother, under whose rabid hatred of whites the prisoners now were suffering. The Tiger evidently was no mean hater himself. His sole remark from the stocks was that if he lived to be free the seven men under the bamboo would be crucified by the Tiger's own hands. He was a guest of the little father until a day in the middle of April when a single gun once more boomed from the river. A few hours later, the Tiger was released. The little father told them he had been appointed to fill Bandula's place as commander-in-chief, for Bandula had been killed in battle!

The following day, Lanciego was brought in, his finger-tips dripping blood. The torture of the cords had been applied to his wrists by order of the new commander-in-chief. The fact that his wife was sister to the second queen could not save the Spaniard longer from his enemy the Tiger, now in control of the army. The little father fastened Lanciego to the bamboo beside Adoniram.

He told them that Bandula's brother, who had brought word of the general's death, had had his head cut off instantly. After this relief to his feelings, the king had sat dazed and the queen had beaten her breast and cried, "Amé! Amé! Who will venture, since the invincible Bandula has been cut off?"

None knew better than the queen that the common people were whispering of rebellion in case more troops were levied. For as yet they had borne the brunt not only of the fighting but of the cost in rupees thereof. Not a tical had been taken from the royal treasure-chest.

Their majesties were talking, panic-stricken, of these matters when a message came from the Tiger. If released from jail, he would undertake to raise a new army by offering a bounty of one hundred ticals to each soldier, the money to come from the still unexhausted tax funds in the public treasury. Before the king had begun to consider the offer, the queen sent her own bullock-cart for the Tiger.

All was bustle again in the capital, while the new army was raised. And the little father relaxed his vigilance to the extent of permitting Ann once more to come to the door of the prison, and to look in on the bleached faces of the bamboo prisoners. What it cost her to gaze into that limbo not even Adoniram fully knew. But her face was as the face of an angel to men lying in the pit of hell. She alone kept their hope alive, burning with however feeble a spark. She was their one reliance in a Burma gone amok. She stood like the cobweb across Bruce's cave, just so delicate, just so completely efficacious. Even Constantine learned enough English to bless her dear, tender face.

One morning in late April, when the pain in his festering ankles was more than usually difficult for Adoniram to support, one more familiar figure was thrust into the stocks near by. The missionary stared at the wrinkled face, at the austere yet kindly eye, and for a blissful moment forgot the prison. He was sitting in the zayat beside the lotus lake, with the southwest monsoon making heaven of the heat, while he drew a map and told the story of the Pilgrims.

What could have happened? It was almost unprecedented for a monk, a gaing-ôk, to touch such ignominy. To be sure, the old man was no longer wearing the yellow robe. Only a paso of faded green covered his loins. Was this the disgrace the gaing-ôk had foreseen? Adoniram's first impulse was to call out to him, to ask him whence and why. But immediately he warned himself not to add to the old man's anguish by identifying him to his fellows. He would get at him more subtly, make himself known by indirection. And after a moment's thought he began to recite as if to himself:

"Here are no gadflies—so said the herdsman Dhaniya. The cows are roaming in meadows full of grass and they can endure the rain. Then rain if thou wilt, O sky!"

Although the room was full of the sounds inseparable from the herding together of a hundred men, the commingling of voices was subdued. No one happened to be under torture or to be dying too painfully, and so Adoniram's rich tones penetrated to the gaing-ôk's ears. The old man started and stretched eagerly forward. He could not place the voice, and after a moment he replied, tentatively:

"I have made a well-built raft—so said the Blessed One. I have crossed over. I have reached the further bank. I have overcome the torrent of passions. I need the raft no more. Then rain if thou wilt, O sky!"

"My wife is obedient,"—Adoniram took up the dialogue; "she has—"

But the gaing-ôk had found him. "So you lie there, O my enemy!" he exclaimed.

"I lie here, O my enemy friend," replied Adoniram. "Is it because of me that you are here also?"

"In the beginning, yes," grunted the gaing-ôk. "I would not absolutely deny that your God was antecedent to the Buddha. Thus one catastrophe led to another, which I wouldn't care to repeat to this multitude, but my first trouble came from pleading with the lord of white elephants to save Maung Shway-gnong from torture."

"Poor, ill-starred fellow!" ejaculated Adoniram. "Where is he?"

"Somewhere in Ava. I know not where. His friendship for you and Jesus Christ brought him to disgrace. I know not the details. But he sent me a message."

The two men looked at each other, one from the filth of the floor, the other from the cramped ignominy of the stocks. And there was curious sympathy and liking in each man's eyes; the Burman's black and calmly sad, the American's hazel and still filled with wistful fire. It was impossible to continue the conversation with any satisfaction, for the jailers brought in a respectable-looking matron and her four daughters, and put them in stocks, and a pandemonium of protests and ribald salutations greeted the women. But Adoniram watched the old man and pondered heavily on his own share of responsibility for the monk's misfortunes.

Finally an idea came to him, and when the little father arrived for his mid-afternoon visit, Adoniram asked to speak to him confidentially.

"Do you remember once, O father, offering me a hut in the yard for a hundred ticals?" queried Adoniram.

"You must know, monkey, I can't do that now!" snarled the little father.

"Certainly, I know. But that wouldn't prevent you from taking the flowered silver for helping another man to be freed of this place? Especially if by doing so you acquired as much merit as by building a pagoda?"

"Tell me!" gasped the little father, with enormous eagerness. "For who has such need of merit as I?"

"No one on heaven's green footstool," returned Adoniram amiably. "O father, yonder in the stocks sits a mistake that will place in deepest hell-pit the man who made the mistake. The old man yonder is a gaing-ôk."

The father stared with goggling eyes. A sweat broke out on his dreadful forehead. "I thought his face was known to me. . . . Do you realize that a monk's person is sacred, O foreign teacher?"

"I realize," replied Adoniram, entire complaisance in his voice.

"But I'm not the Buddha Gautama! I'm not the fountain of all wisdom," urged the father, ferociously. "Could I know by touch that he was different from the beasts sent me here? Is there any one in the golden kingdom who has more on his mind than I, with every member of government ordering me: Starve me this man, torture me that, let me out the bowels of so-and-so?"

"We all have our peculiar difficulties," agreed Adoniram. "In the meantime, who sent him here?"

"I don't know. He was one of a batch I let in at the gate. As you say, some one has made a mistake."

"Let him go and my wife shall bring you the silver," whispered Adoniram.

"Do you think my merit would be greater if I didn't take the money? . . . No, I'm poor . . . I'll balance taking the money by informing him it was the foreign teacher who had the thought and not I."

"No!" ordered Adoniram. "He may refuse to be contaminated by my favor."

"He's human, if he is a monk," grunted the jailer, out of a vast disillusionment. With which philosophical remark he moved off.

A little later, Adoniram saw him stoop over the gaing-ôk and whisper in his ear. The old man's head jerked up and a painful red suffused his yellow cheeks. He stared at Adoniram while carefully, not touching even the monk's paso, the jailer unlocked the stocks. The gaing-ôk withdrew his hands and feet painfully, sat immovable while circulation became normal, then hoisted himself to his legs; and all the time he gazed at Adoniram.

The missionary smiled and quoted, "The stakes are driven in and cannot be shaken—so said the herdsman Dhaniya. The ropes are of holy-grass, new and well made. The cows cannot break them. Then rain if thou wilt, O sky!"

The old man's voice broke. "Like a bull I have rent the bonds—so said the Blessed One. Like an elephant I have broken the ropes. I shall not need to be born again. Then rain if thou wilt, O sky!"

They smiled uncertainly at each other. Then, followed reverently by the little father, the old man limped out.

CHAPTER XXIII

UNBROKEN OF HEART

ANN paid the jailer the ticals from her fast-diminishing hoard without protest. But when, a short time after, Adoniram was afflicted with his recurrent fever, she used the transaction as a lever to pry a favor from the father. She begged him to allow Adoniram to go into one of the yard shelters for a holiday, as it were. Spotted Face for once yielded with decent grace, and Ann and Maung Ing half led, half carried, Adoniram into the open air.

Here he lay by day, returning to the inner prison by night, for a week. But one hot morning at the end of that time the privilege ended abruptly. After the so-called breakfast-hour, all of the bamboo prisoners were hurriedly dragged out to the familiar granite block in the center of the enclosure. Certainly they were a tragic sight, as they stood blinking painfully in the unaccustomed light: emaciated, feeble, with matted hair, sunken eyes, covered with sores, blanched after the year in semi-darkness.

No one spoke while the fetter expert, working with great rapidity, struck the chains from their ankles. Hope flickered up. Then, as they were tied two and two, like children playing at horse, each pair with a jailer as driver, it died again. They took it for granted, as they were urged out into the streets of Ava, that they were headed for the execution-place, just beyond the court of justice. But they passed this evil spot, and were herded onto the road to Amarapura.

Young Gouger and Dr. Price were linked together, Lanciego and Rodgers. Adoniram was team-mate to John Laird, who offered the sick man his shoulder for a short way. But this was too much for the remnant of the Scot's

UNBROKEN OF HEART

great strength, and at the end of the quarter of a mile he told the missionary to shift for himself. They all were bareheaded and bare-footed. The road cut their feet to pieces before they were out of the environs of Ava. Constantine could not walk after they left the shade of the city streets and the jailer freed him from Arakeel and dragged him. The others were halted on the bridge crossing the little river that swung out of the Irrawaddy half round Ava, to wait for the Greek. Adoniram's fever had flared up again. He felt his brain going.

"Laird," he exclaimed, looking down at the loveliness of flowing water, "Laird, let's end it! Drowning is a pleasant death. Come, Laird, for God's sake, come!"

The captain stared at the missionary from startled, sunken eyes. Henry Gouger put a feeble arm round Adoniram.

"He's off his head, Laird. Never tell him this thing he's said."

Laird grunted. The spotted face jerked impatiently at the ropes and the procession started on. Constantine was dead.

All that Adoniram knew now was that they were on the old road, under tamarind and palm and fig and passing the zayat by the lotus lake. Sometime during the trip, as he was about to sink, his lacerated feet quite done, Henry's servant ran up, pulled off his turban, and dividing it between his master and Adoniram, tenderly wrapped their bleeding soles. In the afternoon, they were halted in a shed in Amarapura. A long debate followed between the spotted faces and the police to whom they gave the whites in charge. It was obvious they could walk no more. The spotted faces were in favor of dragging the prisoners. But the police pointed out that, for some reason, they must be kept alive for a few more hours. They were allowed to sleep, finally, where they had sunk to the ground. The next morning, a cart was produced and the prisoners loaded into it.

Their new guards told them they were headed for Aungbinle, a little village four miles beyond Amarapura, where they were to be again imprisoned. The slow-moving buffalo brought them to their destination about two o'clock, when they came to pause before a solitary, ruinous building standing alone in a vast rice-field. The building was roofless and doorless, and entirely unoccupied. There was no stockade and the only traces of the village were a few huts and palms a quarter of a mile away. Men came shortly and thatched the roof with palm-leaves. The prisoners were then led into the building, and after their feet were placed in stocks they were left to the tender care of the single jailer in charge of the prison.

This individual was much irritated at being called from his paddy fields, but his face did not bear the dreaded murder brands, and the white men dared hope that he might prove to be a human being.

There was no food for the prisoners that night, but Gouger's servant appeared the next morning with a bag of biscuits he had baked. And, O blessed phenomenon! there was plenty of water to be had. The prisoners drank and made shift to wash themselves, and were grateful when they were led into the open air, and, though still chained two and two, permitted to sit in the shade of the building and watch a gang of men at work erecting a fence around the premises.

Late in the afternoon a bullock-cart creaked up and paused before the prison. In it sat Ann with her baby, Koo-chil and little Abby and Mary Hasseltine, surrounded by various pieces of household impedimenta. The prisoners set up a feeble cheer and Ann smiled wearily but triumphantly. She had overcome insuperable difficulties in leaving Ava, but had not hesitated, when Gouger's servant had told her of Aungbinle, to leave the mission in charge of Ma So and Maung Ing and move to the new location.

"You look as if you'd come to stay, O crazy foreign woman!" exclaimed the jailer, desperately.

"I have, O jailer of beautiful paddy fields," returned Ann,

who, Adoniram could see, was sinking with exhaustion.

Price spoke loudly. "You had better return to Ava, Mrs. Judson!"

The three Britishers hooted at him, and Ann gave Adoniram no chance to join either party. She went hastily to confer with the jailer's wife, who was gaping from the veranda of her hut across the road. It was only a paddy shed of two rooms, into which the jailer had moved his family that day from the village. Ann rented one of the rooms, still half filled with paddy, and watched by the admiring line of scarecrows under the eaves of the jail, she settled in with her three children, while Koo-chil built himself a palm-leaf lean-to against the prison fence.

Certainly conditions now looked favorable for the prisoners to recover their health, and, indeed, all, even Adoniram, began to gain strength. The moist air did not help Dr. Price's cough, but he gained weight in spite of that. If their minds could have been relieved, they might have been able to await with comparative content the apparently inevitable arrival of the British army. But death still stalked them. Their jailer divulged to them, after a day or so, that they were the guests of the Tiger, and this was enough to destroy all sense of actual reprieve. They tried to get further facts from the paddy father, as Gouger named him, but nothing of value came forth until they'd been in his care for a week. Then he burst out with information that paralyzed them.

He was to preserve their lives carefully, because the Tiger proposed to sacrifice them before his army of 50,000 men, as a gesture of defiance and prophecy to the British. Aungbinle was the Tiger's birthplace. It was many miles out of the army's line of march. Still, some of the sentiments must be retained, and the Tiger had a pretty fancy for performing the ceremony there.

Mercifully this particular agony was not to be long-lived, for three days after the paddy father made his disclosure

Gouger's servant panted in, having rushed with all possible speed from Ava and gasped out the glorious news that the Tiger was dead!

The queen had heard that he was dreaming of the golden throne, and had had the Tiger seized and his house searched. There, it was said, were found not only royal investiture robes but half of the money drawn by the Tiger from the public treasury with which to pay the bounty to the new-raised troops. Without further inquiry or trial, he was sent to the elephants and trampled to death.

For all save the Judsons there now ensued a period of calm, during which Ava apparently forgot them. But, as if fate was determined there should be no let-up to the scourging of the missionaries, Ann came down in June with a heavy attack of fever. Koo-chil sent into Ava for Ma So, but the messenger returned with the sad news that Ma So had died suddenly of cholera. It was a hard blow, not only for Ann's sake, but because they all had loved the vivid little Burmese woman.

Koo-chil, as usual in sickness, forgot caste and became a tower of strength and he and the jailer's wife nursed Ann under Jonathan Price's directions.

Adoniram sweated blood. His helplessness would have driven him to frenzy had it not been for tiny Maria. On the second day of Ann's illness, Koo-chil brought the baby to the prison yard and peremptorily bade her father do something about finding food for her. Adoniram clutched the wailing, blue-eyed atom, and looked helplessly at his fellow-scarecrows. They gathered about him, sympathetically. Laird and Gouger suggested buffalo milk. Jonathan David, a wet-nurse.

Adoniram asked the paddy father to procure a wet-nurse.

The Burman rubbed his belly reflectively. A snake tattooed in blue was represented most realistically as emerging from his navel, and in moments of doubt, the paddy father consulted this apparition. He looked down at it now and muttered a word or two, then gave his opinion:

"The foreign female brat has no karma. It should be allowed to die. No Burman woman must lose merit by feeding it."

Adoniram flushed angrily, but controlled himself to say, "Only a holy one must pronounce on a human creature's karma. How many ticals a day will the paddy father charge me for permission to take my child to the village yonder to be fed?"

"One tical a day!" replied the jailer, promptly.

"Good God, what brutality!" ejaculated Laird.

"It's the only way, I cal'late," said Price. "See if you can leave her in some good woman's care, Judson."

"Have you lost your memory, Price?" demanded Adoniram, impatiently. "Do you not recall the filth and ignorance in which they nurture their children? And you heard what this brute said—that she ought to die? How long would my baby survive in yonder village?"

His emotion was not all indignation with Jonathan David. It was partly mortification. The new crisis robbed him of the last dignity of fatherhood. To go to those cheroot-smoking pagans yonder and plead with them to suckle his daughter! Surely this was his most exquisite moment of chagrin. His friends, sensing his feeling of shame, turned away, and in utter silence, Adoniram set out along the path through the fields to the village.

It was a tiny hamlet, set under the deep shade of fig and palm, the huts close-huddled to a white pagoda. There were the green bronze paddy round about and many little gardens with onions and capsicum and turmeric and scarlet tomato vines. Adoniram shuffled slowly along the street, followed by staring brown children, until he reached the village water-tank, where gossiping women always were to be found. And there he made his petition to a dark-eyed Burman who, crouched on the moss-grown steps, was nursing a child. Other women gathered close to hear and see.

Adoniram did not dream that even after the many months in prison there was still that within him which women-folk, without regard to race, understood and by which they were touched. Clad only in shirt and trousers, bare of foot, wrists galled and manacled, careworn, feeble, there still was indestructible beauty in eye and lip and voice. To his astonishment, as he made his plea, tears flushed to the eyes of this madonna of the leaf-thatched huts, and without protest she took little Maria gently to her breast.

And so for many weeks, thrice each day, Adoniram made his unprecedented pilgrimage.

During all this time, he talked with none save the women. But, late one August afternoon, when he was returning from his last visit for the day, with his little daughter replete and sleeping on his breast, a man stepped from a bamboo clump and called to him to halt.

"Maung Shway-gnong!" gasped Adoniram.

The teacher nodded, gazing at him sorrowfully. "O best of pupils, what have my countrymen done to you?"

"You see!" answered Adoniram. "But what brought you here? Where is the gaing-ôk? Is this safe?"

"One question at a time, lord teacher!"—with the familiar lighting of the tragic eyes in the specter-like face. "Let us sit like Buddha in the shade of this fig-tree and talk."

They were on the edge of the village, in plain sight from the prison. Adoniram hoped the paddy father would be patient, and seated himself beside his friend.

"The gaing-ôk," said Maung Shway-gnong, "came to see me soon after you talked to him about your country, and asked me many questions. I must have convinced him that you were a fountain of pure wisdom, because he went back to Ava and told his royal pupils the world *might* be round! For this, the chief queen had him removed from teaching, and he returned to the monastery at Amarapura. When the British took Prome, in the spring, I retreated with other Burmans, and, as my ill-fated karma would have it, was one of those held accountable for the defeat. I was brought up to Ava and put under examination. The gaing-ôk had ruined my reputation with the lord of white elephants years ago, you will remember, and it was decided I should be tortured. The gaing-ôk tried to interfere, with the result you know."

"What were they going to torture you for, O best of teachers?" asked Adoniram, looking at his friend sadly.

"Strangely, O Lord teacher, not because of any connection with the evacuation of Prome, but because I would not deny I had embraced your religion."

"And thus?" Adoniram drew a deep breath.

"And thus, they gave me the wrist torture,"—holding up his scarred and still swollen arms, "but, O upholder of the Cross, I did not recant. It would seem that Jesus Christ at last had made a man of Maung Shway-gnong."

"A man, indeed!" cried Adoniram. His hazel eyes turned from his friend to gaze with new perception on the paddy fields, reeling in green-gold beauty, at the violet sky curving in vast stillness over the tiny prison, at the hut in which Ann had suffered so long, and he felt like a man who had returned from a visit to hell. Spiritual strength swept through his soul with a force so tangible that the Burman wondered at the flush which suffused the missionary's hollow cheeks.

"O friend of my days of truth," exclaimed the missionary, "you're a better man than I! But, thanks to God for His unspeakable patience, you have shown me my terrible weakness. It's not too late. . . . Dear old friend, if I am proud of my disciple, what must our Lord Jesus Christ feel!"

"My greatest difficulty is not to be proud of myself," returned the Burman, ingenuously. "You don't know what it is to be turned from a trembling rat into a fighting bull-elephant!"

"I only wish I could know," ejaculated Adoniram, with a little smile.

"You!" Maung Shway-gnong stared at the missionary as if for the first time he perceived to the full what the past fifteen months had done to him. Suddenly he covered his eyes. "My pupil! My best of pupils! Jesus Himself didn't suffer more than you."

"I haven't borne it like a fighting bull, though," said Adoniram brokenly. "I've been no credit to Him, O my pupil in Christ."

Maung Shway-gnong laid a still livid hand on Adoniram's. "The chief jailer at the Hand-shrink-not told the gaing-ôk that the other Europeans fed on your will as the cubs feed on the dam; that he could not break their hearts, short of torture, so long as your heart remained unbroken. What say you to that, O great of will?"

Adoniram looked into the cadaverous face sadly. "I say that I don't deserve it, for in my deeps was despair, O Maung Shway-gnong. I've fallen from grace these many months. You must pray for me."

"Always I've prayed for you, lord teacher. Ever since I learned you'd been placed in the Hand-shrink-not, my prayers have wrapped you like the perfumes of jessamine and heliotrope."

Neither spoke for a moment. Children's voices drifted from the village. Then Maung Shway-gnong said, "When the Tiger was killed, they freed me and I retired to Dr. Price's house. I've been holding Christian services there. So far I've been unmolested. As soon as I'd recovered from the torture I came hither to see if I might help you and to tell you I wish to be accepted as a preacher of the Gospels."

"You shall be, indeed, as soon as I am able to prepare you!" cried Adoniram, joyfully. "Tell me, my brother, have you news of Rangoon? We have heard nothing since we left. And, too, what of the gaing-ôk?"

"The gaing-ôk has retired to do a work of merit, of what nature I have no knowledge. Of the Rangoon church I know nothing," replied the teacher. "I shall return there as soon as my strength permits and teach in the zayat. All must be well, with the British there, and if our God continues to will it, they should soon be here."

"Where are they now?" asked Adoniram, eagerly.

"They are said to be twenty miles above Prome. It's rumored that the golden presence has asked the British what terms they will demand for leaving the country. But I doubt this, for his majesty still has an army of thirty thousand Burmans and eight thousand Shans, under Prince Meng-myat-bo. The British have had a terrible bowel-sickness this last rainy season, it is said."

Adoniram drew a deep breath. A little more of patience and of trust in God, and surely the dreadful months would be forgotten! He rose. "You will go soon then to help keep the little church together at Rangoon, O Maung Shway-gnong?"

"I will, lord teacher; but what may I do for you here?"

"Nothing more can be done save to release us, O friend."

They parted with a smile of mutual regard and love, and Adoniram bore his baby back to Ann's side with a lighter heart than he'd known since he had been taken prisoner. Ann, lying white and spent on her mats, heard his hurried tale with deepening gladness in her dark eyes, but there was no chance for comment. The paddy father rushed upon them and drove Adoniram back into the prison with shrill execrations that had in them, however, more of sound than of fury.

No further news reached the prison for many days after Maung Shway-gnong's report. They all were heartened by it, but to Adoniram the encounter had been little less than a meeting with the Evangel. He was invigorated, uplifted, rededicated. And as Ann regained her feet and resumed her care of the baby and of the prisoners, and her efforts to convert Koo-chil, he felt that life was swinging toward actual cheerfulness.

CHAPTER XXIV

THE SENSE OF HONOR

ONE morning in late October, a soldier on a stout little pony jogged up to the prison gate and shouted to the jailer to open. It happened that at the moment, the paddy father was standing on the prison veranda, protesting violently against the activities of his charges. Under the leadership of Henry Gouger, they were conducting a campaign against the snakes—cobra capello and karaits—which had sought sanctuary from the wet paddy fields on the slightly higher ground of the prison. The jailer was outraged as only a Buddhist and nat-worshiper could be by the spectacle, and the soldier-messenger pulled his pony to its fat little haunches, appalled. But the prisoners continued their unholy work. They had had little sleep the night before, with the creatures crawling over the floor of the house.

The paddy father hailed the newcomer with delight. "You are witness, O fighting-man, to the indecency of these foreign animals. Why should I cherish them when they cherish nothing but their own faded skins?"

"One of them, at least, you'll be rid of immediately," said the soldier. He bore the king's message-case—the tip of an elephant-tusk, slung from his shoulder. He abstracted a bit of palm-leaf from this and handed it to the jailer.

The paddy father perused the message, then shouted to Adoniram, "O foreign teacher, you are to go at once to the golden presence, taking your belongings with you."

Adoniram, who had just dispatched a particularly large specimen of the tiny, deadly karait, scraped the end of his bamboo club in the sand and made his way slowly to the two Burmans by the gate.

THE SENSE OF HONOR 243

"For what am I wanted?" he asked.

"Does the lord of air and earth confide his purposes to his dogs?" demanded the jailer, impatiently.

"Who's a dog?" The messenger slapped his knife ferociously.

"Come, no monkey chatter," exclaimed Adoniram. He had long since finished with a patient forbearance with these assassins. "Where are you to take me, O soldier?"

"To the court of justice," answered the messenger, with a reluctant sort of courtesy that was distinctly encouraging.

"Send for my wife and child, my paddy father," ordered the missionary, "and take me off these chains."

The messenger burst into a roar of laughter. "He fancies he's the lord white elephant because his skin's the color of wet clay! Run quickly, O jailer!"

"Let him talk like a mountain; he'll fall the further," grunted the paddy father. "How will you take him? On a lead-rope?"

The other prisoners now had drawn near. Lanciego, leaning heavily on his bamboo staff, his brown skin hanging in heavy furrows on his face, his double-chins reduced to a wattle, recognized the soldier as one of his former clerks.

"Why is Maung Judson wanted, Maung Lo?" he asked.

The soldier dismounted and sheekoed. "The lord of white elephants, it is said, cannot believe the evidence of his golden eyes and ears as to the peace terms offered by the enemy. He wishes the foreign teacher to translate."

"But why the foreign teacher?" cried old Rodgers, his palsied hands on his ragged hips. "Have I not served him faithfully for forty years?"

"But you're English, Rodgers. You've never let me forget that in the thirty years I've known you," sneered Lanciego. Then, to the messenger, "You're sure he said nothing about me, Maung Lo?"

"Show the lord collector the writing, O jailer," said the soldier.

The fold of palm-leaf was handed from one prisoner to another.

"If you feel sick, I'll go in your stead, Judson," suggested Price.

"It says Maung Judson, the foreign teacher, and it's Judson I bring, and deliver," shouted the soldier irritably.

"Also my belongings," said Adoniram, quietly. "My wife and child."

"Not so,"—the paddy father rubbed the blue snake on his navel reflectively. "They stay and pay rent as usual."

Ann, who had been standing for several minutes behind the soldier's pony, gave Adoniram a knowing glance from her dark eyes, gathered up her dragging tamein and disappeared. The argument at the gate was still heated when she returned in the jailer's bullock cart, her three children, her mats, her bedding and clothing piled higgledy-piggledy behind her, and Koo-chil driving the buffalo.

"O paddy father," she called, "there is ngape in my room and pickled tea and a week's supply of venison. They are yours, in case I am not here to eat them."

The argument was stilled as by magic. Adoniram, though with wrists in chains, was not hindered otherwise from crawling into the cart, and with the half-wistful, half-anxious gaze of the scarecrows following them, the two set off on the next act of their drama.

They reached Ava at dusk. The soldier took Adoniram in hand at the court-house and Koo-chil drove Ann on to the mission.

There was a tripod lamp burning near the familiar dais. The flickering light fell on the dark faces of the half-dozen officials seated there. The night was cool and they wore their robes. They looked curiously at the white man in shirt and trousers. None of them knew him, nor had he seen any of them before.

"Maung Judson, the foreign teacher, as ordered by the golden presence, O noble lords," announced the soldier.

THE SENSE OF HONOR

A Burman, who by the cords across his breast was a privy councilor, spoke courteously:

"Come closer, O teacher."

"Not with the manacles of a felon on my hands, my lord. It would be unseemly," replied Adoniram.

The official gave a quick order, and the soldier unfastened the chains that for eighteen months had burned and galled Adoniram's wrists. He walked to the edge of the dais.

"I am here, O lords of Burma," he said, hoping that they would not observe the heavy pulse which fluttered his linen shirt.

A hatchet-faced Burman, chewing nervously, leaned toward him. "What do the English mean, O teacher, by telling us they wish to treat of peace and at the same time saying they will take from us the west coast, beyond the Arakan Yoma, and the west coast of the country we took from Siam, which is ours, also two crores of rupees?"

"I am not English. I am an American," declared Adoniram.

"You are white," insisted the privy councilor, "and a certain monk has told us that you have great wisdom and that you are like a monk in that belongings mean nothing to you. Tell us what you think."

So the gaing-ôk was back of this! A little of confidence dawned in Adoniram's anxious mind. He prayed for the right word, standing very still, the six pairs of black eyes upon him. After a moment, it seemed to him that, as a man of peace, it was his duty to try to help these people toward resigning themselves to the inevitable British occupancy, which, after all, they had brought upon themselves.

He spoke carefully. "The Burmans began this war, thinking to take vast territory to the west. The British already had taken that territory for themselves. They found it a difficult mouthful to chew, requiring all their strength, yet you would have war. Suppose now, they move away from Burma, requiring nothing from you, will his majesty agree to leave Bengal alone and will he keep that agreement?"

"Why should a great king keep an agreement?" asked the councilor. "Of what use to be king, then?"

"Just so!" agreed Adoniram. "The British understand this feeling of the lord of air, therefore, they say, we will take these strips of land from you and if that doesn't teach you to leave us alone in Bengal, we will return and take yet more strips."

"But how do we know that if—of course he won't, but *if* the lord of earth and air gives up the Arakan coast, the British won't come back with more soldiers and take Ava?" A minister with a face more scarred than poor Laird's said this.

"If the British general agrees, he will keep his agreement, absolutely and finally," declared Adoniram.

"But he has beaten us. Why should he keep his agreement?" All six were staring at the missionary in helpless bewilderment.

"Because a Christian keeps his promises, and General Campbell is a Christian," was Adoniram's answer. "One of the basic laws of our religion is, Thou shalt not lie. No true Christian will break a solemn promise, for that would be turning his own word into an untruth."

"It's as little to be understood as a pariah dog baying the moon," groaned the councilor. "And if we can't understand, how hopeless that the golden presence—"

"The golden presence," interrupted the smallpox gentleman, "as you very well know, would end the war to-morrow. But the first queen—"

There was a silence full of heavy breathing. After a time an elephant trumpeted remotely and, roused to his duty, the councilor said to Adoniram, "What would you say the British plan to do next, O teacher?"

"First, I must know what was your reply to the terms which General Campbell gave you, my lord."

"The golden presence procured forty days in which to consider. During this time, he gathered a mighty army of a size ten times the enemy's. Then—it was yesterday, to be exact—he sent word to the British that it was unknown to Burmese wisdom to give up territory or to pay money and they must think of other terms. Now the army under Prince Meng-myat-bo is beginning to close round the enemy, and if the British wish to treat, they must treat under fire."

"But you've answered your own question, my lord," said Adoniram, sadly. "If you fire on the British, it's an invitation to them to fire on you, and they will continue their progress up the Irrawaddy."

The Burmans shook their heads and he with the pitted face cried triumphantly, "They can make no progress against this new army, O teacher. They will send shortly with new terms, and that is where your usefulness begins. The lord of life sends you down the Irrawaddy to-morrow to Prince Meng-myat-bo's headquarters at Melun, where you will interpret and translate for us."

"But I have no wisdom for this!" protested Adoniram, aghast at the responsibilities, the impossible difficulties, of such a task. "Send Mr. Lanciego. He is not English and you know him to be astute."

"We are astute, ourselves. That's not the quality we need. We must have some one who speaks truth—nay, more, who can recognize it."

Adoniram thought of Jonathan David and how he would delight in the job. "Send Dr. Price," he pleaded.

The Burmans laughed.

"Don't chatter like a parrot," protested the councilor. "You are to be fed by the king's bounty. Twenty ticals will be given you and you will leave to-morrow." He beckoned the guard. "You will be housed near by." He rose, indicating that the audience was over.

Adoniram was shut into a neighboring hovel. It was cold and damp, but he managed to snatch several hours' sleep, although it was hard to adjust himself to unfettered wrists.

He was led to the mission-house at dawn and given a half-hour in which to eat, dress and make a bundle of clothing and bedding. It was a mad half-hour, but he and Ann dared to be almost happy as it flew. The sun was only fairly above the tree-tops when he was led aboard a dispatch-boat which set off immediately.

Three days later, he sighted the glittering beach of Melun, where a vast temporary town had overrun the sands and the pagoda-crowned cliffs as far as the eye could sweep from the water. Adoniram had been treated with fair decency on the way down, but as soon as the boat was beached, he was put under guard and marched to a hut which had been prepared for him. It was without windows, and when they had thrust him within and barred the door, he found himself in darkness. Protests were unheeded. The heat was intense. Mosquitoes blanketed him, and twelve hours of this combination brought on an ague attack. When, the morning after his arrival, the door was opened and a Burman officer entered with a copy of a Calcutta newspaper which he wished to have translated, he found the missionary unconscious, nor would kicks bring a coherent response from him.

There was an indignant conference then, in Prince Meng-myat-bo's presence, and reluctantly it was decided to move the prisoner into light and air. Higher up the beach was a cook-house. The eaves of this were elongated by the help of a mat supported on bamboos, and Adoniram was carried thither and placed under a mosquito cloth. In a day or so he was in comparatively good shape again. The Burmans watched his recovery with complaisance, but he was treated still as a prisoner and not permitted to leave his shelter.

As a matter of fact, Adoniram was little tempted to wander about. Not only was the heat on the beach intense but the camp under Prince Meng-myat-bo was disorderly and dirty beyond the imagination of one who did not know the Burmans, and there was nothing in it to tempt Adoniram into a sightseeing tour. Sitting on his mat behind the

THE SENSE OF HONOR

cook-house, he watched the beautiful war-boats dashing up and down the river, and heard, to the south, the pounding of the British guns and recognized, as the wounded dragged themselves across the sands, that the Burmans were in a state of almost complete funk. It was going to be very hard to appeal to their reason. Nor was this feeling limited to the common soldier. On the third day after his arrival, Adoniram was honored by a visit from his former patron, Prince Meng-myat-bo.

He was like the king as to features; had the abnormally receding forehead and the pleasant wide mouth, but his eyes were more intelligent. Yet he had none of his majesty's physical restlessness, for he was a cripple. Both his legs and arms were partially paralyzed. He was brought to the missionary's shelter in a padded arm-chair, and an especial awning was immediately set over his head. It was impossible, of course, for him to compromise his royalty by sharing Adoniram's shade.

The two men stared at each other for a long moment; then Adoniram sheekoed and the prince said:

"You have been ill, O interpreter of the starry systems!"

"Illness is a new name for the Hand-shrink-not, O Prince!" replied Adoniram, with a little smile.

"It was not my doing, lord teacher," protested the prince, with great earnestness. "I was always your friend."

"Always? No, not my friend in adversity, which is the only true test of friendship." Adoniram shook his head. "But in Burma, one never looks backward. Did your lordship come to talk of Copernicus?"

"I only wish I might!" exclaimed the prince. "But that must wait. I have come to ask you if you do not think it advisable for us to retreat now to Ava. These British eat human flesh, and while mine certainly couldn't tempt a gourmet, still I'm not tempted to risk what I have."

"But that's a child's saying, O prince of the stars! The

British are white, and abhor the very thought of eating human flesh."

The Burman eyed the missionary doubtfully. His attendants leaned forward eagerly. "You'll deny also that their doctors can sew a head or a leg on so that only a scar remains?"

"Yes, I deny that quite as emphatically," was Adoniram's answer.

"Will you deny this:—that they obey their officers absolutely, going straight into gunfire or leaping into a thicket of spears?"

"That is true. They are obedient even to death, as all well-disciplined soldiers must be," Adoniram nodded.

"Ah!" The prince drew a long breath. "Don't you realize, O lord teacher, that their blind obedience to command is more terrifying to a Burman even than their flesh-eating, for it means that they will go as far as their commander sends them. And General Campbell has his eyes fixed on the golden throne."

Adoniram rubbed his chin thoughtfully. The prince was frightened, physically frightened, and he must be quieted. A frightened Burman was always and imminently a butcher. The prince might turn the camp into a shambles with the next report of misfortune at the front.

"The British, O prince of the stars, don't want Burma. Sir Archibald Campbell doesn't want the golden throne. If you will sign his peace terms, he will retire to Rangoon and there wait for your money payments, just as it says in these papers." He laid a thin hand on the documents which had been given him to translate, that morning.

"What makes you think he will do so?" The prince spat out the cheroot an attendant had placed between his lips. "There is nothing on earth between him and Ava, for we Burmans are to the British as an army of butterflies."

"The endeavor of Christian peoples is to keep the signed word," said Adoniram. "If General Campbell makes you a

THE SENSE OF HONOR 251

promise in writing, he will keep it, and so will his king."

"But why, why, why?" shouted his highness. "What has religion to do with it? We are Buddhists and our religion is built on the teaching of not taking life. But the history of Burman kings is a history only of war and killing. Religion, O lord teacher, is one thing and living is another."

"Jesus Christ's mission on earth was to prove to men that if we would win to eternal heaven, our living and our religion must be one. It was for that He went to the Cross. And since that day, the people who gave His name to their religion have tried to make His teachings and their living one and the same."

"Tried!" snorted the prince. "Lanciego is a Christian, and old Rodgers, and these British soldiers. Did your Christ teach war?"

"He taught peace," replied Adoniram, sadly. "He taught us to love our enemies, to do good to those that hated us and despitefully used us. We fall far short of that, O prince, far, far short. But there are other things He taught that we make our own more and more with each generation. About some things we are truthful, and taking us in the large, we keep our word, even to our own disadvantage."

This was the sort of ethical discussion the prince had loved best, in the better days, and Adoniram believed that not only might it assist the prime business at hand but that it would calm his highness. And watching him closely, he saw the prince's dilated pupils slowly return to normal and the familiar speculative lift to his eyebrows give his round face its old charm.

"Then, though General Campbell repudiates his Christ in that he's a killer of men, he follows Him in that he will keep his word not to take away more than our sea-coast?"

"That is truth," replied Adoniram, a little heavily, as he caught a glimpse of Christianity's history through these pagan eyes.

"There is this always to be remembered,"—the prince

gave the missionary a clear look—"that we have known one Christian here in Burma for twelve or more years, and he has spoken truth when he believed it would send him to the maul. He who was a gaing-ôk told me that, not long ago. And there is always the chance that we may find that some of the British have also this habit."

"We call it a sense of honor," said Adoniram with a little smile for this reminder of his enemy friend.

"What is that?" exclaimed the Burman. Adoniram had used the English word, and the prince repeated it, awkwardly.

"It is the inability to lie," replied Adoniram. "No man can be a Christian who doesn't acquire it."

The two men listened to an all-too-close shrieking of mortar shots; then the prince looked up at a pagoda rising in its chaste beauty from the wooded cliff above them.

"Lord teacher," he asked, "have you ever thought of what it might have meant to their disciples had your Christ and my Buddha met and talked together?"

Adoniram's hazel eyes deepened. "Yes! And it would have changed the whole history of the world had the Buddha Gautama been with Jesus Christ during the last forty-eight hours of His life."

"I wonder!" breathed the prince.

He meditated on the thought for an interval, then with a smile for Adoniram, directed his attendants to carry him to his quarters.

The following day, Meng-myat-bo sent for Adoniram. Prisoners had been brought in from the front. Adoniram found them loaded with chains—several sepoys and a British soldier, grouped before the prince. Their Burman guards were trying vainly to force them to kneel.

"You'd better give in," suggested Adoniram to the angry Britisher, "and tell the sepoys to do so. What advantage is there in affronting these people on harmless matters of etiquette? Waggle your thumbs or your ears, if it will please them." He dropped to his own knees as he spoke.

The Britisher, a grizzled old warrior, gave the missionary a grin, compounded of surprise and pleasure.

"Sir, it's a great happiness to see you. We've all heard of you. Are you Mr. Price or Mr. Judson?"

"I'm Judson," replied Adoniram.

"Come," interrupted the prince, irritably. "This isn't a village play, O teacher. Ah, I see"—as the prisoners reluctantly squatted—"you were teaching them manners. Ask them how many men now fight behind General Campbell."

For an hour Adoniram interpreted. It was not easy. The prince was surrounded by government officials and officers who were sulky and ugly. They insisted that the prisoners were lying. But, curiously, never did they doubt Adoniram's word. And when, at the end of the hour, he said, "There can be no doubt, O supporters of the golden throne, that the British will be at Melun within a week," they were convinced and one of the Burman generals cried, "All is lost! What shall we do?"

"Sign the peace treaty," said Adoniram, grimly.

"Tell them that that big body of Shans they had protecting their right flank took to the hills yesterday," said the English soldier. "We were holding some of them prisoners and let them off to join the flight."

Adoniram translated.

"Now that I will not believe!" shouted the prince. "See, here comes a runner. We'll prove these pariahs to be liars."

A sweating, panting Burman in a breech-clout flung himself on his face before the group on the dais.

"The Shans, O shadow of the golden presence, have refused to continue our march of victory and have withdrawn to their own country to the east."

"Kill me this liar!" roared the prince.

A general in a pea-green coat leaned from the dais and

caught the unresisting messenger by the topknot. Adoniram covered his face with his hands. A moment later, he said, eyes averted from the horror on the floor:

"He did not lie, poor fellow. You must face your defeat now, O prince, or face total disaster later."

"Get out of here, croaker!" cried Meng-myat-bo. "Take him back to his hovel," to Adoniram's guards.

Adoniram gladly obeyed the royal command, but he paused at the tent door to say, pointing toward the still kneeling prisoners, "You must not forget, O brother to the lord of white elephants, that for every prisoner you slay, Sir Archibald Campbell will demand bitter payment."

"What is that teaching of yours, O Jesus Christ's man," sneered the prince, "to the effect that Christians return good for evil?"

"The one Christian virtue that I've guaranteed you'll find in the British military is the sense of honor," was Adoniram's reply. He turned and followed his guard out from the shade of the teakwoods, down the path to the reeling white sands where his shelter was set.

Day after day, now, runners flung themselves before the dais and met a bloody fate. Day after day Adoniram struggled to prepare these minds, so strangely blended of childishness and of mature intelligence, for the inevitable disaster. But it seemed an impossible task. They were being asked to think thoughts, to understand ideals, utterly alien to the Burmese mind.

It was curious that they never accused Adoniram of being unfair to them or of being over-friendly to the British. Absurd as they considered truth-telling, during these weeks of inexorably approaching ruin, the one anchor to which they clung was the sense of honor in this foreigner, this missionary. The officers left off all formality with him and crowded his mats as had the inquirers after Christ, in the old Rangoon days. And difficult as was his physical situation, Adoniram found his unique task extraordinarily stim-

THE SENSE OF HONOR 255

ulating. The last of the prison miasma of doubts and fears, lifted. He again saw life crystal-clear.

It was on the 7th of December that the advance lines of the Burmans retreated to Myede, just below Melun, and Sir Archibald Campbell once more sent peace terms. They duplicated those which the Burmans earlier had repudiated. There was tremendous excitement in the camp. The stockade on the bluffs was strengthened and a picked force of 4,500 men garrisoned in the fort. But the prince continued his refusal to negotiate, until he awoke one morning and beheld across the river, here about four hundred yards wide, a sudden eruption of white tents and red coats. Then his bearers brought him on a run to Adoniram's shelter.

"You behold the pestilence yonder, O teacher?" shrilled the prince, his face twitching.

Adoniram, wrapped in a ragged piece of blanket, for this was his "chill" morning, looked from the documents in his shaking hands to the unhappy prince, and said gravely:

"You must appoint commissioners to meet the Brahman whom General Campbell has sent as messenger, O right hand to his majesty. The time has come for you to meet the sword with the written word."

"But, my brother— I shall be crushed between the lion across the river and the elephant at Ava."

"The British will protect you, if you ask them to," suggested Adoniram, "after you have signed the treaty."

The Burman's jaw dropped. He puffed furiously on his cheroot and then said, "The louse crawls to the dog's back to save his life! I shall send you to the boat the British propose to anchor in mid-stream, as neutral ground, in an hour, lord teacher."

"That is well!" Adoniram spoke cheerfully, but he did not for a moment believe that Meng-myat-bo meant what he said.

But for once Adoniram's reading of Burman character was at fault. Late in the morning, a canoe was made ready and Adoniram, with three Burmese officials, was ordered aboard. They were at once rowed out to an empty rice-boat anchored in the middle of the Irrawaddy, where the emissaries of the British awaited them.

It was an extraordinary scene and situation. The glorious river here was set in hills, deep-wooded and crowded with white pagodas. The shores of both the British camp on the east and the Burmese on the west were thick-set with craft of every description guarding their respective headquarters. And squatting under the umbrella of the chief Burman commissioner was the American missionary whom the British twelve years before had hounded out of their East Indian possessions, and on whom the success of the negotiations depended.

Pale, now shivering, now burning with fever, in his threadbare clothing, his galled wrists bandaged, his festered ankle still making normal movement impossible, Adoniram gave his utmost to the task so singularly imposed upon him. To the sound of rushing waters and of screaming king crow and sea eagle, hour after hour, gently but persistently he urged on the uneasy Burmans the hopelessness of delay. He translated and expounded sentence by sentence the terms of the treaty, which was a model of simple brevity, until he as well as every man present could repeat it word for word.

Each day, under the anxious eyes of the commissioners, the fleet on the British side was augmented by armed boats of every sort, but it was not until a steamer, snorting fire and terror from its long stack, paddled in an enormous circle around the treaty boat, that the last stronghold of the Burmans' *morale* was leveled. They signed the treaty before the *Diana* made anchor.

Fifteen days' armistice was granted by the British for the treaty to receive Bagyi-daw's signature. Adoniram had no hope of being returned to Ava before the time-limit was up, for he knew that Prince Meng-myat-bo shared his own doubts as to the reception the treaty would receive from his

THE SENSE OF HONOR

majesty. He did not see the prince on the afternoon the treaty was signed, although immediately on his return to the cook-house shelter, he sent a request for an audience. He received no reply to this for several hours, and was made a little uneasy thereby. And although he constantly assured himself that nothing the Burmans could show in the way of fickleness could surprise him, still he was stunned by the nature of Meng-myat-bo's answer when it arrived at last.

He was eating his belated supper of boiled plantains when a guard of three soldiers came in and showed him an order signed by the prince. "We have no further use for Judson. We therefore return him to the golden city."

His protests were of no avail. Chains were replaced on his wrists and ankles. He was dragged to a boat and lay all night on the deck, shivering and staring up at the tender beauty of the great stars.

CHAPTER XXV

AVA AT BAY

THE voyage back to Ava consumed ten days. The humiliation of the return to fetters and the irony of his position with both the Burmans and the British were fairly well balanced by Adoniram's quiet sense of success. He had brought peace to beautiful mad Burma, a peace which would at least in all portions under British control assure a foothold to the Christian faith. The two years in prison, the travail of body and of spirit, were justified. He thought of Jeanne Marie Guyon's lines:

> "Long plunged in sorrow, I resign
> My soul to that dear hand of thine—
> The Cross! O ravishment and bliss
> How grateful every anguish is,
> Its bitterness, how sweet."

Even were Bagyi-daw to order him back to prison, this much was done and done because God had sent Adoniram Judson to Burma. Even though Rangoon would not be under English control after the several payments of moneys were completed, still the English would be too close at hand in Arakan and lower Burma for official Burma to continue its program toward Christian converts. He and Ann and baby Maria would return to Rangoon—back to the familiar mission yard, grown how dear in memory! and there with the blessed Maung Shway-gnong and Maung Ing and Maung Nau rebuild the church on a foundation of rock!

No, during those ten days, the splendor of the great river was no greater than the splendor of Adoniram's thoughts of the Cross in Burma; nor than his thoughts of Ann! Deep as had been his gratitude toward her, his pride in her, his dependence on her during the two years just past, his misery, mental and physical had been too great for him to appreciate to the full the marvel of her as a human being; what she had endured, what she had accomplished. He told himself, as the multiplying toddy palms and ricefields announced that they were nearing Ava, that he had lost so much of his manhood in the Hand-shrink-not that he had taken Ann for granted as a boy does his mother.

A thousand pictures of her floated between him and the sweating rowers:—Ann in her white bonnet with the pink rosebud for which she apologized, making her first call on the viceroy; Ann with baby Roger in her lap and Ann's face drowned in tears asking, "Where is my baby now?"; Ann with Madame Guyon under her arm looking at him with brown eyes of unfathomable understanding; Ann, ravishingly lovely on her return from America and on the trip up the Irrawaddy, when she was in renewed truth his darling, his darling, his bride! A great sigh broke from him and his heart was flooded by an overmastering love for this woman who was essential to all that was true, was virile, was fine, in his nature, a love that was nobler and deeper, more overpowering, than all he had felt for her before.

When at last they disembarked in the starlight at Ava, he begged his guards to take him, if only for five minutes, to the mission. He offered them every bribe he hoped would move them. But the Burmans were adamant. They durst not. The order was to take the teacher to the court house. And to the ill-omened court house he was taken. The officials there were the same as those who had sent him to Melun but they appeared not to know Adoniram. They were panicky and distrait. No one knew the king's will of him and in spite of threats, bribes and cajolery, he was taken to an outhouse and chained there with orders that he be returned to Aungbinle on the morrow.

Then they forgot him for twenty-four hours! Somehow,

this was worse than anything that had gone before and Adoniram fairly wept with chagrin. Shouts brought no one. There was neither water nor food. But on the second morning, a fat brown face was thrust anxiously in at the window. Maung Ing, at last!

Ann had heard of his arrival and had sent Maung Ing to comb Ava until the teacher was found. It had been a slow job. But now, here were rice and chicken and fruit and a message from Ann; her love; and he was to send a note by Maung Ing to the governor of the north gate, their only influential friend in the city. Adoniram hurriedly wrote the note and faithful Maung Ing rushed off with it. After he had gone, Adoniram wondered why Ann had not herself written to the old governor with whom her prestige was so much greater than his own. Then the thought came to him that after all, it was he who had brought about the signing of the treaty and Ann was of course using the kudos he may have gained thus.

The day dragged and night closed down breathlessly. Drums were beating at intervals and pagoda gongs were struck continually. The city was troubled and reckless and it behooved him to be thankful that he was not in the death prison. He slept a little after this thought came to him and at sun-up a guard arrived who turned him over to a liveried servant. The governor of the north gate wanted him.

The old man was sitting on his veranda as Adoniram shuffled up. He stared at the missionary with growing wonder in his sunken black eyes. After a moment, tugging at the rope of hair on his chin, he said:

"Beautiful women invariably have strange tastes in husbands, eh, lord teacher?"

Adoniram looked at the clothing he had been unable to change for two weeks and rubbed the beard he had not been permitted to shave.

"Strange, indeed, my lord," agreed Adoniram with a grin.

"Sometimes one thinks of the mating of the ruby with a daub of clay."

The governor chuckled, showing broken black teeth. Then he said gravely, "Every second day for over a year, the exquisite dak-blossom, your wife, came to us here to plead for you and your foreign friends. Not that she stood on the door sill whining like a leper, you understand. No, she came with a smile and sat with us and at my request instructed me in the knowledge and ways of America until I came to understand her mind and yours and to think with shame of Burma and what Burma dreams and does. Thus, O Jesus Christ's man, has the dak-blossom pleaded for you and my heart has unfolded as the lotus after the rains. I cannot do all that I would wish for her. Were I younger," with a flash of heat in eyes and voice, "I would show her the difference between what pale devotion like yours must be and the passion of a *man*. But I'm only a dried seed waiting for the next turn of the wheel. Another life, another opportunity—" He looked beyond Adoniram at the peacock parading full-spread on his garden wall, and at its reflection in the blue pool below. "Beauty is of itself a merit," he murmured, "and accumulates in one's karma." Then his voice changed and he said in his official manner, "This much I have done, O lord teacher, I have gone bond for you, that you will not leave the city. I have obtained permission for your chains to be struck off and, that being done, you are free to return to your monastery on the river. But I advise you to walk softly as the cheetah and with neither voice nor eyes." He motioned to the guard. "Take me off those chains, fellow."

Adoniram stood motionless and speechless during the governor's monolog and while the guard liberated his agonized wrists and ankles. Then after biting his lips as the freed circulation roweled him with pain, he said huskily:

"With all that which is within me, I thank you, O governor of a mighty heart and of a merit great as the building of the Shwé Dagôn."

He lifted a hand stained with blood and pus to touch his hollow cheeks thoughtfully and then he added, "All that you say of my beautiful wife is true. I am blessed in her far beyond my merits. But, O friend of the unhappy, in spite of your wisdom, you have not measured adequately how deep she is folded in my heart."

Hazel eyes locked with black. The peacock, ravished by his own reflection, drunk with his own vanity, fluttered down to embrace himself Narcissus-like in the sky-blue pool. In the confusion of raucous cries and beating wings that followed, Adoniram sheekoed and made his escape. . . .

Ann! Ann!

Reeling on his uncertain ankles, he rushed out of the gates and along the tamarind-shaded road to the mission and burst in at the door. There was a fat, half-naked Burmese woman crouched by the fire box with a filthy wailing baby in her lap. Through the open bedroom door, he saw Ann, in bed. He hobbled to her side and stared in speechless horror at a ghastly shadow, so depleted, so wan, that for one terrible second as he gazed, he thought she was dead. He dropped to his knees and with a great sob laid his cheek to hers. Ann stirred and lifting a transparent hand, rested it upon his head.

"God heard me," she whispered.

"Nancy! What happened, Nancy?" he begged, raising his head and looking, revolted, at the dirt and disorder of the bed and the room.

"Spotted fever, dearest. You oughtn't to be touching me. I had only Koo-Chil as nurse, until Dr. Price was released last week. I'm convalescing now."

"Convalescing!" Adoniram wrung his hands.

But there was no doubting the assurance and reassurance in Ann's sunken eyes and Adoniram, with hope revived, rose to his feet. Here was a task to his hand that permitted no

AVA AT BAY 263

intrusion of business of state or church. Five minutes later, Koo-chil, coming in with a bowl of broth, found his master putting clean sheets on his mistress' bed.

Dr. Price's treatment had had one sane element. He had found Ann refusing all nourishment and he had ordered Koo-chil to force food upon her. The faithful Bengalese had obeyed implicitly and, beginning with wine, dropped teaspoon at a time between her semi-conscious lips, he had now progressed to bowls of broth and rice. The rest of Jonathan David's treatment filled Adoniram with mingled wrath and consternation. He had shaved Ann's lovely head and applied blisters to her skull and to her feet! The doctor was expected, Ann told him, to come over from Sagaing that day to apply leeches.

"Over my dead body, Nancy," muttered Adoniram, grimly, as she told him this, late in the afternoon.

He and Koo-chil and the Burmese woman had been at work all day and Ann lay in a room which was sweet with cleanliness, her baby daughter beside her. Adoniram had bathed them both and arrayed them in the night clothes the Burmese woman had laundered under his eye. He smoothed the plain muslin cap on Ann's head, disapprovingly.

"It's unnecessarily ugly, dearest," he protested.

"I was grateful even for this, 'Don, darling. It's one of Dr. Price's night caps."

"One consolation, your hair is already coming in, so you won't need any head covering long," said Adoniram, consolingly.

Ann looked pleadingly up into his face. "Can you, will you, keep on loving me, even thus, Adoniram?"

"Didn't you loathe me in my filth at the death prison?" demanded Adoniram, fiercely.

"Certainly not!" Ann's eyes were indignant. "But with a woman—her looks are more important."

"You vain, flattery-seeking peacock!" touching her wan cheeks tenderly with his now clean-shaven lips. "Nancy, even Jonathan David's night cap can't entirely quench your loveliness. And in saying this, I've paid you the highest compliment possible in human language!"

She laughed weakly and, drawing her baby into the hollow of her arm, fell happily into slumber.

All Ava went softly now, awaiting the king's next move. The consultations in the palace were continuous, as day after day slipped by and the limit of the armistice approached, was reached and passed. Adoniram as he watched Ann's strength flow back under his skillful nursing wondered with ever-increasing unease if, after all, his work at Melun had been futile. He was following the governor's orders and confining himself to the mission yard. Maung Ing brought him garbled reports of which he could make little. Maung Shway-gnong had gone back to Rangoon. He would have been a reliable source of information.

But the suspense of ignorance was ended on a morning late in January when a servant wearing the royal livery appeared at the mission with an order for Adoniram to repair to the council room. He would wait only for the missionary to put on his broad-brimmed straw hat before hurrying him out into the dusty road. He would not talk except to say that Dr. Price also had been summoned and Adoniram followed, sustaining himself with the thought that if the king had meant mischief he would have sent soldiers for him and not one of the household servants. Moreover, one who has been in prison may not enter the king's presence without a pardon. Perhaps Bagyi-daw had wiped the slate!

On a very low throne sat Bagyi-daw, with several civil officials in their long robes kneeling before the dais. Back of the ministers knelt a dozen generals and their lieutenants and back of these three astrologers, in white robes, star embossed. Dr. Price in a marvelous new suit of bright blue silk made in the best interpretation of European style by a Burmese tailor sat behind the astrologers with his long legs doubled under him. Adoniram squatted beside his confrere

AVA AT BAY

and the two smiled ruefully at each other. What now?

A guard brought in an Englishman in uniform and thrust him toward the Americans. The newcomer's eyes lighted when he beheld white faces and he dropped beside Adoniram with alacrity.

Bagyi-daw pointed his little sword at the latest arrival. "You in the British uniform, were you at Melun? Ask him, Judson."

Adoniram repeated the question in English. The Englishman made to rise but Adoniram pulled him down.

"Remain as nearly on all fours as you can," he whispered.

"I was captured after the bombardment of Melun, as I was binding wounds. I am a doctor, Mr. Sanford by name," said the Englishman, bowing his head obediently.

"And what will General Campbell do next?" demanded the lord of air.

"He will continue to march toward Ava. He found the treaty signed by your majesty's commissioners lying on the floor of the prince's tent. He had supposed that the armistice was for the purpose of procuring your majesty's signature and was much chagrined at finding the document."

"Good heavens!" ejaculated Adoniram. He gave Dr. Sanford a startled look, then interpreted in a bitter voice.

"What need was there to send me a treaty I wouldn't sign?" asked Bagyi-daw, reasonably. "Then Melun is now garrisoned by the British devils and the British general continues his way toward the golden city?"

"Yes, your majesty," was the doctor's answer.

Bagyi-daw bit his nails and gnawed at the hilt of his little sword alternately.

"It's not to be understood how when the enemy has taken the whole of the valley of the Irrawaddy, they will give it up—at any price," he said. "But Judson says they will and we'll let it stand. Still this the enemy must be made to understand. It is impossible for us to pay so great a sum of rupees. They must take less. We can pay but a third of the rupees. And we must have some proof that the enemy will leave the country after the money is paid. Therefore, it is my golden will that the teacher, Judson, and this enemy devil doctor shall go down to meet General Campbell and persuade him to acquire merit by a gentler chastisement."

Adoniram raised his head and would have burst forth violently in protest had not the golden voice forestalled him by going on in sudden passion.

"Why, oh, why!" shouted Bagyi-daw, "did we begin this war? Who first gave me this unseemly advice?" He glared savagely about him. There was a soft rustling of silks as every bowed head cowered closer to the floor.

Adoniram whispered to Jonathan David: "It will be fatal to undertake this errand, for it's doomed to failure and the Hand-shrink-not is ready for the next emissary, white or brown, who fails him. I'm going to try to get out of it and you do the same if he turns to you."

"Nonsense!" whispered Price. "It's a good chance to get back into favor."

Adoniram gave him an exasperated glance but set his teeth. The doctor was hopeless when it came to court favor.

"You have heard me, O Judson?" roared Bagyi-daw.

Adoniram sat back on his haunches. "I have heard, O great king!" he replied, his soft full voice very firm. "But in the kindness of your heart you have forgotten that I did not win concessions from the British at Melun. I would only fail you again, try as I would. O lord of white elephants, send this English doctor to treat."

"How do I know he'll return?" demanded Bagyi-daw, staring at Adoniram, who returned the gaze frankly.

"If he says he'll return, so he will do," replied Adoniram. "He is a Christian and to such as he a promise is sacred."

"I'll go in place of Maung Judson, O lord of air," suggested Dr. Price suddenly.

"You are not a monk such as he nor do you know the Burmese mind as he nor is your brain as large as his," was the king's succinct reply. "How do I know you'd be faithful?"

The prime minister raised his head from the floor. "Well, monkey face, what is your thought?" growled Bagyi-daw.

"O lord of existence!" said the minister, "give Maung Price a title and a position in your service and nothing will tear him from you."

The king gazed from one to another of his advisors not unlike, Adoniram thought, a badgered animal. Finally, he said, "Will you offer your body, Maung Judson, to be forfeit in case the English doctor does not return, unless he is killed on the errand?"

"I will, O golden majesty," replied Adoniram.

Dr. Sanford turned his sunburned face toward Adoniram and the two men exchanged a little smile.

"Maung Price," said the king, "shall be given the title of agent of the royal education. He shall carry one umbrella of pink and he shall instruct the sons of the king and the high nobles in astronomy and medicine. He and the enemy doctor must leave within the hour to tell General Campbell he must give us easier terms. One hundred ticals will be given to each man and a golden dispatch boat made ready."

The king rose as he spoke and with a kick of irritation at the rug which draped the throne, he strode behind the curtains leading to his apartments.

The audience came to its feet with a sigh of relief. Dr. Sanford thrust a warm hand toward Adoniram. "I am your obliged servant, Mr. Judson. We knew of your efforts at Melun. What a fiasco!"

Jonathan David, his broad face flushed, exclaimed excitedly as he shook hands with the English doctor: "Well, well! I cal'late I've received something to be proud of, eh? What do we do first, doctor?"

"Get the hundred ticals," suggested Adoniram, dryly. "I had twenty. It lasted me for a month, with great care. When it was gone and I asked for more, they accused me of extravagance and set a guard to watch and check my disbursements. A tical is only two shillings, you know."

"I know," nodded Sanford. "But money goes further here than at home. I shall send half of mine to poor Henry Gouger. Can you assist me there, sir?" turning to Adoniram.

"Yes, I can reach his servant, a faithful fellow, a Bengalese. He's baked biscuit for his and Gouger's living ever since Gouger's money was confiscated."

A white-robed minister now interrupted them. He handed Price and Sanford each a little bag of flowered silver and ordered them to be at the official landing place within the hour. Sanford immediately divided his quota with Adoniram who set off at once in search of Gouger's servant.

Ava was in a state of indescribable confusion. New stockades were being erected and houses and trees removed to make way for trenches and ambuscades. Buffalos, elephants, men, women and children mingled in a mad effort to save the golden city from the enemy. When Adoniram reached the mission gate he found a guard posted there who informed him that he would have to move. The new stockades which were to be erected without the city walls would pass directly through the mission. The Judsons had until the following day to find new quarters.

Thankful that Ann could be moved safely, Adoniram without delaying to tell her of the new ill fortune to the mission hurried back into the city to seek the governor of the north gate. They would require a permit from him to settle within the city walls.

He found the old gentleman superintending the removal of several chests of documents from his house to a waiting bullock cart. He smiled grimly but not unkindly when Adoniram made his request.

"You're a man of many misfortunes, O lord teacher. You have been given great opportunity to win merit. Where will you live in Ava? There are not houses enough to go round."

"I will build a bamboo hut with my own hands, never fear, sir," replied Adoniram.

"But the hot season is coming and the dak-blossom should be within brick walls. Bring her and her child to my house, O teacher. I long to know your theory of the stars and you shall instruct me, daily." He rubbed his tattooed thighs reflectively.

The quick tears stung Adoniram's eyes. "O lord of the kind heart," he said, brokenly, "I shall ask God daily to bless you for this."

"The merit is less because of your wife's beauty," said the old man, frankly.

"But our gratitude is not less," replied Adoniram. "We shall bring gifts to you and to your wife." He looked from the old governor to the house with its beautiful formal gardens, its shade and fruit trees and its veranda trellis with grape vines and roses intermingled and he thought of the herdsman Dhaniya. "You remember the perfect dialogue, O friend! '. . . I am living with my comrades near the banks of the great Mahi river: the house is roofed, the fire is lit— then rain if thou wilt, O sky!'"

"Nay! I know it not," ejaculated the governor, his dark eyes suddenly eager. "I have heard you were deep in the Pali. When you return, I will hear more, eh?"

"Yes, if you desire, my lord!"

Adoniram sheekoed and as he started back toward the mission, his heart was warm within him.

CHAPTER XXVI

SIR ARCHIBALD CAMPBELL

ADONIRAM, with the help of Koo-chil and Maung Ing, moved Ann, little Maria, and the adopted children that afternoon. This was no moment to waste mourning over the defeat of his great effort at Melun. By the time his little family was happily established in the governor's house, the prime minister had sent for the lord teacher and he was hurried off to the council room, there to answer endless questions with regard to the work at Melun and the probable plans of the British. And when toward sunset, he was dismissed and returned to the new refuge, he found the governor waiting for an exposition of the theory of Copernicus. He was kept in this state of mental activity during the entire absence of the two doctors.

The brick house in the mission yard was razed and the beautiful garden destroyed to make way for trench and road and cannon emplacement but protests or regrets were worse than idle and Adoniram was glad that Ann's rapidly reviving strength enabled her to take the loss of their home philosophically.

Price and Sanford returned earlier than they had been expected. As word flashed through Ava that the golden boat was in sight, hundreds of Burmans rushed to the river bank and, as the canoe was beached, demanded news. But Jonathan David knew the etiquette of the occasion well. He strode through the crowd in majestic silence, Dr. Sanford following. No one must hear the verdict before the king had heard. Adoniram, who had not gone to the landing place, was called hurriedly to the council room as soon as the doctors reached the palace, to hear the report. It was not a long one. General Campbell would make no alterations in the terms except that the money could be paid in four installments. But the first payment must be made within twelve days, and all prisoners must be given up, including Mr. Judson and his family and Dr. Price. If so much as a hair of the heads of any white prisoners was hurt, the general promised to lay Burma waste. In twelve days, the army would continue its march. The doctors had left General Campbell near Pugan.

The king shouted excitedly, "Price is now a royal slave, as are Laird and Rodgers and Lanciego. They are Burmans and cannot go. Judson also is mine. That wild boy Gouger can be freed and the Armenian Arakeel. Tell that to the devilish Campbell and let the nats destroy him." He lifted his spear and waited for some one to speak. There was dead silence in the council chamber. He then addressed Dr. Price. "Lord of royal education, go back to the British and tell them what I say."

Adoniram lifted his head. "O gracious king, the British never will moderate their terms. Cannot the golden mind perceive that the bravery of the Burmans is only forcing General Campbell to take the golden city?"

"And do you want to go back to the Hand-shrink-not?" roared Bagyi-daw.

Adoniram felt the chill of utter fear on his flesh, but he forced himself to say steadily, "Your golden person will not be sacred to the British cannon when they shell the golden city, O feet of lotus. Mortar balls do not recognize majesty, however supreme."

For a moment, it looked as though this were Adoniram's last second on earth. Bagyi-daw frothed at the lips as he glared at the missionary. But his gaze finally shifted under the white man's eyes and he turned to Jonathan David to snarl:

"Go back to the British devil and demand that the total fine be lowered to six hundred thousand rupees. Take with you Gouger and the Armenian and this devil doctor. That ought to satisfy him as to prisoners."

Adoniram gathered himself together to make one more protest but he was forestalled by a pleading voice in the rear of the room. A Burman general, on his face, assured his majesty that he could so fortify Pugan, if given opportunity, that the British army of only one thousand eight hundred men would destroy itself against its defenses.

Bagyi-daw smiled for the first time in many days. "Go, O great blood drinker! I give you a title. You shall be called lord of the setting sun. Go, conquer and win the great peace!"

The council was dismissed on this note of cheer.

A week later, the lord of the setting sun raced into Ava like a frightened fallow deer. The British had taken Pugan. The great blood drinker demanded more men. Bagyi-daw scarcely heard the demand through before ordering the poor man to be crucified and the excited spotted faces beat the lord of the setting sun to death on the way to the execution place.

Dr. Price was rushed off to persuade Campbell to lower the amount of money demanded. He returned in two days with the intelligence that General Campbell was furiously angry, had refused to communicate with him and was within three days' march of the capital.

The chief queen now took a hand. She ordered that one-fourth the sum required in the first payment be raised at once. She set the entire city as well as the palace in motion. Gold and silver vessels and ornaments were melted and brought to the king and queen to be weighed. Messengers ran through the streets, seized on hapless Burmans who were known to have concealed their treasures and dragged them to the court house, where their possessions were made forfeit to the national emergency.

And in the midst of this confusion, an embassy arrived from the king of Cochin China.

SIR ARCHIBALD CAMPBELL

A halt was called in the rounding up of rupees and feverish preparations were made for a proper reception of the embassy in the gorgeous audience hall. Here at last, was help against the British! Their majesties were jubilant.

But, alas, the king of Cochin China knew of no war in Burma. His mind had been fixed on an old tribute arrangement with the ancient kings of the golden throne. He had sent to demand a white elephant and a princess.

Bagyi-daw was momentarily speechless with disappointment, then he hurled his spear at the dignified Chinaman in his magnificent blue embroidered robes. Fortunately, anger disturbed his majesty's aim and the spear entered the shoulder of a Burmese minister.

"A white elephant!" shouted the king. "Never! As for a princess, we've none on hand! Go back and tell your emperor that I fight the world while he dreams forgotten dreams."

It was a short audience.

A half hour later, as Adoniram walked slowly along the street after a look at the Chinese camp, a panting officer in a bright red leather hat caught him by the arm and told him that the king had ordered the teacher to take the treasure to General Campbell. He was to go aboard the boat at once. Adoniram protested violently but was allowed only to send a message to Ann before he was hustled to the river.

They reached the British lines, thirty miles below Ava, the next morning. Adoniram did not believe that Sir Archibald would receive him, still there was nothing for it but to make the effort. The patrol boats allowed him to land, under a white flag and, a solitary figure in white linen, carrying a Chinese umbrella, he crossed the beach before the first sentry accosted him.

"I am an American missionary," said Adoniram, "with a message from the king of Burma to General Sir Archibald Campbell. Will you send word to him that Mr. Judson has a great desire to speak to him, personally?"

The sentry stared at Adoniram stolidly, then called to a passing drummerboy and gave him the message. In five minutes an orderly appeared who saluted and led Adoniram at once to a little grove of toddy palms where a tent was set, a short distance from the river bank. General Campbell rose from a camp table at which he was writing and the two men looked each other over.

Campbell was a tall, heavy Scotchman with dark blue eyes and tight-curling chestnut hair. His round face was smooth shaven; a pleasant, wise-looking man with a shortish nose, fine, small mouth and a fighting chin.

"This is a distinguished pleasure, Mr. Judson," he exclaimed as he shook hands. "Why did you send Dr. Price in your stead before?"

"I knew it would be a futile errand, General," replied Adoniram. "I would not be here now were it not that I'd been forced to come." He told of the conditions at Ava.

Sir Archibald listened with eagerness. When the story was done, he seated Adoniram and ordered tea.

"What is your advice, Mr. Judson?" he asked.

"I don't like to give advice, sir," replied Adoniram. "You saw what came of my weeks of advising at Melun!"

"I saw the neglected treaty, Mr. Judson. But before that I'd learned that whatever hope we had of bringing the Burmans to their senses, lay in your wisdom, with our guns behind you."

"My position has been difficult. I'm a man of peace and the horrors of the two years past have all but wrecked me." Adoniram gazed thoughtfully from the general to the precise and orderly encampment. The picture of chaotic Melun was vivid in his mind and of pathetically confused Ava, with the palace a mad house. He suddenly realized that the Burmans were preordained to be a conquered people. In spite of all he had suffered, in spite of the hope it gave Christianity, there was tragedy in this realization. And yet, because of the hope it gave Christianity, he must abet this British peace.

"General Campbell," he said, "I have with me in the king's boat yonder, six lacs of rupees as a first payment, that is, only a quarter of your required first payment. But you see, sir, they still don't understand the nature of a negotiation with a European government. Sending you even this much money is a desperate experiment on their part. They fully expect you to take it and also to continue your march on Ava."

"They must be taught, Mr. Judson. The British have been singularly fortunate in having a gentleman of your extraordinary character and intellect to interpret their ideals of honor to these pagans. I could only wish that our history justified all that you said to them. I received detailed reports of your sessions aboard the boat at Melun. We shall hope to thank you adequately some day."

Adoniram in his shabby linens bowed. This was a pleasant tribute indeed and for a moment he warmed himself at its glow. Then he said with a little smile:

"I'm afraid I don't deserve all your gratitude, Sir Archibald. What I did was for the cause of Christ in Burma. I merely took advantage of an unparalleled opportunity to explain Christian ideals to men steeped in Buddhism."

The general chuckled. "Oh, I recognized that from the first, my dear Judson! Nevertheless, it was the English you were using as an exemplar. I only wish," he repeated with sudden sadness, "that we were more worthy as models."

"Who is worthy?" asked Adoniram.

They looked at each other with understanding. Then Sir Archibald said, "You agree with me that to soften terms now would be to undo all? The Burmese philosophy would interpret it as cowardice?"

"Yes, General Campbell, having begun you must stand firm as a rock. What message shall I take back, sir?"

"Tell his majesty, if you will be so kind, that I refuse the six lacs of rupees, and that I shall continue my march. But that if the full quarter of the total sum demanded reaches me before we arrive at Ava, I will not fire on the town. I commission you also, Mr. Judson, to collect the foreigners in Ava of whatever country and ask them in the presence of the king if they wish to leave Burma. Those who wish to leave must be delivered up at once or peace will not be made. Give my most admiring compliments to Mrs. Judson, O lord teacher—you perceive I've been learning in my two years here!—and tell your lady I will offer her all the hospitality this camp affords when she honors us with her presence."

"Thank you, Sir Archibald," said Adoniram. "And now can you give me news of my fellow missionaries at Rangoon, Mr. and Mrs. Wade, Mr. and Mrs. Hough?"

"Yes, I can, sir. They received rough but not serious treatment when we appeared in the river, two years ago, but we rescued them and sent them to Calcutta."

"That's most grateful news, General!" exclaimed Adoniram. "We've heard nothing, all this while. With your permission, sir, I'll take my leave."

They shook hands and bade each other God speed and Adoniram returned to his boat, weighed down with responsibility but with new strength drawn from the decision and sureness of power that radiated from the personality of the general.

On board the golden boat, the three ministers received Adoniram's message with stupefaction. A human being had had six lacs of rupees within his grasp and had not taken them! When they could get breath they demanded why of the missionary.

"Because it was not according to the terms of the treaty," said Adoniram patiently.

And all the way back to Ava, under the glory of the sunset and afterward under the moon, the Burmans wrestled with this not-to-be-understood decision of the British general.

They reached Ava at midnight and reported at once to the council room in the palace.

All the rest of the night Adoniram sweated to persuade the king that the terms of the treaty must be met and kept as scrupulously by them as by the English. As dawn lifted over the white pagoda spires which made an enchanted city of Ava, Bagyi-daw, who was marching up and down the council room, his bandy legs trembling with weariness and apprehension, paused before Adoniram.

"O teacher," he said with a curious mixture of the child and king in look and voice, "O truth telling, Jesus Christ's man, are you so sure that the English will cease their march and go back to Rangoon if we fulfill their terrible treaty terms, are you so sure that you will agree to be crucified if they don't?"

"I am that sure, O emperor of many doubts," replied Adoniram.

His majesty stared into Adoniram's tired hazel eyes. Then he turned to the panic-stricken ministers and paid Adoniram the greatest compliment he ever had received in his life.

"I believe the teacher," said Bagyi-daw. "Let the terms of the treaty be fulfilled to the last tical."

A great protesting sigh burst from the group but without a murmur its members dispersed to their several tasks.

"Maung Judson," said Bagyi-daw as Adoniram reached the door, "after you have carried the money to the British, return to me here and I will make you rich and great as I shall Dr. Price."

"I must go back to my old home in Rangoon, O golden king," answered Adoniram.

"How long do you wish to stay there?" asked his majesty.

"All my life," replied Adoniram.

"That is good!" The king smiled complacently.

There was no more vacillating now on the part of the

Burmans. That day, the remainder of the twenty-five lacs was collected and while Maung Ing and Koo-chil packed under Ann's direction, Adoniram marshaled the prisoners of the bamboo into the golden presence. The group at Aungbinle had been augmented a few months previous by the Portuguese priest. He and Dr. Price alone voted at once to remain in Ava. Poor old Rodgers, palsied and ill, wept and said it would be like heaven to return to England and the Surrey Downs. Then, his son, to all appearances a Burmese lad of fifteen, pleaded with him to remain in Burma and the old man, with a full pardon from the king, gave up his dreams of home.

Adoniram urged Dr. Price to curb his absurd appetite for honors at the hands of Burmese royalty, pointing out Lanciego and Rodgers and Gouger as examples of the royal fickleness. But Price was obdurate.

"Judson," he said with admirable dignity, "you've never understood me. Not that I've blamed your irritation. My own mother said I was like a yearling calf to live with. Yet a man can't change his nature. But I'm a doomed man. I have a slow consumption that will finish me in a few years' time. In less than that if I leave Ava. I shall be doing God's work here, for I shall teach the children of the royalty the Copernican system and once its theory of the Universe is done, Buddhism must go. And I shall hold Christian services every Sunday for such as wish to come. I shall practice medicine only among royalty, however, at his majesty's orders."

Adoniram put out his hand and said with emotion, "God bless you and keep you, Price. I shall see you when these unhappy times are over."

"You are of finer metal than I am, Brother Judson," was the doctor's last remark.

That evening, under a magnificent moon, a little fleet of boats set off down the river to Yandabu, where Sir Archibald was now encamped. On one of the boats were the required lacs of rupees, and the Judsons with their children and their servants and the moiety that was left of their belongings. In the other boats were the liberated prisoners and the commissioners who were to sign the treaty.

There was wind on the river and the rushing waters were ruffled in a thousand glorious tints.

The very peace of God descended on Adoniram's heart and on Ann's, as the swift boats got under way.

CHAPTER XXVII

JOHN CRAWFURD

THE Judsons remained two weeks in the British Camp while Adoniram assisted in completing what is known to history as the treaty of Yandabu. They were during that fortnight the recipients of a hospitality from Sir Archibald Campbell and his officers, unique in their experience, a hospitality which never could be repaid in kind.

Gouger and Laird sang the praises of the two Americans until they begged them to desist. Henry then relieved his surcharged feelings by writing a long letter to a Calcutta paper in which he told of Ann's unparalleled devotion to the prisoners and paid Adoniram a high compliment by saying that Judson was worthy of such a wife. He added naïvely, that Adoniram was possessed of a quick, chivalrous sense of honor which made him a noble representative of the English character!

Ann, so slight, so frail, yet so lovely, with her small transparent hands still too weak to hold little toddling Maria, sat dreamily all day long under the veranda of her tent and became, as Adoniram said, a sort of wayside shrine to the officers in the camp. They were starved for the sight of a white woman and Ann was an exquisite sample of the ladyhood that was precious in their memories of home.

After the years of contumely this was very good for their souls.

The treaty was signed on the 24th of February, 1826. On the 6th of March, Sir Archibald evacuated camp and started back to Rangoon on the gunboat, *Irrawaddy*. The Judsons and Gouger accompanied the general. The British were to occupy Rangoon until half the payments of the ten million dollar fine had been completed and Henry Gouger was made happy by the general's appointing him police magistrate of the Rangoon district.

They landed at Rangoon on the 26th of March.

Some of the fiercest fighting of the war had taken place around the Shwé Dagôn and although the golden beauty of its spire remained, the splendid trees, with the shrines about its base, had been blasted, utterly.

The Judsons had expected to find Maung Shway-gnong at the mission but the house had been gutted and the huts in the yard were empty save for Maung Shway-ba's dwelling which showed signs of recent occupancy. They hoped the old pagoda builder was only off on a visit. Maung Shway-gnong, of course, was always a law to himself and always turned up eventually. Poor Maung Nau, they heard, had been killed in the war. Although all its furnishings had disappeared, the mission house was still habitable, and they moved in directly from the ship. They would live Burmese fashion on mats until Adoniram could find furniture in the town. Their bedding had been in such bad condition that they had left it at Yandabu.

"I'll see if I can't buy blankets and pillows from some of the naval officers," said Adoniram.

"I can lend you a pillow, O lord teacher!" exclaimed Maung Ing with a twinkling grin. "It is a precious memento, I assure you." He held up to view the matting-covered roll which the spotted face had acquired that dreadful night of threatened execution at the Hand-shrink-not. "It was so hard that the spotted face couldn't use it"—the Burman went on eyeing the two astounded faces before him triumphantly—"and, by the grace of God, I discovered it on the rubbish heap behind the prison the day we left Ava. I have awaited a propitious moment, O most loved of teachers!"

Adoniram, with little Maria on his shoulder and Ann's gentle hand on his arm, felt the room reel about him and saw Maung Ing's round face duplicate itself in a shining circle. When he could safely do so he put the baby in her mother's arms and held out his hands for this other precious burden, the child of his brain and his soul.

The mat covering was fearfully soiled but when cut away it revealed the great pile of manuscript, mildewed but otherwise unharmed. Adoniram clasped the pages to his heart and dropped to his knees. Maung Ing and Ann knelt beside him while, in a voice broken with sobs, he offered thanks to Almighty God for this unspeakable gift beside which even the blessed return to Rangoon was insignificant.

The delivery of the Bible translation was, of course, Maung Ing's chief triumph. But he had also a lesser which brought a chuckle from the missionaries. Mr. Beg Pardon, in a new dress of yellow strips, was hung in the veranda before Maung Ing followed Adoniram to the wharf to purchase bedding.

It was not difficult to buy blankets and pillows of sorts, and by sunset Adoniram was leading the way back to the mission with a line of coolies behind him. Ann met him at the gate.

"Let Maung Ing attend to this," she said quietly, "while you come with me, dear 'Don."

He gave her a quick, uneasy glance. "Something more serious than the devastated garden?" he exclaimed.

She did not reply but taking his hand led him to the shadows under the casuarina tree. There was a third grave beside Roger's and Mrs. Price's, a grave with Burmese characters on the headstone. Adoniram read it aloud. "Maung Shway-gnong, the beloved disciple of the great teacher. He giveth His beloved sleep."

"Oh, Ann! Ann! Not this!" groaned Adoniram.

"I know! You loved him, my darling!" whispered Ann.

"He was my friend!" cried Adoniram. "Oh, Shway-gnong, friend of my heart! Oh, Shway-gnong!" He wrung his thin hands.

"He is happy now!" murmured Ann.

"You don't know, even you don't know, what he meant to me! All those dreadful months when you were away—he knew me—knew my weakness and my strength—O Shway-gnong!"

It was deep twilight when the nightingale, sobbing in the branches above his head, brought Adoniram back from the desolated world in which he wandered and, with Ann's hand warmly in his, he returned to the house.

Adoniram's nerves were in bad condition, ill-fitted to bear this new shock, and during the days that followed, Ann watched him with growing concern. The excitement and responsibility of the position forced on him by Bagyi-daw after his release from Aungbinle had buoyed him up for many weeks. But now it looked as if the inevitable reaction had set in. She dreaded it for him, mentally and physically.

He tried, as soon as the house was settled, to begin work on the Bible but found it impossible to concentrate on it. Whenever he retired to his study and picked up his pen, some unspeakable scene of torture would come between himself and the sacred pages and his imagination would grovel in horrors from which he was powerless to rescue it.

Maung Ing cleaned out the zayat and spread Adoniram's mat invitingly. But a tiger bedded itself on the mat within an hour after Maung Ing had finished his work. The jungle had made great inroads in Rangoon in the two years of war. A tiger was shot in the bazaar, the day after the Judsons' return, and snakes made of most of the water tanks a deadly menace. Maung Ing begged to be permitted to begin public worship. But after a week only two of the former eighteen converts had dared to appear in the mission yard; these were two women who had been living on the river during the war. They had followed the Judsons downstream. Maung Shway-ba came back early in April.

Adoniram's first question was of Maung Shway-gnong. The Burman wept as he told the short story.

"He lived only for Christ, O lord teacher. When his wife was killed by the bullets of the enemy and his children were lost or stolen while he was detained in Prome, he said that he had the more thought to give to God and to you. He was full of the church he would have ready for your return. Two weeks ago he was smitten with cholera. He said to me that I must promise to carry on his work and to tell you this: 'I have forgotten passion, I have lost desire, I have achieved the great peace: Then rain if thou wilt, O sky!'—It was I, Maung Shway-ba, who buried him as a Christian should be buried."

Adoniram went into the yard and stood long under the casuarina tree, after Maung Shway-ba had told the sad little history, trying to put into endurable philosophy the mystery of this too-early withdrawing of the man who would have been of inestimable value in the Christianizing of Burma. Ann watched him uneasily from her bedroom window, but dared not go to him. She could only pray for an interruption to what she knew was a disintegrating reverie.

And her prayer was answered shortly by the arrival of a strange white man at the mission gate. Ann welcomed him and sent Koo-chil to call Adoniram. The new-comer was John Crawfurd who had been appointed civil commissioner over the province of Tenasserim, ceded to the British by the treaty of Yandabu. Tenasserim embraced a strip of country along the coast above the Malay peninsula, 500 miles long and forty to eighty miles wide. Crawfurd wished Adoniram to accompany him to Tenasserim to find a suitable location for a capital.

The commissioner was a tall blond Englishman, smooth shaven and suave and he wore a monocle, through which he examined Adoniram with critical interest.

Adoniram, whose mind was still under the casuarina tree, ran his fingers through his chestnut hair and replied to the invitation absently.

"I must beg to be excused, Mr. Crawfurd. I would be of

JOHN CRAWFURD

no use as an explorer. And I hope henceforth, frankly, to have nothing more to do than my work as a missionary here in Rangoon."

"But, my dear Mr. Judson," protested Crawfurd, "Rangoon will be a shambles as soon as the British leave. Bagyidaw has warned the citizens here that he'll retaliate on them because they let us pass up the river. You had much better settle in Tenasserim. There are many Burmans there now, and there'll be thousands more escaping from the king's tortures."

"Why not accompany Mr. Crawfurd, my dear husband?" asked Ann, eagerly. "Perhaps we may find it best to leave Rangoon."

Adoniram looked at her in speechless astonishment.

"Thank you, Mrs. Judson," exclaimed the commissioner. "You see, my dear sir, you made yourself far too famous as a diplomat at Melun and Yandabu for us to forget you! And we now hope to draw on your profound knowledge of Burma to help us begin our governing of these people with wisdom. We shall of course compensate you financially to whatever reasonable extent you desire."

"I have no present need for money," said Adoniram.

"Oh, my dear!" gasped Ann.

Adoniram looked from the Englishman, in his handsome white linens, to Ann, in the pretty flounced dress she had contrived from Burmese jacket muslin since their return. He had known that Ann was troubled about him but how troubled he had not realized until this moment—to send him away after their prolonged separation—almost four years of it actually!

And yet, he acknowledged to himself for the first time, a profound ennui, a paralysis of ambition had been growing on him for days. Prayer had not helped. Attempts at meditation, attempts to place himself in harmony with the Infinite Purpose, had resulted only in barren stupor. And two years had gone by since the ceasing of mission effort in Burma.

A great bitterness engulfed him and was reflected on his face in a sadness so profound that Ann leaned forward and touched his knee.

"My dear, we're not trying to coerce you," she murmured.

Adoniram straightened his shoulders. "I know!" Then he turned to the commissioner with a smile. "I don't like to admit it, but my wife is nearly always right! There's no one like her."

"No man is as wise as a wise woman," agreed Crawfurd. "Mrs. Judson knows that you look ill with nerves, sir, and that an interesting bit of exploring will set you up, wonderfully. You Americans are born explorers, you know. Do come with me if only for a week, Mr. Judson! I'm convinced you and I'd get on famously together."

"You might be disappointed as to that," said Adoniram. "As a matter of fact, I'm a crabbed, broken-down missionary whose work has been a failure and I'm not good company, even to myself."

The Englishman smiled. "Sir Archibald Campbell told me that he never had met a man who could talk so well on every subject, religious, scientific, metaphysical. And young Gouger said that your companionship in prison sweetened even that foul air. He said—"

Adoniram, pale cheeks flushed, raised a deprecatory hand. "Please!" Then as Crawfurd would have continued, he cried, "If only you'll stop, I'll go!"

They all laughed, Adoniram with a sudden release from depression that was almost exhilaration. Two days later, a guard of red-coats was placed at the mission to protect Ann during her husband's absence and Adoniram set off on this really intriguing expedition.

The exploring trip proved important for many reasons but the prime reason for Adoniram was that for the first time in fourteen years he formed a deep-seated friendship with a white man. He had liked most of the missionaries well. He was fond of Henry Gouger. But none of these had been his mental equal, none of them filled the need Maung Shway-gnong had filled. Crawfurd was a man after his own heart. And so during the short trip in which they founded the town of Amherst, Adoniram and Crawfurd also founded something which proved to be far more permanent. This was their friendship.

He was back in Rangoon by April 10th, clear of purpose once more and fully determined to remove the mission to the salubrious climate, the fine strategical position—from the mission angle—of Amherst. Ann was glad to go. Baby Maria had sickened immediately on breathing the miasmic air of the Rangoon swamps and Ann had already undergone a bout with ague. Adoniram's account of Amherst, high on its rocky promontory with its noble view of the Gulf of Martaban and the mouth of the Salween River, pleased her immensely and she began preparations for the migration with high hopes.

Maung Shway-ba and Maung Ing tore down the zayat and shipped it to the new site. Adoniram had a deep attachment to the rest house and would not leave it to rot in the jungle. The four disciples and Koo-chil were only too eager to accompany the missionaries and in June, the removal was accomplished. Ann wept with sheer relief when, from the decks of the *Phœnix,* she saw the British flag fluttering above the cluster of houses that already marked the site of the new town.

Crawfurd gave them their choice of locations for the mission and Ann selected a site near a huge hopia tree, standing on a bluff edge above the sea. Until the mission house was finished, Crawfurd insisted on vacating his own, for the Judsons' use, and Ann moved in with thankfulness.

The commissioner welcomed her and then prepared to leave. But on the veranda he paused. "Mrs. Judson," he said, "before I go and while your husband is inspecting the zayat, will you tell me if you will object to my urging him to accompany me on an embassy to Ava? I must go there shortly to negotiate the commercial treaty the Burmans agreed to make, when at Yandabu. I don't see how it can be negotiated without Mr. Judson's help."

Ann, seated in her precious American rocking chair, looked up at the Englishman with thoughtful brown eyes. She knew that while Adoniram was better he still was a sick man.

"I'll be frank with you, Mr. Crawfurd," she said, slowly. "My husband needs a companionship now that I can't give him. I'm still too much depleted mentally and spiritually. No one but his wife knows what he suffered in prison. He has an inborn refinement that has made certain aspects of even his mission work deeply distasteful. You can imagine what prison meant to him! He is a man of most ardent and tender affections. He saw men beside him disemboweled, starved, their flesh torn from them— His moral nature has received a profound shock and his spiritual nature staggers under the impact. I *know* that he will revive with a nobler spirit than ever. But I can't bear not to be able to help him. Mr. Crawfurd," clasping her hands, "do you feel enough interest in him to help him?"

Crawfurd polished his monocle and put it back in his eye, then cleared his throat. "Interest? Dear Mrs. Judson, in the ten days we were together, I learned to love him! Will you beguile him into going with me? The trip will require perhaps two months of time."

"Thank you, Mr. Crawfurd! I'm sure he'll go, although he'll protest. But in his heart he knows he's not fit for mission work, just now."

Adoniram did protest, violently. Not only was he unwilling to leave the new mission, but he was very loathe to leave Ann. He dreaded Ava again. He thought it extremely unlikely that Bagyi-daw, now that the pressure of Sir Archibald knocking at his door with mortar balls was removed, would negotiate a commercial treaty of any value. But Crawfurd finally made a point he could not ignore. The commissioner offered to include in the treaty a clause guaranteeing religious freedom to Burmese subjects. Against this he had no defense and at last, overcome by Ann's urging, he agreed to go.

Crawfurd had been gathering together an interesting group of men; a geographer, a botanist and a geologist, Englishmen from Bengal, and in early July, in spite of the fact that it was the rainy season, the start was made. Adoniram said good-by to Ann and little Maria on the veranda of Crawfurd's house. Ann in her ruffled full-gathered skirts, her hair in curls over her ears, looked like a girl and the baby was growing pretty too. Adoniram loved his little daughter dearly but he put her aside when the last moment came and folded her fragile mother to his heart.

Later, from the stern of the *Phœnix,* he saw them under the hopia tree waving their handkerchiefs and looking tiny, so tiny against the sky of Burma.

The trip was to be one of leisurely study of the people and the country of the Irrawaddy: an expedition after Adoniram's own heart. And after a day or so of homesickness for Ann and the mission work he gave himself over to the work of the embassy with absorbed interest.

They did not reach Ava until the first of October and did not obtain audience with Bagyi-daw until three weeks had passed. The lord of white elephants was quite unchastened and subjected the embassy to every vexation of spirit he could contrive.

Dr. Price had moved into Ava at the king's order and the chief members of the embassy took up quarters in his house at Sagaing. Jonathan David was prosperous and, in spite of ill health, very happy. He devoted himself to propitiating Bagyi-daw on Crawfurd's behalf, but it was a footless task from the very start. The Burmans were entirely ignorant of their own interests and they were as much afraid now of the wisdom of their late enemies as they had been of their prowess in war. And so, after weeks of effort, instead of a treaty of twenty-two articles which would have placed the two countries on the most liberal and friendly footing, the treaty as signed included only four utterly insignificant items. The king refused the bargain offered by the British for the return of Tenasserim and he declared point-blank that he would not tolerate missionaries in Burma.

And so on a day in mid-November, Crawfurd gave up and began preparations for the return to Amherst.

CHAPTER XXVIII

ANN

ADONIRAM heard Crawfurd's decision, given in the audience hall, with relief and at once left for Sagaing to make the final translation of the farcical treaty terms. As he entered the house a messenger from a British dispatch boat called his name and Adoniram turned to receive a letter with a black seal. The youth, as he delivered it, said hesitatingly:

"We are very sorry, sir, to have to inform you of the death of your child."

"Little Maria!" ejaculated Adoniram.

He went sadly into the house but as he broke the seal in his own room, he murmured:

"Our heavenly Father, if death had to visit my family once more, I thank thee that it was the baby and not the mother, Thou called."

Then he opened the letter:

"My dear Sir: To one who has suffered so much and with such exemplary fortitude, there needs but little preface to tell a tale of distress. It were cruel even to torture you with doubt and suspense. To sum up the unhappy tidings in a few words, *Mrs. Judson is no more* . . ."

Adoniram gave a great cry. "God! God! God!" and all the world went black around him.

When he came to his senses, there was a candle lighted in the room and Crawfurd was bending over him, holding his hand in a warm grasp.

"I'm here, my dear fellow."

"Ann!" whispered Adoniram.

"I know. I had a message by the same hand, the assistant commissioner at Amherst. What can I do or say—or—"

Adoniram freed his hand and rose from the mat on which he lay. "Leave me alone, dear Crawfurd, to read the rest of this terrible letter."

The Englishman hesitated. Then he put his hand for an instant on Adoniram's shoulder and left him.

". . . Early in the month she was attacked with a most violent fever. From the first, she felt a strong presentiment she would not recover and on the 24th of October, about eight in the evening, she expired. Dr. R. was quite assiduous in his attentions, both as friend and physician. Captain Fenwick procured her the services of a European woman from the 45th regiment and be assured that all was done that could be done to comfort her in her sufferings and to soothe her passage to the grave. We all deeply deplore the loss of this excellent lady whose shortness of residence among us was yet sufficiently long to impress us with a deep sense of her worth and her virtues. It was not until the 20th the doctor began seriously to suspect danger. Before that period the fever had abated at intervals but at its last approach, baffled all medical skill. On the morning of the 23rd, Mrs. Judson spoke for the last time. She said, 'The teacher is long in coming.' The disease had then completed its conquest and from that time up to the moment of dissolution, she lay motionless and apparently quite insensible. Yesterday morning, I assisted in the last melancholy office of putting her mortal remains in the coffin and in the morning, her funeral was attended by all the Europeans now resident here. We buried her near the spot where she first landed and I have put up a small, rude fence around the grave to protect it from incautious intrusions. Your little girl, Maria, is much better. Mrs. Wade has taken charge of her and I hope she will continue to thrive under her care."

Only repeated efforts, broken by long intervals of suffering, forced Adoniram through the letter. It was midnight before he had assimilated the last word. He then folded the sheet carefully, put it in his breast pocket, and slipped deep into the abyss of agony.

Just before dawn Crawfurd came in with a steaming cup of tea. He slid a gentle hand under the head bowed on the table, lifted it and said:

"Dear Judson, you must keep your strength."

Adoniram, his eyes bright and hard with unshed tears, looked at the tea with horror. "I, to drink tea and Ann new in her grave?"

"What would—Ann—" hesitating at the familiarity but repeating it firmly, "what would *Ann* wish you to do?"

At the sound of the loved name Adoniram's lips quivered and quick tears softened his eyes. "Tea was her sovereign remedy. She might have been English." He tried to smile.

"Her grandparents were English." Crawfurd held the cup to Adoniram's lips as if he were a little boy. "She was an honor to the English race."

Adoniram drank the tea. Crawfurd renewed the candle and sat down opposite him with the evident intention of remaining. The river rushed below the window—a sound of many waters. The Englishman watching Adoniram's face reflected its expression with a scowl of pain. He adjusted his monocle and murmured:

"It was God's will."

"How do you know it was God's will?" demanded Adoniram. "Do you know where God is? Have you heard the still, small voice? . . . Forgive me, Crawfurd . . . I'm a charnel house, within . . . Give me a little time."

Still watching the tragic face opposite, Crawfurd said,

with set jaw and deliberately, "She was very beautiful. I remember the first time I saw her. I thought that if one of the early painters had seen her he would have used her for his angels. She was pale, very pale, yet you could perceive the deep, vigorous mind within that frail body. Her brown hair was parted over her holy brow. Her hands, small, lily hands, were lovely, so lovely! And when she talked, I thought I never had been privileged to listen to language of such beautiful and energetic simplicity. But I felt, I knew then, dear Judson, that so fragile a flower as she, had but a brief season to linger on earth. She was so graceful, but so emaciated, so ethereal—"

Adoniram put out his hand protestingly and burst into tearing sobs. Crawfurd, with a look of relief in his own tear-wet eyes, rose and left his friend alone with his dead.

After a long interval, Adoniram was conscious of an oriole's entrancing melody in Price's garden and then of the soft reverberation of gongs from the monasteries. He had been lying despairingly on his bed, utterly oblivious to his surroundings. But when at last the tender music of bird and gong penetrated to his brain, he rolled from the couch to the floor and on his knees uttered that most poignant cry known to man's history.

"My God, my God, why hast thou forsaken me?"

There was no reply and yet as Adoniram waited with distorted face lifted blindly toward the source of light, there slowly permeated his mind, subtly, all but intangibly, a sure knowledge that there was purpose back of this chastisement. There was little of comfort in the conviction, yet its presence gave him back his self-control. He rose and after steadying his trembling body for a short time against the table, he made his usual immaculate toilet and at the breakfast hour was able with pale set face to join the others.

Dr. Price had heard the news and appeared immediately after the meal. After all, the doctor was deep versed in the ways of human suffering. He said little but he locked

Adoniram's arm in his and walked with him up and down the tiny garden and talked of baby Maria's charms and of the sort of care she would require from her father. Adoniram found solace in the firm embrace of that lean, hard arm. Yes, little Maria was flesh of Ann's flesh. It would be good to clasp her to his breast . . .

They had walked for an hour when a servant came running to the doctor. His wife, tiny Ma Noo, had been smitten with a sudden, violent illness. Adoniram insisted in accompanying Price back to Ava.

Ma Noo had cholera. Jonathan David would not permit Adoniram to enter the sick room but ordered him to go home to bed. So Adoniram wandered out into the streets of Ava, Ava so filled with life and color and laughter that he fled from it quickly through the east gate to the Amarapura road. He was smitten with a sudden desire to sit in the zayat by the lake. He thought of Colman and of the gaing-ôk and was conscious of a curious yearning to see the old man and talk to him. He even talked to a passing monk and questioned him. The monk replied that after much trouble, the gaing-ôk had returned to the yellow robe and had gone down to Prome.

Adoniram passed on. After all, what could the gaing-ôk have given him? He was a celibate, a man who had foregone love. . . . "I am free from substance, from care, so said the Blessed One. I am abiding for one night near the bank of the river. My house has no cover. The fire of passion is extinguished—"

The zayat was unchanged. The little green pigeons fed in the fig tree. The turtle doves cooed. The lotus lay in beauty on the waters of the lake. Life went on. But what was life? Who had defined it? Whither did it lead? *What was life?*

He did not pause in the zayat. With burning eyes and aching throat he turned from it and went back to Sagaing.

Little Ma Noo died the next day. Adoniram urged Price

to go back with him to Amherst but the doctor was adamant in his determination to remain in Ava.

Adoniram, had he been free to consult his own wishes, would have returned at once to Amherst. But he felt obliged to remain with the embassy until all essential translation and transactions had been completed. The obligation was a blessing, perhaps, as work always is under such circumstances.

It was late December before the departure was made. To his surprise several of the Burmese officials expressed regret at Adoniram's going, notably the old governor of the north gate and Prince Meng-myat-bo. The prince actually made him a parting gift of a jewel-set betel box and spittoon.

On the 24th of January, 1827, Adoniram reached Amherst. He went directly from the ship to Ann's grave, solitary on the bluff edge, under the hopia tree.

What was life? Aye, dear Christ who suffered both, what was life and what was death?

CHAPTER XXIX

BARE TO THE BUFF

THE Wades were settled in the dwelling Ann had almost completed at the time of her death. She had built also a little bamboo schoolhouse and had begun her loved vocation of teaching Burmese girls to read. Mrs. Wade was carrying on this work, beside caring for baby Maria who, poor mite, was obviously doomed to follow her mother at any moment. There was another member of the household left by Ann. This was a little dog of the general shape and size of a fox hound who had attached herself to Ann and Maria immediately after their arrival at Amherst. Her name was Fidelia. Maria called her Fidee. As soon as he reached the house, Adoniram took over these two pathetic but living legacies of his wife. They were an extraordinary comfort to him.

The Houghs had not returned from Calcutta with the Wades. George Hough had left the missionary work and gone into the employ of the British government. But the American Baptists had not been idle during the two years' intermission of church work in Burma. The year before, George and Sarah Boardman had arrived at Calcutta on their way to Rangoon. While the war continued they had remained in Bengal studying the language and had not crossed to Amherst with the Wades because they were awaiting the birth of their first child. Jonathan and Deborah Wade were convinced that no finer material ever had been sent out by the Board of Foreign Missions than these two young people from Maine. They assured Adoniram that a new era of missionary success was certain to begin with the arrival of the Boardmans in Burma.

Adoniram listened to these rhapsodies with his usual courtesy but without a spark of enthusiasm. He wondered if he revealed to Jonathan and Deborah the awful apathy toward missionary effort that was making an utter blank of his old burning desires, would they be able to rekindle him. Or would he hurt irreparably their faith in him and in the validity of his ideal? He dared not risk it.

He could not realize how obvious his state of mind was to these, his close associates, and how troubled they were concerning him. Yet they could not gather courage to speak to him. During the long fourteen years in Burma, Adoniram had developed the dignity peculiar to one bearing the Cross and suffering had for the moment submerged the humor and the tender demonstrativeness that had made him companionable to so marked a degree.

Not that he neglected the requirements of his work. Immediately on his return, he took his place as head of the mission and began to hold daily worship. He appointed Maung Ing a preacher and teacher of the Gospel, though without power to administer the ordinances and sent him down the coast to Tavoy to start a native church there. Maung Ing was the first Burman preacher ever sent forth. Adoniram believed that this was the most important single step ever taken toward the Christianizing of Burma. He had learned that a nation could be evangelized only by means of its own population. He and his fellow missionaries could establish native churches. But it was from these churches that preachers must be taken to carry the Gospel to their brethren. He blessed Maung Ing—and yet saw him depart without a thrill.

He set to work on the Bible translating, but it had become a dry grind. Nothing was real. Little Maria faded day by day and died in his arms, early in April. He laid her empty body down, a dream baby born of the passionate love of a lost illusion.

He told himself that he was mentally, physically and spir-

BARE TO THE BUFF

itually bankrupt. The work of twelve years in Rangoon was wiped out. His health was shattered. His wife, his children, his friend—were dead. He was empty, stripped to the buff, at thirty-eight years of age! This was the man who twelve years before had called himself a novice in affliction.

What incentive was there to begin life anew? God had cast him aside like a broken crock. . . .

George Boardman's initial job on reaching Amherst was to make a coffin for baby Maria. Adoniram's first intimation of his arrival was the tap-tapping of a hammer next to the room he had not left for a week. The sound annoyed him and he strode to the doorway to protest, but paused with a jerk.

Two of the most beautiful people he had ever seen were at work on the little box. The man was tall and slender, with a transparent complexion and a mild blue eye that harmonized perfectly with the serene gentleness of his face. His features were not regular. His beauty lay in the extraordinary fineness of character expressed in every lineament.

The woman was of a loveliness without flaw; rich golden hair which she wore in a Grecian knot, great violet eyes, delicately flared nostrils that gave pride to her face, and lips that curved like Psyche's. She wore a blue muslin dress, full skirted and ankle length in the new fashion. Once upon a time, Adoniram had permitted himself to love daintiness in a woman's dress.

They came toward him as he stood motionless in the doorway. "I am George Dana Boardman, dear Mr. Judson, and this is my wife," said the young man.

"You are most welcome." Adoniram bowed gravely. He looked from the hammer in Boardman's hand to the length of white cloth in Mrs. Boardman's. "This shouldn't have been asked of you."

"We wished to do it, sir. Your work has been a part of our lives for many years. When the newspapers told of Colman's death I was studying at Waterville Academy. I said I'd take his place and I went to Andover to prepare." The young man's eyes were fixed on Adoniram's, pity and awe contending in them.

His wife smiled gently as she said in a peculiarly low contralto voice: "When I was a little girl and read of baby Roger's death, I wrote a long poem about it and dedicated it to his mother. You won't forbid me doing this for her daughter?"

"Some day when my brain has cleared I'll thank you," sighed Adoniram. "Now I see you both only dimly; the beautiful creatures of a Greek play."

He went back into his room.

John Crawfurd came on from Rangoon in time to attend the funeral and after it was over took Adoniram to his own house on the excuse that the government needed expert advice. What the commissioner actually told the other missionaries was that unless Judson's mind was distracted, he'd go insane and the anxious associates agreed.

Not that the request for advice was wholly a subterfuge. After Crawfurd had forced some curried chicken and chutney down Adoniram and had settled him in an armchair which commanded a magnificent view of the sunset over the sea, he said briskly:

"Now, my amiable friend, riddle me this. Sir Archibald Campbell has fixed his headquarters at Moulmein, twenty-five miles up the Salween River, opposite Martaban. He insists it's the best military station although the river isn't navigable and although this is the better port and the more salubrious climate. That is the reason we get no more immigrants from Burma and why there is already a population of 20,000 at Moulmein. Query: Do John Crawfurd and Adoniram Judson join in a memorial to the government protesting against the absurdity of General Campbell's action? What a pig-headed Scot he is!"

Adoniram made a determined effort to rouse himself.

BARE TO THE BUFF

Here was a matter that would affect the future of the mission. He must give it intelligent attention. This was less difficult than he had anticipated, the reason being, he told himself, that the question was one of intellect and not of spirit.

"Have you talked with Sir Archibald?" asked Adoniram.

"Certainly not! The man's arrogant beyond belief. If I go to him he'll take it as an acknowledgment of his superiority." John adjusted his monocle and glared at his friend.

"Well, suppose he does! If you succeed in showing him he's wrong, what do your personal feelings matter? Your English stiffness on precedence and form is amazing. It hampers progress. You remember how absurd I insisted your attitude on the sheeko was at Ava? I'd sheeko to the moon or to a nat house if I would advance my Cause. Is it decided that the British will keep Tenasserim and Arakan?"

"Yes, sir," replied Crawfurd. "The Burmese government has behaved so ill since the war in not complying with the treaty terms that we can't restore the provinces and the difficulty of erecting them into independent kingdoms or of transferring them to neighboring powers seems impassable. We'll have to keep them though we don't want them. At any rate, this climate is the most salubrious in India."

"I'm glad for any reason that keeps you here, Crawfurd," said Adoniram.

Crawfurd smiled, then said, "The question is, am I to be here? You can help answer that query, my dear fellow, if you will go to the General and tell him what's what. He'll listen to you more willingly than to any man in India."

Adoniram looked far out over the Bay of Bengal. There was a white-winged ship sailing westward, westward to America. Nostalgia swept him like an illness. His mother and father, his sister and brother, still were in Plymouth. At thirty-eight, he could begin life anew there—a safe white-steepled church with bells ringing at ten on the Sabbath morning.

Crawfurd spoke more urgently. "You don't want Amherst to be supplanted, do you, Judson?"

"This was my wife's abiding place. She called it her safe haven," said Adoniram. "Yes, I'll go to see Sir Archibald, Crawfurd."

"Good chap! I'll have a boat ready for you to-morrow at any time you say," cried his host.

Adoniram smiled at the unwonted precipitancy. "Say at seven in the morning, Crawfurd."

"And now," said the commissioner, indefatigable in his determination to distract Adoniram's mind, "I'm going to read you the first portion of my report on our embassy to Ava."

Two hours later Adoniram went home through the moonlight, vaguely refreshed and glad of to-morrow's trip.

He reached Moulmein after a twenty-four-hour journey. He was astonished at its growth. What had been a year before a tiny village was now a city running along the Salween River for two miles. The long narrow hill a quarter of a mile back of the town was dotted with new pagodas and a wide road was being thrown to its summit. As Adoniram walked along the single street of the city toward the garrison, he passed a bazaar, thrice the size of Rangoon's, thronged with Shans, Chinese and Bengalese as well as Burmans. Even America would have found such mushroom growth miraculous.

Sir Archibald's house was of Burmese type but large and furnished in European comfort. It looked like luxury to the missionary's famished eyes. Lady Campbell and Sir Archibald were at breakfast and Adoniram found himself eating toast and tea and marmalade, the recipient of a welcome that somehow filled more than the void in his stomach.

The general and his handsome wife made no attempt to conceal their pleasure in their guest.

"I hope this means you're going to look for a site for the mission, sir!" cried Sir Archibald. "You can have your

BARE TO THE BUFF

pick of Moulmein. I suggest an acre or two next to the old pagoda!"

"I came to bring you back to Amherst, General!" laughed Adoniram.

"You do well to laugh," retorted Sir Archibald. "Did you see our new shipyard, as you passed? Five thousand tons on the ways now and more waiting. Teakwood bottoms, begad! I'll show Crawfurd a thing or two. No tonnage to pay on vessels, no duty on merchandise and minimum pilot charges."

"But your harbor's no good, Sir Archibald, and you live neighbor to the Burman thieves' paradise at Martaban," protested Adoniram. But he spoke without conviction. Moulmein was already the chief city of Tenasserim with or without government sanction.

"Don't talk tosh, my dear Judson!" The general accepted his fourth cup of tea. "The Burmans are going to flock to the place that gives them military protection. And I'm here with my garrison at the strategic point for military headquarters in the new province. Just take my word for that, sir. Crawfurd will have to see it my way."

"I'm sure Mr. Judson already sees it your way," said Lady Campbell, settling her white cap strings, archly. "If not, stay a few days while we pay court to you."

Adoniram liked her intelligent dark eyes and although her curls were streaked with gray, their dark gloss reminded him of Ann. "I must return to-morrow, dear Lady Campbell. Will that give you time for an effective effort?"

"That remains to be seen! My dear," turning to her husband, "you must take Mr. Judson to the officers' mess for tiffin and I'll have in some people for dinner."

Sir Archibald nodded. "And I'll just show you that plot next to the big pagoda, myself, Judson, and one by the river, too."

It was very pleasant. For the first time in six months, Adoniram was taken out of his fog of grief. He liked the

English. There was a deep zest in discussing the future of Burma, of Bengal, of Siam, of China, with these people who knew whereof they spoke. It was very pleasant to share his knowledge of Burmese history and literature with them, to make them see that this nation, which they had conquered so easily, was not savage, but pagan. It was amusing after the horrors of Ava to appear as the sympathetic and not always unadmiring friend of the people who fathered the Hand-shrink-not.

Before he left to go down to Amherst, Adoniram had decided to send the Boardmans to Moulmein to open a Baptist mission church. George would not be ready to preach for another two years. But there were translations from the New Testament and tracts which were sufficient to use as a beginning.

He found himself, as he lay in his little boat going home with the drive of the tide, thinking of the far-flung talk at the Campbell's dinner table from another point of view. If trade were promising in Siam and China, why was not missionary work promising? Why limit one's efforts to Burma? His imagination took fire and he began mentally to draft a letter to the Baptist Board. They must send men and more men to Moulmein and the place would become the disseminating point from which the Gospel would be sped to the entire heathen world. Yes, Moulmein, vigorous and full of mental stimulation, not stagnant Amherst. Poor John Crawfurd! He would feel that Adoniram had deserted him.

The commissioner, who met Adoniram at the landing-place, was bitterly disappointed. He stared at this friend in whom he'd placed his trust as if the missionary were in very truth a traitor.

"The general seduced you!" he cried. "I didn't think it possible!"

Adoniram looked at the huddle of deserted huts that clustered around the idle bazaar Crawfurd had laid out so proudly the year before.

"The general needed to bring no pressure, dear Crawfurd," he protested. "As soon as I saw Moulmein I knew where my duty lay. Already the place offers a new and wide field for missionary work. Why should I seek to destroy Moulmein? Why not extend the Amherst mission to cover it?"

"Didn't you even *try* to influence Sir Archibald?" cried Crawfurd.

Adoniram shook his head. "Not even my love for you could blind me to the fact that the mountain had come to Mahomet. The king drove the Cross from Burma. Burma was deaf to your call, but at Sir Archibald's, Burma has come to the Cross. Why not bow to the inevitable, dear Crawfurd, and take up your headquarters in Moulmein?"

Crawfurd fixed his monocle in his eye with a sudden fierce gesture. "You don't understand," he said angrily. "I, too, have my duty. Not to Sir Archibald Campbell nor to the governor-general of India but to England. New provinces should not be overshadowed by the military, by the show of force. We supposedly learned that from the American mistake. If I give up Amherst and go to Moulmein, it admits this a military, not a civil occupation of the coast. The Burmans themselves must administer this province. The military will not teach them to do so. It will absorb them. We have no right to blot out a race . . . And Amherst . . . See that harbor God made, Judson, and breathe deep of this air—the only decent breath to be drawn on the three coasts! Do you remember the scriptural quotations you made when we founded the town? I shall never forget! 'The abundance of the sea shall be converted unto thee. Violence shall no more be heard in thy land, wasting nor destruction within thy borders?' And now it's all ended—ended! The jungle's already taken half the town back again."

Adoniram was much perturbed by the Englishman's unwonted display of emotion. He saw dimly ideals of which he had no knowledge, a conviction of a destiny for which he had no yearning. But he could not bear that Crawfurd should so suffer.

"Don't give up, Crawfurd. Go up to Moulmein and fight for your dream. After all, such a fight is all there is in life. Dreams are the only permanency. Go and put the military where you think it belongs."

Crawfurd dropped his monocle. "No one has ever won that kind of fight against the military in the world's history," he said. "Nor ever will." He turned on his heel and strode off along the jungle path that led to his house. Adoniram moved sadly on toward the mission.

The enthusiasm which had fired him the night before had faded during his interview with Crawfurd. This friend too was to be taken from him. Fidee ran up to him as he paused beside Ann's grave. He took the little dog in his arms and kissed her shining white head, then set her to her feet and dragged on to the house. Sarah Boardman met him at the gate with her five-months-old baby over her shoulder.

"We saw your boat and were coming to meet you. *Is* Moulmein so great and beautiful? Come and tell us! You can't think what a gap you leave in the mission when you go!"

She was only twenty-three. Not so girlish as Ann at her age and yet her youth made him think of Ann. The warmth of her welcome cheered him. He took the baby in one arm and offered the other to Sarah. They walked slowly to the veranda where the others were awaiting him.

The idea of the new mission was received with enthusiasm. Jonathan Wade was troubled for a moment about funds for the venture. But Adoniram was prepared. "I received $3,000 for my services to the British," he said, "and Lanciego sold the ruby-set betel box and spittoon Prince Mengmyat-bo gave me for $1,000. I shall send the $4,000 to the agent of the Baptist Board at Calcutta as a free donation. I think we may draw against the sum for the building of a house and zayat at Moulmein."

"I wish we had something to give!" cried Sarah Boardman, wistfully.

"You are giving something priceless," said Adoniram. "Your youth!"

"Indeed, yes!" agreed Deborah Wade. "I feel sad to look at your bright beauty, sometimes, dear Mrs. Boardman." Her pale, gentle face, on which four years in the Orient had written its story of physical depletion, was wistful.

"Don't talk like a grandmother, Mrs. Wade," protested Adoniram. "You're all mere children compared with me."

"No one can ever give as you have!" said Sarah.

"Every stroke that befalls me only proves that I've not done enough!" Adoniram's voice was grim. He brushed his hand across his forehead and began to speak of his vision of broader activities. His audience listened breathlessly and with rising enthusiasm. They wrote the letter to the Board that day, pleading for five more missionaries for Burma and still five more for the great world of the East. Adoniram added a postscript:

"Siam is a noble field for missions. The capital, Bangkok, is only twenty miles from the sea and is itself a port. Constant communication is maintained with Singapore, just at the extremity of the Siamese and Malayan peninsula.—An American missionary would be less suspected in China than an English one. The Chinese perfectly understand the difference between the two nations and trade with America is direct, furnishing means of constant communication."

The following week, Adoniram went up to Moulmein with the Boardmans and baby Sarah. They found lodging in the married quarters of the garrison while seeking a location for the mission. Sir Archibald welcomed them with great satisfaction and, when he offered them a site about three-quarters of a mile south of the cantonment, commanding a noble view of the Salween and of the beautiful mountains of Bilu island opposite, they hesitated not a moment in taking it. Adoniram found a builder whose lucky day coincided with the date it was possible to have teakwood and bamboo delivered and then left George to superintend the erection of the house. He longed to return to Amherst. All his supreme faith in heaven could not wean him from the feeling that Ann was under the hopia tree.

He found a letter from Crawfurd awaiting him when he reached home. The commissioner had gone to Bengal and Adoniram was never to see him again, though they never ceased to correspond with each other.

CHAPTER XXX

DESIRE SHALL FAIL

THE rainy season was settling in and Maung Shway-ba induced several Burmans on the eve of moving to Moulmein to take shelter at the mission, postponing their migration until the rains were over. Adoniram found thus a half dozen men and women in the zayat for morning worship and took up the old work of instruction. None of them showed the keenness of Maung Shway-gnong, but at least there was less hostility to the idea of the atonement here than in the early Rangoon meetings. After the morning in the zayat, Adoniram each day, without regard to weather, withdrew to Ann's grave and there, with Fidee shivering against his thighs, knelt in communion with his dead.

He lost track of time while thus employed. Mrs. Wade would come for him when her anxiety overcame her reluctance to intrude on his grief and would lead him home for his supper, which he would eat, talking to them with the utmost composure. Then back to the hopia tree. Jonathan Wade finally gathered his courage together and gave Adoniram a salutary shock. He did not mean to be brutal but embarrassment made him so. He and his wife had sat alone during one evening when the rain had held off and Adoniram had tarried on his visit at his grave, until they were half distraught. At last Jonathan leaped to his feet.

"I'm going to give him a talking to, Debby! Some one has to or we'll lose him." His kindly blue eyes were half exasperated, half frightened. He lighted the candle in a lanthorn and rushed out.

He found Adoniram with Fidee asleep on his lap, sitting beside Ann's grave. "Behold thou art fair, beloved, behold thou art fair," Wade heard him murmur. "Thou hast dove's eyes."

"I tell you what, Mr. Judson," shouted Jonathan Wade, "if you'd translate the Song of Songs into Burmese instead of reciting it to empty ears, you'd be doing your duty instead of performing a heathen blasphemy!"

Adoniram looked up, astounded. He never had heard Wade raise his voice before. He was a man of utter reticence. He could see Jonathan's face but dimly and was glad of that. It must be contorted from its usual set quiet.

"Why, Brother Wade!" gasped Adoniram.

"You act," the other cried, "as if you were the only man who ever lost a wife. We all know your loss. The loss to the mission was great too when she went. But are you acting the part of a man, sir? And are you showing the confidence our revered leader should show in the righteousness of God's act?"

Adoniram came to his feet angrily. "Do you realize what you're saying, Wade?" he asked in a low voice.

"God forgive me, I do," replied Wade firmly. "You must be brought to your senses . . . We await your leadership, sir, while you lag under His chastisements." His voice suddenly broke. "She isn't here, dear Mr. Judson. She's with Him."

"Is she, Jonathan?" asked Adoniram, as simply as a child. His anger died within him. He came close to Wade and, putting a hand on the other's sturdy shoulder, bowed his head upon it. After a moment he whispered, "I know she's with God. And if I can find God, I'll find Ann."

"You must leave all that, sir," Wade shifted the lanthorn to take Adoniram's hot fingers in his. "You must leave it. If you can't do so in Amherst, you must go to Moulmein and I'll carry on here. It's certain to my mind that Moulmein needs you more than this sad jungle does." He began to lead the way back through the bamboo thickets to the house.

DESIRE SHALL FAIL

An immense mortification enveloped Adoniram as they walked. That he should have deserved this!

"I'm sorry and ashamed, Wade," he said. "You must try to forgive me."

"Forgiveness isn't mine, you know, sir. And we all realize that you have suffered in the degree that dear Mrs. Judson was angelic. But our love for you overcomes all natural reluctance to intrude on your sorrow. You must come back and kiss the rod. What of the translating, sir?"

"Not the Songs of Solomon, certainly," said Adoniram grimly. "The Psalms should be my task just now."

"Begin them, sir, begin them! But not here. In Moulmein." Wade did not add that he was convinced that there could be no concentration for Adoniram in the neighborhood of the hopia tree.

They were mounting the steps to the veranda now and Deborah's pale, anxious face peered at them from the sitting room. Adoniram went straight to her and held out his hands.

"I'm sorry and ashamed, dear Mrs. Wade," he repeated. Then as her gray eyes became suffused with embarrassment he added in his old whimsical manner, "And very hungry. Do you think we might make some tea?"

It was the last time his friends saw anything of morbidness in Adoniram for many months.

The mission house at Moulmein was finished shortly and he joined the Boardmans in August.

He at once took up the zayat preaching in the Rangoon manner. This zayat fronted not on a pagoda road as had the first but on a busy street leading from a native village to the Moulmein bazaar. Women passed bearing great baskets of lacquer-ware and men bearing delicately carved ivories. An old man who made tiny images of the Buddha from marble rested his tray of little figures on the veranda edge daily and listened to Adoniram with gaping jaws. English soldiers, red coats unbuttoned, strolled by on leave, paused to sneer and remained bare-headed to pray.

Across the road from their huts and little gardens, the leisurely Burmese householders eyed him through the rain respectfully. He was under the protection of the flag that fluttered over the red-coats' garrison. Beyond the huts to the east stretched bamboo thickets set up the wooded slopes of the hill which backed the town and still farther to the east lay mountain peaks, soft as the heavens they touched. It was very peaceful. But Adoniram dared not open his mind to that gentle invitation to relaxation lest instead of peace the dread memories of the past three years crowd in. He was developing a technique by which to protect himself from anguish. He found that he could close the door on memory so long as he kept his mind filled with the present. He threw himself feverishly into the mission work.

When he was not pushing this forward he was responding to the constant attentions of Sir Archibald and Lady Campbell and others of the English circle in Moulmein who found the American missionary a brilliant acquisition. One of Adoniram's characteristics as a young man had been his sociableness. Burma had given this but slight outlet until the beginning of his association with the British in the embassy to Ava. And now when again they began to draw him into intimacy with their work and those of their social activities in which his conscience would permit him to share, he drank greedily from the cup so stimulating to his mental faculties.

Outwardly he was returning to normal. The ravished look left his hazel eyes and the lines that Ava and Amherst had written on cheek and brow were softened and their shadows remained only to add sweetness and character to his face. His dark hair with its ruddy tints was still untouched by time and as health was renewed ague bouts became more and more infrequent and his slender body returned to its old erect bearing. Not strange that the Burmans as well as the British found him an arresting personality.

George and Sarah Boardman offered him a sort of hero-worship that was as delightful as it was subtle. George never got over his shyness before this hero of his boyhood and showed his feeling only in the fidelity with which he followed Adoniram's slightest wish. Sarah set herself the task of carrying on all the work that Ann had planned and when Adoniram told her that his wife had been learning Karen and Siamese, she at once took up the study of these languages.

Adoniram watched her progress with interest. She was a brilliant student with a fine gift of expression. Long before George was ready to speak in the Burmese vernacular, Sarah was writing short sermons in Pali and translating them to her women inquirers; sermons which Adoniram had helped her to prepare but which she grasped and used with remarkable intelligence. She had not Ann's gay practicalness but she had a great mind and a gallant attitude toward life that made Adoniram think of young Colman.

In November, the Wades came down from Amherst. The town was quite deserted now, save for one or two families and Adoniram sent Maung Ing up to minister to these. They built a second zayat in a thickly populated section of the town for Mr. Wade and Mrs. Wade organized a second school for girls. In a third zayat, Maung Shwayba was established to read the Gospel aloud half of every day. There were no baptisms to record for the year but Adoniram could well look on his organization with satisfaction.

Early in the new year, Adoniram decided that the Boardmans were sufficiently well trained to establish a mission on the south coast at Tavoy, where Maung Ing already had broken ground. It was hard to send them away but he was convinced that a strongly centralized mission was not the type that spread the Gospel. So in the spring of 1829 the two young missionaries with their blue-eyed baby girl set off into the wilds.

The evening after their departure the house felt forlorn and Adoniram extended his walk to the hill back of the town in dread of returning to the mission's new loneliness. He paused long at the top near the Uzima pagoda, eyeing the entrancing view—the beautiful frontage of Moulmein, where the waters of three rivers met, set with wooded little isles and with the greater and mountainous isle of Bilu, with Martaban to the northwest, beautiful with its pagoda spires.

For months now his mind had been drugged with work and with the intellectual wine of his social intercourse. During all this time, not once had he given himself over to speculation. But the loveliness of the view put him off his guard and he said aloud, " 'Whatsoever things are lovely—think on these—and the God of peace shall be with you.' " He rubbed his forehead as if to clear away a fog and gazed anew at his surroundings. He was standing near a recumbent statue of the Buddha, the dying Buddha. The artist had done his work well. There were sublimity and perfect peace in the marble face.

"You have your beauty, O blessed one," said Adoniram, in Pali, "but it is of the earth and not of heaven."

"Heaven doesn't interest the Lord Buddha, O lord teacher," said a quiet voice.

Adoniram turned. It was the gaing-ôk in yellow robes, his wrinkled, kindly face rosy in the sunset light. The missionary strode toward the monk with outstretched hands. "O friend of my friend," he cried, "did you know that Maung Shway-gnong is dead?"

The gesture must have seemed strange to the Burman but he gave the missionary a sharp look, then dropped his rosary over his wrist and grasped Adoniram's fingers firmly as though he was holding him above menacing waters.

"Yes, I knew," said the gaing-ôk. "Let us hope, O Jesus Christ's man, that he has found peace."

DESIRE SHALL FAIL

"The peace of God which passeth understanding!" Adoniram's voice broke. And clinging blindly to those kindly hands, he felt all the world of words which he had built so carefully for the past year collapse about his head while into his brain rushed all the waiting agonies. As if through a raging monsoon he heard the gaing-ôk's deep voice.

"You must empty your soul or go mad, O my rescuer. Let me save you as you once saved me. Tell me what oppresses you." He drew Adoniram to a seat in the sand beside the Buddha. "Tell me, O friend!"

And Adoniram, still clinging to that kindly hand, emptied his heart of its biting grief; told of Ann to this man who had cut himself off from all human love that he might help his own soul toward nigban. It was dusk when he had finished and bats circled low over the shadowy Prince Gautama.

The old man said, softly, "Do you recall, O man who has loved a woman as few men love—and she was a noble woman, I grant you, for Maung Shway-Gnong told me—do you recall what the Blessed One said when he became Buddha?"

"Tell me!" whispered Adoniram, out of a great exhaustion.

"He said, 'Looking for the maker of this tabernacle of my body I have run through a course of many births. And painful is repeated birth. But now, Maker of the Tabernacle, Thou hast been seen and Thou shalt not make up this tabernacle again. All my rafters are broken, my ridgepole is sundered, my mind, approaching nigban, has attained to extinction of all desires.'"

"Did he mean that he had seen God?" gasped Adoniram.

"To him there was no God. I know not what or whom he addressed. But I do know that he found peace by having all desire taken from him. O lord teacher, one by one your earthly joys are being removed. Were you of my faith you would see in that the means for sloughing off all that divides you from communing with Truth."

Adoniram thought of Madame Guyon's oft-reiterated statement. "It is only by a total death to self that we can be lost in God." What, he asked himself bitterly, had he been doing ever since coming to Moulmein but feeding and indulging his own ego? Was this what was to come of dear Ann's death? It was unthinkable. What could God have meant unless He meant to draw Adoniram toward Himself, to teach him how to find Him, by this removal of all earthly joys. He bowed his head on his knees.

"God forgive me!" he groaned. "I didn't understand! And You found an instrument in this man of mistaken faith." Then he added, in Burmese, "'For now I am persuaded that neither death nor life nor angels, nor principalities, nor powers, nor things present, nor things to come, nor height, nor depth, shall be able to separate us from the love of God.' And from this hour forth, I go to seek Him."

"Those are mighty words!" exclaimed the monk.

"They were spoken by a man of mighty faith," said Adoniram. "You have done me a great service, to-night, O friend. You have rescued me from a prison as dreadful as the Hand-shrink-not."

"I am glad," returned the old man, getting slowly to his feet. "We must have been together in dangers in many another life. I am living in the monastery beyond the chief Moulmein pagoda, O teacher. If you need me, I am there."

"And I am in the mission house near the river. It looks like the house in Rangoon. If you need me, I am there."

The gaing-ôk's yellow robes merged with the night. For a long hour Adoniram was too much exhausted to move. But it was a cleanly weariness. All the sense of tensity, of turgidness of brain, was gone. In its place was quiet, if tragic, purposefulness. He would have liked to spend the night there under the stars. One was nearer the heavens here than below on the river. But he knew that the Wades must already be concerned about him and shortly he set off down Sir Archibald's new winding road.

The following morning, immediately after breakfast, he waited on General Campbell. He found him smoking a cheroot in his garden, walking slowly with his wife along the border of heliotrope and lilies that was developing into a maze of beauty under Lady Campbell's skillful direction.

Adoniram, slender in his immaculate linen, was a violent contrast to the corpulent soldier, who was in brilliant regalia for the reception of a visiting grandee from Bengal. Sir Archibald greeted him cheerfully and Lady Campbell affectionately.

"You are coming to meet the governor-general, to-night, dear Mr. Judson, don't forget!" said Lady Campbell.

"I have not forgotten, Lady Campbell," returned Adoniram, quietly, "but I shall not come, if you will forgive my brusqueness."

"What's the trouble, Judson?" asked the general, eyeing Adoniram keenly.

"I don't think I can make you understand. Yet I wish very much to do so," replied Adoniram. "You see, I have found that my social activities are interfering seriously with my religious duties. So I'm making this call my valedictory, to tell you that I'm going to give up everything that has not to do with the mission or with—with my religious problems."

"Oh, come, Judson, why not return to a monastery and be done with it!" protested Sir Archibald.

"I'm not trying to be ascetic," said Adoniram, earnestly. "You have been so extraordinarily hospitable I thought it your right to know that I've resolved to give up all fashionable intercourse and I shall not dine outside the mission again except in the course of my work."

The two Britishers stared at him speechless. Lady Campbell in her white muslin morning robe, fluted and ruffled from hem to waist, set all her little flounces rippling as she opened her rose-colored sun-shade and said, half in sorrow, half in irritation:

"You have turned fanatic, sir. It's most regrettable," and she moved off along the flower borders that were swooning in the hot spring sun.

Sir Archibald put a hand on his shoulder. "I think you'd better see Dr. Richardson, Judson. Let me take you to his house, now."

"You think my troubles have unbalanced me!" Adoniram laughed ruefully. "You force me to the long explanation I wanted to avoid. Sir Archibald, true religion doesn't consist in attachment to any particular church nor the observance of any particular forms of worship. Nor does it consist in merely not sinning or in being honorable. True religion consists in the reunion of the soul with the Omniscient Being. And that is what your form of life will not permit one to accomplish."

The general shook his head. "You're over the head of a simple soldier now, my friend. I go to church as I was taught in babyhood and I find my spiritual needs well fed." He hesitated, then looked long into Adoniram's deep eyes with his own of piercing blue. He knew men and he knew Adoniram. "You must find peace where you can, Judson. I've feared for a long time that you were headed for this breakdown. Go your ways—with this reservation. I shall look you up when I feel the need and the desire—and that will be not infrequently." He shook hands, patted Adoniram's shoulder and as his horse appeared at the gate, left him with a certain embarrassed relief.

Adoniram felt like a little boy whose confession has been smiled at and whose resolve to be good has been found unimportant. He could imagine how sarcastically his renunciation would be talked over in the small society of Moulmein. Well, and did that matter? he demanded fiercely of himself as he swung through the Campbells' gates out into the fresh paved street, new planted with palm and acacia. Did any-

DESIRE SHALL FAIL 319

thing matter to Adoniram Judson save that he do the task for which God had sent him to Burma? That the task had ramifications and soul searchings far beyond the accepted ideas of missionary work, he could not expect his British friends to see.

He returned with set lips to the mission house, where Mr. Beg Pardon hung neglected under the eaves beside his window, and wrote a letter to the secretary of the Baptist Missionary Board.

"Rev. and Dear Sir: When I left America I brought with me a considerable sum of money, the avails of my own earnings and the gifts of my relatives and personal friends. This money has been accumulating at interest for many years until it amounts to twelve thousand rupees ($6,000). I now beg leave to present it to the Board or rather to Him who loved us. I am taking measures to have this money paid to the agent of the Board and the payment will I trust be effected by the end of this year."

He did not tell the Wades of this letter but a little later he made a suggestion to them. He said that since it was to be ascribed to the want of money rather than of men that the American Baptists were making such feeble effort to send the Gospel through the world, why shouldn't missionaries show their sense of obligation more than any other class?

"Let us, dear Brother and Sister Wade, so simplify our living that we can relinquish each, one-twentieth of the allowance we receive from the Board each year. And let's write to the Board and propose that a like proposal be made to the Baptist ministers in the United States, agreeing that when one hundred clergymen have agreed to follow our example, we'll relinquish a second twentieth of our allowances?"

The younger missionaries looked at him, thoughtfully, then at the mission sitting room, bare of all save necessities and at their worn clothing. But if they felt that Adoniram's request demanded keen sacrifice, they did not show it.

"If you'll draw up the letter, I'll sign it, sir," said Wade. "You ought to give the Boardmans the same opportunity."

Adoniram nodded. "I'm going to take but one meal a day for the next week, Mrs. Wade."

"You'll unfit yourself for work, Mr. Judson," she protested.

"You mean, I'm going to fit myself for clear thinking," he retorted as he returned to his study, to write more letters.

One was to the corporation of Brown University, his alma mater, declining the degree of doctor, which it had bestowed on him. He had taken a peculiar pleasure in receiving this attention. He now saw in that pleasure a survival of his old overweening desire for fame. He cut it from him. He had received many letters from Americans and Englishmen who wanted to write his biography. He now destroyed all of his correspondence as far as possible, including a letter of thanks for his services toward peace from the governor-general of India.

He wrote to his sister in America, resigning all interest in his father's property, stipulating, however, that in return for this she must destroy all his old letters in her and their mother's hands. He at the same time returned to her twenty dollars which she had sent him.

"I have no occasion for the money, my sister, and I return it to you but on the express condition that you appropriate part of it to the purchase for yourself of the Life of Lady Guyon. And I hope you will read it diligently and endeavor to imitate that most excellent saint so far as she was right. I shall never need any pecuniary aid from either you or mother. I thank you for your kind offers but you can help me in no other way than by your prayers. My dear sister, I shall never forget our days of childhood. Perhaps if mother should be taken away before you, you might scrape together

DESIRE SHALL FAIL

your little property and find your way out to me. I should exceedingly rejoice to be once more in the old mansion house at Plymouth and sit and talk with my own dear mother and sister; but that time can never come—I believe absolutely in God but I cannot find Him— With ever enduring love to dearest mother and to you, I am, your affectionate brother—"

He had made during the fifteen years many translations of Burmese literature, chosen with his scholar's taste from that great and exquisite treasure-house of art. These he read again, his face flushing as he thrilled to this undying loveliness. Couldn't this be sent westward to rouse interest in Burma? He fingered the pages wistfully. Once before, he remembered, he had had strength to answer in the negative. Again he told himself that as a missionary he had no right to disperse his mental forces over the wide surface of scholarly pursuits. He must know nothing among the Burmans save Christ and Him crucified.

With tears running down his cheeks, he tore his manuscripts to shreds.

CHAPTER XXXI

SARAH BOARDMAN

THE withdrawal from the English was not as simple as Adoniram supposed it would be. Sir Archibald Campbell called on him regularly and the new civil commissioner took it for granted that he could drop in on the missionary whenever a problem arose which Adoniram's knowledge of Burma would solve. In spite of every effort, Adoniram found himself looking forward to these visits until later in the year Sir Archibald was transferred to Bengal. With the civil commissioner he never took up a social relation.

Interest in the zayat teachings were on the increase and Adoniram gave more and more of himself to these. Five Burmans were baptized during the summer. This was glorious, but curiously enough, as his work took firmer and firmer foothold, Adoniram felt his unrest increase. It seemed almost impossible to get himself into the mood for meditation. Fasting only lessened his power of clear thinking. The solution he thought he had found left him only more spiritually forlorn than ever.

At last, late in August, he faced the ultimate truth. More fundamental even than his devastating grief for Ann was the fact that he had not found a satisfying relationship with Omniscience. Until this was done he must be increasingly uneasy and unhappy. He had completed the stripping of himself which life had begun with the dread experiences of Ava. This was to be of no avail unless he followed it with a persistent search for understanding.

The day after reaching this conclusion, he left the zayat when the rain ceased at four o'clock and made his way northeast where the jungle pressed on the town. At the end of two hours' hard going he paused. He was deep in the jungle, in a twilight of bamboo and tree fern, with thick undergrowth of twisting vines. Here he knew lived wild hog and tiger, water buffalo and sambur and innumerable snakes. But he was beyond physical fear. He had brought an ax with him and began at once to cut bamboo with which to build a hut. Here he would make a hermitage for his soul.

He worked until darkness descended, then he picked his way home by the light of his lanthorn. Two weeks were required to complete the house. It was a quaint affair of a single room, standing on four-foot stilts well roofed with dennees, palm leaves stitched on rattan, which he bought in the bazaar. The floor was of whole bamboos, the walls of mats.

When the hut was finished, he dug a grave close beside it.

The Wades were aghast when, on the day he was ready to move, Adoniram told them of his purpose. He would live in the hermitage, fending for himself, coming into Moulmein each day to attend to his missionary duties, but he quietly demanded that no one intrude upon him in the jungle. He listened to their pleas and protests courteously, but without reply, as he packed up a few necessities he had not already removed.

It was the second anniversary of Ann's death, October 24. A remnant of the summer monsoon was disporting itself on the coast. Its wild twilight followed Adoniram along his solitary path, shrieking and rattling among the palms, high overhead and dropping leeches on him from the twisting fern trees. His lanthorn showed him the trail but uncertainly. He stumbled and fell and rose again and again, moaning to himself, "O Ann! Ann! Ann!"

Surely the God he sought with such agony of endeavor was watching over this tragic figure that night for in the pestilential darkness he did not lose his way nor did the bloodthirsty creatures of the jungle, beyond the leeches and mosquitoes, molest him. He reached the little house, breathless but unscathed. He scrambled up the ladder, lifted the mat, entered and hung his lanthorn on the waiting hook. A curious thumping noise greeted him. He controlled his jumping nerves and wiped the sweat from his eyes to stare at the corner in which lay his bed roll.

It was occupied.

Adoniram gave a sudden glad shout, "O Fidee, you villain!"

It was Fidee, indeed! Fidee too busy to rise to greet her master for she was nursing a litter of puppies. Adoniram dropped down beside her to investigate. There were nine of the little creatures of every imaginable color. Fidee lapped them indiscriminately and banged the floor with her tail and smiled her dog smile at Adoniram.

He rubbed her head and chuckled. "So here is where you chose to have them! The jungle will get them, you idiotic female, and really I can't share my bed with you and your nine children. But, oh, dear little Fidee, I'm glad to see you!"

He did share with her the supper he had brought, cold boiled plantains and fish. Then he moved her and her family to another corner and undid his bed roll. As soon as he lay down, however, Fidee began to carry the puppies over beside him. He protested, humorously, but she wagged her tail and whined and had her way. And so Adoniram passed the night staring sleepless at the roof but with this palpitating little heap of life warm against his legs to keep him in touch with earth, to bring him back from borders which no man ever has passed and come back again to reality.

At dawn he fell asleep, waking only when a water buffalo crashed through the thicket at mid-morning, setting Fidee to barking. He rose then and, leaving his breakfast for the little dog, went to his day's work in the mission and in the late afternoon returned to the hut.

The Wades were in despair. They tried to keep their

leader's strange activities a secret but they, of course, became known and the whisper went round among the English that Judson had a touch of insanity. Among the Burmans there was no such talk. To a Buddhist there was nothing but holiness in a man's withdrawing himself for meditation on sacred things. Adoniram acquired merit with them immeasurably by his new plan of living and the earnestness of the inquirers increased.

Adoniram himself was quite conscious of what was being thought and said. He was sorry but unmoved. When he was not preoccupied with answering questions in the zayat, he was preoccupied with fighting nameless fears, dreads and longings in the hermitage. These were the only two worlds that counted.

For many weeks, much of his thinking in the hut only covered the old baffling ground so often traveled in Rangoon and Ava. If only he could refine the consciousness of his body until it could record for him the motions of the Over Soul! But always as of old at the moment when his consciousness was about to make the splendid contact, his silly body reported some trivial reality to him: the belling of a sambur, the far primal howl of a tiger, little Fidee growling at her puppies, the scent of fern—

Constantly when he subdued himself to utter quiescence to receive God's message as Madame Guyon bade him, melancholy, tender thoughts of Ann intrigued him or some dreadful memory of death in the prison house brought the sweat to his lips.

For months, he continued the effort, ceasing only when exhaustion claimed him.

In the meantime, work went on well in the mission. From Tavoy came both good and bad reports. The Karens were responding wonderfully to George Boardman's teachings, but the baby, little pink-cheeked Sarah, had died.

"Aye, the Cross—at a price," sighed Adoniram.

A Burman named Maung Thah-a made pilgrimage to

Moulmein from Rangoon. He was one of Maung Shway-gnong's converts, a deep-eyed man of fifty-seven. He came to report that he had gathered together a secret church of a dozen members in the deserted mission at Rangoon and begged to be made pastor over the little flock. Rangoon! Adoniram could have laughed and wept at once over this new echo from the sad silly town. He established the old gentleman in the mission house and he and Jonathan Wade began to examine and instruct him.

Word came from Ava that poor Jonathan David Price had died of consumption.

During all these months no one visited Adoniram at the hermitage, save Koo-chil, whom he had finally to forbid so firmly that the poor fellow was heartbroken. But one morning near the third anniversary of Ann's death when a Burmese holiday made zayat work impossible, he did not go into Moulmein but planned to give the day to his devotions. Toward noon, he was sitting on the doorstep staring unseeingly at the little trail through the bamboos which led to town, when he was roused by Fidee's barking and the yipping of the new litter of puppies. A tall figure was coming toward the hut, a slender woman in white wearing a broad-brimmed sunhat. It was Sarah Boardman! Adoniram rose and walked gravely to meet her.

"I know I shouldn't intrude," she cried—and he saw that her blue eyes were tragic, "but we've had such shocking news as only you could help us to support. We came up yesterday to consult Dr. Richardson. He confirmed our fears. Mr. Boardman has consumption of the lungs and the doctor gives him only a year."

Adoniram drew a deep breath. Death! Was there no escape from the thought of it, even for an hour? Then his flagging will rose to meet this most recent demand. He clasped her fingers strongly in his own and said:

"Evidently God means that you and I shall see life as it

really is even if He breaks our hearts. My darling Ann, your beloved George! Come over to my veranda and let's prepare the armor with which to meet the new defeat—if it is defeat."

He had made a rude bamboo bench beside his cooking place before the house and to this he led Sarah. It touched him, her coming to him for help in defiance of the many things that should have kept her from intruding on him. She was always gallantly independent. She sank down on the bench and he stood before her.

"God will enable," he began, "God will—" Suddenly, the familiar phrases died on his lips. Had such words comforted him, had they meant anything? He swept his arms wide and threw his head back. "Face it, Sarah Boardman!" His great voice boomed through the jungle. "Stare at your agony until its every outline is bitten into your consciousness. And then when it's become a part of every breath you draw, seek the reason from God for your chastisement."

Sarah grasped the edges of the bamboo with her long slender fingers and gazed up into his face. She had come to beg for spiritual support. Had the Wades been correct when they told her that this spiritual giant had none to give her? She twisted her hands together and with a little groan turned her head away. Her eyes fell on the open grave.

"Good heavens, what is that?" she cried.

"That's my effort to face death," replied Adoniram. "I sit on the edge of it and picture my body rotting in its embrace."

"But why," whispered Sarah, "dear Mr. Judson, why!"

He set his teeth and confessed to her what he had not expected ever to confide to mortal being.

"Sarah Boardman, ever since I lay for a week next to a man who was being slowly disemboweled by a spotted face, I have suffered from a horror of what death will do to my body—the mildewing and moldering in the damp corruption of the earth. I am forcing myself to face it until my self-love is worn out."

He needed help—aye, more deeply than Deborah Wade's quiet imagination or Jonathan Wade's devotion to facts could encompass. But, Sarah told herself, *she* knew how deeply—somehow, strangely *she* knew as clearly as though the beloved Ann were whispering in her ear.

She returned his agonized gaze quietly and said, "You are braver than most men. After you have trained yourself to face the horror, dear Mr. Judson, then what?"

"My last remnant of concern for the welfare of my body will be gone and I shall be that much closer to God," he answered, hoarsely.

"Then you don't think we should conserve our health carefully, that we may carry the Cross farther?" Sarah asked. "You think that my husband is right when he refuses to seek a dry climate but says he will continue with his Karens in the festering jungle till he drops?"

"With an incurable disease I'd do precisely what George Boardman is doing—glorious fellow!" ejaculated Adoniram. "You don't understand my attitude on the body, Mrs. Boardman."

"Perhaps not!" Sarah walked over to the grave and looked at it coolly. There was something boyish in her posture as she stood with hands clasped behind her back, her short skirts revealing the firmly planted feet. "What I fear for you is, Mr. Judson, that Buddhism has tainted you and that you have become too much interested in the welfare of your own soul. All this"—she tossed her head toward the hut and glanced again at the grave—"all this means that you are giving the intensity of your thought to your own body and not to that body which hung upon the Cross to save you from all the doubts you're experiencing now."

Adoniram flushed deeply. He did not observe that Sarah's hands were clenched and that her whole body was trembling violently. She did not wait for him to speak but gathering herself together went on in the deep contralto that was one of her many charms.

"You've been here so long, dear lord teacher! Do you realize that over a year has passed since you moved into this place and that while you give all your days to the mission, the fact that you have ceased to give your nights is a source of weakness to us all!"

"In all my years in Burma there never has been such interest, such response as now," thundered Adoniram. "The more I slough off of mortality here in the jungle, the surer becomes my ability to reveal Christ to the Burmans."

"That is because they feel your leaning toward the asceticism of the Buddhist," declared Sarah firmly.

"Sarah Boardman," Adoniram controlled his hurt with difficulty, "will you please return to Moulmein at once. I am sorry that you don't find my spiritual consolations fit for your need."

"Oh, you've given me much, much, Mr. Judson!" Sarah's eyes were full of tears but she kept her chin up, intrepidly. "You are an object lesson in bravery—the bravest man I ever knew. You dare to try to look on the face of God— which God Himself forbade us doing."

She did not offer to shake hands but she bowed and moved with her long free gait across the little clearing to the path. The crickets chirped loudly. A thrush trilled. Fidee whined from the veranda, wagged her foolish tail and drooped her ears. Sarah paused and looked from the little dog to the master, still standing with eyes of reproachful sternness upon her.

Sarah hesitated then said meekly, "The puppy from Fidee's last litter which you so kindly sent us was killed by a snake. Will you not give me one of these for my baby George?"

Adoniram bowed. "Take several of them if you wish, Mrs. Boardman."

"You're sure you won't miss that little black one?" asked Sarah, solicitously.

Adoniram suddenly laughed softly. "I'll bring him to you to-morrow morning, O lady of Tavoy!"

Sarah's eyes twinkled and the corners of her mouth lifted. "Thank God for laughter," she exclaimed.

"Aye, thank Him for laughter," agreed Adoniram. "I shall pray that He will send you and your husband many moments in which you may smile into each other's eyes, in the months to come."

At this Sarah's gallantry failed. A little sob broke from her. She turned abruptly to the path again and Adoniram watched the strong white figure until the shadows of the jungle swallowed it and wished that Ann had known her. She had been utterly wrong, of course, in her attitude toward the hermitage but he would forgive her because of her youth.

And yet her remark about the taint of Buddhism had bitten him. He did not again that day give himself over to meditation but worked until late that night at his translation of Ecclesiastes.

The next morning when he arrived at the mission gate with three choice puppies in a basket for transportation to Tavoy, he found the Boardmans just emerging. They were all ready to embark for home. Adoniram turned the basket over to Sarah and clasped George Boardman's burning fingers.

"Would you like me to come down to Tavoy and give you a lift, dear Boardman?" he asked.

"No, indeed, your hands are full here," returned George, cheerfully. "I'm going into the jungle when I get back and be an itinerate for a while. I find it's the best way to catch these wild Karens."

"That's an idea," said Adoniram. "Certainly we've never been able to woo them into a zayat, have we!" Evidently

George was going to treat his death sentence as part of the day's casual program. Brave fellow! Adoniram added, serenely, "I shall want to know your results at frequent intervals. They are a fearfully dirty lot. I've always felt it would be punishment to have them round."

George chuckled. "They evidently feel the same way about us."

Adoniram joined Wade in helping them into the bullock cart then went on to his zayat. The rest house was empty when he first seated himself and as he opened the New Testament and began to read aloud he quickly lost himself in Paul's words:

"Thou fool, that which thou sowest is not quickened, except it die— So also is the resurrection of the dead. It is sown in corruption, it is raised in incorruption— It is sown a natural body, it is raised a spiritual body— The first man Adam was made a living soul. The last Adam was made a quickening spirit—"

A shadow fell across the page.

It was the gaing-ôk, seating himself deliberately on the mat edge. "To me, O friend of my friend," said the Burman, "what you are reading is most splendid nonsense. Do you pretend to explain it?"

"I know nothing more than St. Paul wrote," replied Adoniram.

"Do you believe what he said, O teacher?" asked the gaing-ôk, running the beads of his rosary through his fingers.

"I do, absolutely," Adoniram answered with quickening breath. Was the monk to follow in Maung Shway-gnong's footsteps?

As if he read the missionary's mind, the Burman smiled, showing teeth long corroded by betel chewing. "I shall not be persecuted, for I am no longer the teacher of the young. I am the librarian of our monastery and my strange taste in friends is tolerated because I bring many precious books to our chests. Neither does this morning call mean that I shall be baptized. Your religion is too sad, O teacher. I would not suffer as you suffer there in your jungle. Granted that there are points of wisdom and beauty in your Christ, He does not bring the peace that Buddha brings."

"That is my fault, not Jesus Christ's," protested Adoniram. "If I weren't so full of sin—"

The old man interrupted. "That's more nonsense. All Burma knows that you are without sin—a man of great wisdom and of incorruptible heart. Surely your Christ doesn't wish you to think of yourself as a bit of offal. Did He talk so of the body He borrowed when He was on earth? Nay, you admit He didn't. Look, O friend who rescued me, you have spent a year in meditation. You are freed of passion. You know the four great truths, you are following the eightfold path. You are ready to achieve the peace of the blessed one's teachings. Come up to the monastery, don the yellow robe and live with me in my library of inexhaustible treasures."

"You are kind, O keeper of Burma's true jewels," replied Adoniram. "But no true Christian ever could become Buddhist."

"And no Buddhist a true Christian," exclaimed the monk. "You will fail here as you did in Burma proper. How much more must you suffer before you give Moulmein, as you gave Rangoon, back to the Buddha Gautama?"

"But I never gave—" Adoniram began and stopped. There flashed across his mind that scene on the veranda the day after he and Colman had returned from Ava. As if he were another entity, he saw Adoniram Judson's young impassioned face raised to God and heard his promise: "I have received your answer, O Eternal God, and now I promise You that I never will leave Burma until the Cross is planted here forever."

"This is Burma!" said Adoniram, aloud and vehemently.

"This is not Burma," retorted the gaing-ôk, pointing with his palm-leaf to the flag that rippled lazily over the distant garrison. "This is something begot by miscegenation between the British and the runaways of India and Pegu. Burma lies yonder on either side of the Irrawaddy." He rose slowly and slipped his feet into his sandals. "Amé! I see I must give you yet another year in the jungle. I am going, O teacher."

"Go then, O friend of my friend," returned Adoniram.

But he read no more that morning. The monk was speaking truth. Moulmein was a hybrid thing. Karens were not Burmans. And Adoniram's pledge was to Burma.

CHAPTER XXXII

AFTER THE EARTHQUAKE, A FIRE

AND yet Adoniram could not bring himself to leave the hermitage. He was willing to grant that he was not fulfilling his promise to God for Burma—though the admission wrung his soul. He was willing to admit that Sarah Boardman had been perilously near truth when she accused him of too great concentration on self. But the accumulated hunger of years for spiritual peace stood like an unscalable wall between himself and the return to a complete missionary life. Clearer, more convincing than the voice of conscience was Jeanne Marie Guyon's poignant voice, bidding him remain in the jungle until the veil was rent—as it would be rent. And so another year crept by with Adoniram leading his two lives: one of an ascetic, the other of a missionary genius.

Of course, his health suffered. He was taut, eyes brilliant with an expectancy that was never satisfied. Inevitably and mercifully the daily agony of Ann's going softened. But the cosmic unhappiness that gripped him was undermining his physical and spiritual vitality. It was only a question of time unless light came to him that he would break and the loved leader change to a tragic fanatic. But it was all subtle—and he was so much the intellectual superior of his associates, his was so much the supreme vision among them that they could have done nothing for him even had he confided in them.

But the work he accomplished in the mission was stupendous this year of 1829-30. Beside his share in the conversion of some fifty-six persons—ten of them British soldiers and eight of them Tavoy Karens, he completed the translation of Psalms and began on Daniel. He prepared a liturgy for the Burman church as well as baptismal, marriage and funeral services. He wrote a tract contrasting the Christian and Buddhist systems and a preacher's guide for native pastors. All of these awaited the arrival of the new printer promised by the faithful American Baptists. He arrived early in 1830; Cephas Bennett, accompanied by his wife and two children.

The Board was learning to choose wisely. Bennett was a stout fellow, physically and mentally, while Mrs. Bennett was an eager-minded, energetic New England girl, with common sense back of her religious zeal. Bennett was a preacher as well as a printer. This fact made it possible for Adoniram to broaden his plans. Maung Shway-ba was made Bennett's tutor-assistant in the printing office which was equipped from the funds made available by Adoniram's gifts. Three months after his arrival, Bennett was running his six little presses with their crude Burmese and Karen type day and night with ten native assistants, all converts.

Late in March, Adoniram ordained Maung Thah-a native pastor to Rangoon. When Jonathan Wade saw the old man's broad back receding among the plantains that led to the landing place, he said to Adoniram with a shake of his head:

"He's a dear, earnest old chap, but think of him trying to fill your place in Rangoon. Rangoon's on my conscience."

Adoniram spoke quickly. "Do you think I ought to go back to Rangoon, Wade?"

"I don't think your health would endure it again, Mr. Judson," replied Wade in a low voice, his eyes on the river, glorious in the sun.

"It's not consideration for my health that keeps me from Rangoon, as you very well know," protested Adoniram, running his fingers round his frayed and much mended linen collar. "If you knew the loathing I feel for myself, Jonathan! Rangoon calls me, calls me, and yet I cannot go."

Wade looked at him now, clearly and gently, from tired blue eyes. "What holds you, dear teacher? Can I help you break the bonds?"

"No one can help me but God," whispered Adoniram. "It's a lonely search, Jonathan—lonely. Sometimes I think I'm the loneliest man on earth."

"I think you are, myself," agreed Wade sadly.

They were silent for a moment, then Jonathan said, "Will you send Deborah and me to Rangoon, sir?"

Adoniram moved his head in a troubled way. "I'll think about it. The Boardmans are coming up to see the doctor soon and we'll advise with them."

This was the Boardmans' first visit to Moulmein since George had received his death sentence. Neither of the two mentioned health in their infrequent letters. The missionaries at Moulmein had expected the worst, but even at that they had not been prepared for the change in Boardman. He was a living skeleton. In his weakened condition it was impossible for him to continue his itinerate preaching in the jungle. He must be content with zayat work in Moulmein; Adoniram told him this flatly.

"I shall be better with a little rest and with a tonic from Dr. Richardson," declared George. "For a little while I'll stay in Moulmein, then I'll go back to my Karens. With your permission, sir," smiling at Adoniram.

They were gathered in the mission sitting room after dinner, taking a moment's breathing spell before beginning the afternoon's activities. Little Elsina Bennett sat in Adoniram's lap. She was his tiny shadow. Small Georgie Boardman eyed her solemnly from his mother's knee. Fidee sat in the middle of the circle grinning expansively. She was enjoying one of her rare periods of freedom from maternity.

"We didn't bring Georgie's dog," his father went on as if he would save the others from the embarrassment of commenting on his physical condition. "He's grown into some-

AFTER THE EARTHQUAKE, A FIRE

thing as large as a Newfoundland but mercifully with short hair. I'm sure Fidee would disclaim him if she saw him."

"I'm glad you saved the old lady's feelings," smiled Adoniram.

"If you could carry on my zayat work for me, Brother Boardman, and Sister Boardman could carry on my wife's work with women, I'd like to go to Rangoon," said Wade, abruptly.

"You'll not go also, Mr. Judson?" asked Boardman, quickly.

"I have a strong pull in that direction but I shan't go," replied Adoniram.

"If you're here with your great strength, I know I could stop the gap for a while," said George. "What is the hope for more help from America, sir?" turning his gaunt face toward Adoniram.

"The Board promises me one or two more before the year's out, but I shall send them to Siam as soon as may be," replied Adoniram. He looked at Jonathan Wade, and his lips were stiff, his eyes full of tears as he asked, "Will you go to Rangoon, then, as soon as you can make arrangements?"

"Gladly," replied Jonathan.

No one spoke for a moment. Rangoon was a hard memory to the Wades as all knew. Adoniram caught a look in Sarah Boardman's blue eyes that was not to be riddled but it caused him to set small Elsina down beside Fidee and to walk quickly out into the yard.

He was standing under the great banyan tree by the zayat when Sarah Boardman came slowly up to him. She was losing her lovely color but she was as gallant in her bearing as ever.

"You are no longer at the hermitage, lord teacher?" she asked.

"I am still at the hermitage, O lady of Tavoy," he answered with his fine melancholy smile.

"That is why you don't go to Rangoon, sir!" she ejaculated; "your health is not the reason."

"I've not given it as my reason, Mrs. Boardman." He lifted his chin and returned the gaze of her violet eyes, unwaveringly.

Baby Georgie toddled up to her and grasped her skirts. She dropped a long, slender hand on his pretty head absent-mindedly, and after biting her lip said in a low voice, "Ever since I was of an age to think, Mr. Judson, I have worshiped you. Our intense admiration for you and your work was what first drew me and my darling George together. But if you turn ascetic—what becomes of the missionary and of the man whom we've served?"

Adoniram's pale cheeks burned. "It's absolutely wicked for you to talk of worshiping me! Nothing more is needed to make my unhappiness complete. I'm not good enough to tie either your or your husband's shoe latchets . . . You nor no one else can understand what a charnel house I am!" He struggled for words and suddenly brought forth Isaiah's cry. " 'What shall I say? . . . The Lord himself hath done it! I shall go softly all my years in the bitterness of my soul.' "

"No!" cried Sarah. "It shall not be. You *shall* see that life is a thing of beauty and holiness."

His eyes held hers for a moment with a fire of consuming wistfulness. Then, silently he turned away.

That afternoon when he had finished his day's work, Adoniram told Deborah Wade that he was feeling the need of rest and would remain at the hermitage for a day or so. She looked at him sadly but did not remonstrate. She'd long since learned that remonstrances were futile.

Adoniram reached his clearing before sunset. He had finished the last quarter mile with a rush in spite of the heat. He was driven by a renewed desire to get away from human associations. He did not pause in the clearing. In the two years since he had first retreated here, Moulmein had crept steadily toward him and his isolation was broken nightly by the sounds of village life.

The time had come, he told himself as he stood breathing rapidly, when he must seek a further solitude. Nay, more, the time had come for him to make a supreme and final effort to end his search. He went into his hut and picked up his copy of Madame Guyon's life, gazed at it for a moment with sad affection, then laid it gently down, and put his worn copy of the New Testament in the pocket of his linen coat. This was his sole piece of luggage as he plunged into the bamboo thicket.

At first he followed a deer trail which lifted gradually to the hills. As the rise increased, the bamboo was elbowed aside by mighty teakwood trees and the beautiful acacia, palm and fan trees, and hopias. As he moved silently, snakes glided lazily across the path or hung motionless from the trees, hogs and buffalo crashed in the shadows. It was dangerous to the last degree but during the two years Adoniram had been absolutely unmolested by a forest creature. Jungle fowl whirred almost in his face, monkeys chattered above his head and the odor of heliotrope beat against his face.

Toward dusk, on the crest of a hill, two or three miles east of the ridge that backed Moulmein, he came upon a small ruined pagoda. Its beautiful white spire was still intact but the platform had been pierced by a banyan tree with a score of trunks and the several Buddha shrines at its foot had been overturned and were vine and moss grown. Nat houses of intricate carving had been broken into and their hidden treasures extracted. Everywhere there were traces of wild animals.

Adoniram seated himself on the edge of the platform and gazed at the entrancing view of Moulmein with its rice fields, its pagodas, its lovely river, all aflame from the dying sun. He laid his Testament on his knee.

Here, he told himself, he could make his last effort to achieve.

Turtle doves murmured in the banyan tree. The dusk came swiftly. Adoniram bowed his face on his hands— The moon, full and burning, sailed above the pagoda. A tiger crossed the platform, on soundless pads. The moon moved steadily down the sky, touching to tragic beauty the motionless figure of the man, giving to the fallen Buddhas the softness of sainthood, rousing to wild cries the jungle creatures on their night prowls.

Moment by moment Adoniram was erasing from the tablets of his mind all that the years had written there. Childhood, youth, father, mother, the ecstasies of religion, the ecstasies of love, the sufferings under religion, under love, the terrors of Burma, and more difficult, the beauties of Burma—life—all life's intricate tapestry—he dropped from the walls of thought, leaving them untraced for God's writing. It was the first time in all the years of trying that he accomplished this.

And then he waited, waited while the moon sank—sank until she had drowned herself in the waiting waters of the Salween. And as her last ray was quenched, darkness and cold pierced through to Adoniram's numbed senses. He raised his head and shivered. Then a great cry burst from him.

"God, You will not speak? I know now, You will not speak! Where shall I turn? What help is there for me?"

He rose to his feet and as he did so the Testament fell from his knee with a soft thud. He picked it up. It was warm from his body. His shivering ceased.

" '—And no man knoweth who the Son is but the Father and who the Father is but the Son and he to whom the Son will reveal Him—' "

Adoniram dropped to his knees and above his clasped hands raised his ravished face to the dusky heavens.

"O Jesus Christ—King of Kings in deepest truth—help

me! If I am not to know what death is, tell me what is life—what is my life that I may go on with it?"

And in the stillness that precedes the dawn, Adoniram's conscience spoke to him and said, Go back to Rangoon!

Rangoon! Rangoon which he never should have left. Rangoon the terrible, the absurd, Rangoon made holy by a thousand frustrated endeavors—his and dearest Ann's. At Rangoon would he find Him?— He did not know. All that he was sure of now was that the years in the hermitage had been futile, perhaps wrong. And that though death lurked in every miasmic shadow he must return to lower Burma. Peace was not yet for him. And still as he reached his resolve, calm—not peace—calm descended on his tortured mind. He laid his tired head on his arm and slept.

On the heels of the sudden blackness that precedes the dawn, a lighting of the eastern sky threw the pagoda and the banyan trees into silhouette. The turtle doves stirred and cooed. As the first long spokes of scarlet shot up the sky, and wings fluttered about the pagoda, a man appeared at the jungle edge from the west. It was Koo-chil. He was carrying little Fidee under one arm. A basket was slung on his shoulder. When he saw the slumbering figure under the banyan, he caught Fidee's jaws, opening to bark, and moved quietly forward.

For a long moment, he stood looking down on his master, his wrinkled brown face working. Finally, he put the dog on her feet and the little creature, with a soft whine, licked Adoniram's cheek. He sat erect at once looking dazedly about him. Then he smiled at Koo-chil.

"Fidee led you to me, O faithful friend!"

"Yes, lord teacher," answered Koo-chil, returning the smile. "I went to your hermitage last night to tell you news but I found only the mother of many puppies in the hut."

"I was afraid a jungle creature would get her if she followed me," said Adoniram, apologetically. "What is the news?" apprehensively.

"Lord teacher," replied Koo-chil, very simply, "for long years, as you know, I closed my ears to my mistress and to you and listened only to Mahomet. But yesterday, I know not how or why, as I cooked the curry and chicken, I knew that your Jesus Christ was the true prophet, and I want to be baptized. You can see, the news could not wait."

"It could not, indeed!" exclaimed Adoniram. He rose to his feet and spoke as simply as had the Bengalese. "You have made me very happy, dear Koo-chil."

The old man pushed his turban back from his sunken eyes and looked at Adoniram attentively. "You aren't happy, O lord teacher. But you are glad for this one thing. Were you ill in the night, lord?"

"I had a knowledge come to me in the night, O friend, that was as bitter as death. But nothing that is left me in life could have made a sweeter awakening than your news."

The two men exchanged a look in which all the long years that had centered around Ann spoke. Then Koo-chil took the basket from his shoulder. "I have brought you rice," he said, "and cold tea."

CHAPTER XXXIII

AT THE FRONT AGAIN

ADONIRAM was ill after this with a low fever which put him to bed for two or three weeks. He told no one at first of his determination to leave Moulmein for Burma proper. But in his renewed concern for Rangoon, he sent the Wades off in late February telling himself that they could hold the fort till he got there.

George Boardman, meantime, had rallied under Dr. Richardson's treatment and soon after the Wades left, the young missionary pronounced himself strong enough to return to his jungle Karens. Adoniram who had recovered sufficiently to lie in a long chair on the veranda and correct proof for Bennett dropped the sheets of the Liturgy when George issued his ultimatum and looked at him. Sarah who was sitting on the steps at work on her translation of The Pilgrim's Progress into Burmese gasped. But George smiled serenely at both and gave them no chance to utter the protests on their lips. He clambered on the back of his waiting pony and rode off to Wade's zayat.

"Mr. Judson," cried Sarah, "you'll assert your authority and forbid him, won't you! Christian martyrdom is one thing and self-murder is another!"

Adoniram nodded. "But I'll assert it indirectly, dear lady of Tavoy! I am going to Rangoon shortly and Brother Boardman will automatically remain until Brother Bennett can take over. That'll be a long time."

Sarah sprang to her feet, pencil, paper and books flying. "You aren't going back to the hermitage! Thank God!" She moved over to his bed-chair and said in a low voice, "Does that mean your search is ended, dear lord teacher?"

"It means that I'm transferring it to Rangoon," replied

Adoniram, looking away from her understanding eyes to the pagoda on the hill top.

"Oh, not another hermitage! Not that!" Sarah implored.

"How do I know?" he asked. "I only know that I live a life of frustration."

"You mustn't go in that spirit!" she cried. "Though my heart is going to be torn out of me in a few more months, I know that still there'll be beauty in the world and I'll thrill to it and as long as one can find beauty, one can believe life's worth the fight, worth living. I'm not afraid of life, are you, dear teacher?"

He looked at her now, so straight, so strong, her yellow hair curling above her violet eyes. "When I was your age, lady of Tavoy, I had so little fear of life that I beckoned it to me with both hands. But now I have all the cowardice of one who is lonely."

She was silent for a moment. Adoniram had confided little in the missionaries since Ann's death. That he should respond always to her efforts to help him with even such limited frankness moved her almost to tears. Her heart beat heavily as she prayed for the right word.

"Do you fear Rangoon, Mr. Judson?" she asked, finally.

"Yes," he replied.

"For every reason, personal and impersonal?"

"Yes, I do! You see, Sarah Boardman, I'm not an admirable object at all, when I give you a peep through the curtain." He changed the conversation abruptly. "You will keep me in touch with your troubles here and if I can help at the last, send for me?"

Her lips twisted with pain for an instant, then she straightened her shoulders and nodded, not trusting herself to speak.

Adoniram looked away again, this time to the yard and suddenly smiled. Sarah followed his gaze.

"There's always a smile where children are," she exclaimed.

AT THE FRONT AGAIN

Little Georgie and Elsina suddenly had appeared under the banyan intent on teaching a disciple's brown baby to walk. Georgie on one side and Elsina on the other were doing their tiny best to support the third baby on its little bare legs. For a few seconds the three would totter and sway then go down in a squirming heap, after which the two white babies, talking Burmese, would urge the brown baby to its feet and the pretty tableau would be repeated.

"There's more than a smile there!" Adoniram's face was relaxed and his deep voice tender. "There's a poem!"

Sarah's eyes were very lovely as she went down to assist in the lesson.

Adoniram was recovered by the end of April and made ready to leave. It was hard to say good-by to the Boardmans. He was certain that he never would see George alive again and he regretted keenly leaving Sarah to go through the dread ordeal with only the Bennetts, comparative strangers, to support her. Somehow George seemed half angel already and one didn't think of offering him spiritual aid. But Sarah was very human and in spite of her intrepid attitude toward pain, her youth made her actually a novice in affliction. Adoniram knew she would need what John Crawfurd had given to him, a warm arm across her shoulders.

And they both clung to him, accompanying him to the boat landing. Adoniram at the last moment held George's dry fingers in his and said, "I love you both dearly, but you don't need me, George, and Sarah does. See to it that she writes to me when it becomes necessary."

"I will, Mr. Judson." The young man returned the pressure of Adoniram's hand. "I do need you, in this sense. I need your promise that you'll look after Sarah and Georgie and make them your special charge. If you promise that, I need no other human reassurance."

"I promise you, George!"

The two men held each other's gaze while Sarah hid her quivering lips in her baby's hair.

Adoniram stood at the stern of the boat watching them, George with his arm around Sarah, Baby Georgie waving his mother's handkerchief, until tears blinded his eyes.

And so, the Shwé Dagôn once more, flashing golden and exquisite above the tree-shadowed, squalid town. All the intervening years dropped away. Adoniram was a boy of twenty-five entering the stockade gates for the first time, high-hearted, frightened, sure, so very sure, that Burma was Christ's for Adoniram's taking—

The illusion was broken by his meeting with Lanciego, who was collector once more. The Spaniard was a broken old man, a shadow of the choleric gentleman who had warned Adoniram of trouble so long ago. Not but what he warned him now as he waved a scarred hand and admitted Adoniram's goods free of duty.

"You're *persona non grata* since you went over to the English, Judson," he said. "If you had stayed at court as Dr. Price did, you might now be preaching every Sunday in the golden audience hall!"

"The greatest imaginative book in the world was written by a Spaniard," smiled Adoniram.

"And Cervantes might have had you in mind as a model for Don Quixote," retored Lanciego.

"Thank you for the complimentary insult," laughed Adoniram. "Henry Gouger is gone?"

"Everybody's gone but me and your two missionaries. They're both half dead with jungle fever. It's taking you a long time to learn Burma, Judson."

"Well, I'm back for another lesson," replied Adoniram, cheerfully, as he followed his coolies out into the street.

The Wades had rented a house near the bazaar and thus far they had not been molested by the viceroy, although inquirers called in considerable numbers. With Adoniram's

AT THE FRONT AGAIN

arrival it was decided to split forces. The neighborhood of the old mission property was now utterly deserted so they erected a zayat for Adoniram, with living quarters attached, in a crowded section, under the shadow of a monastery. But this roused such vehement protest from the monks that the missionaries were bidden by the viceroy to remove the building to the original mission yard.

Adoniram acquiesced in the new arrangement but try as he would he could not force himself to go out to the old mission with its memories. While he was in this uneasy state, the viceroy issued a sudden warning to inquirers to cease their visits to the missionaries. For a short five minutes Adoniram was tempted to employ the old tactics; take a present to the official and placate him. But following this thought came anger. He was through forever with the attempt to *insinuate* Christianity through the barred gates. He was going to carry the Cross openly to the very stronghold of Buddhism and hold it there until driven out by force or until he had worn down the Burmans by stubborn resistance. He was going to Prome.

The fury that possessed him drove out for the time being every melancholy thought, every mystic preoccupation. He ordered Pastor Thah-a out to the new zayat and told the Wades to persist with their work in spite of the viceroy and Satan. Then he loaded himself, Maung Ing and four of Pastor Thah-a's converts into a native boat, filling all available space with tracts, and set off up the Irrawaddy.

It was the rainy season. That didn't matter. Robbers were numerous, mosquitoes made life, outside a curtain, torment, cockroaches and ants fought over the tracts, ague shook and burned Adoniram and the captain of the boat looked suspiciously like a leper. All this was of no moment. Adoniram pushed steadily past the sodden paddy fields, stopping at regular intervals to preach and distribute tracts and felt his heart swell triumphantly at the eagerness with which the people welcomed him. There would be converts here awaiting whomever he might send later to do the harvesting.

It was the end of June when the hills that guarded the ancient town of Prome appeared, with the city on a headland projecting into the red waters of the river. The place had not recovered from the devastation of war. Many of the pagodas were in ruins and most of the houses had fallen into decay. The captain of the boat said there were not more than five hundred families left in the place. Nevertheless, he admitted, it was one of Buddha's strongholds.

The viceroy very reluctantly granted the use of the only available building in town, an old zayat, to Adoniram. But he told the missionary frankly that he wasn't wanted. Since the war, he said, white men had been very unpopular in Burma and Adoniram who had gone over to the English was a marked man. Prome had been ruined by the peace the teacher had made; the city's share of the war debt had been paid only at cost of distress, terror and poverty. The British had recently sent a representative to live at Ava. That undoubtedly meant new oppression.

In vain Adoniram pointed out that by terms of the treaty each nation was to have a representative at the other's seat of government. The viceroy would not understand. He did not, however, at first actually refuse to permit Adoniram to "teach" and so the old zayat was patched up and Adoniram scattered his disciples through the town to preach while he sent Maung Ing into neighboring villages and himself took the zayat.

Burmese Lent was beginning. No one came to the zayat. Adoniram, with set lips, followed the throngs up the hill to the Shwé San-Daw pagoda which all but rivaled the Shwé Dagôn in beauty. On the platform, he seated himself under the shelter which covered a gigantic Buddha and, as crowd succeeded crowd at Gautama's feet, he repeated the old, old cry, "Ho, every one that thirsteth, come ye to the waters—"

AT THE FRONT AGAIN 349

Some were angry. Some listened. Some, looking about them apprehensively, asked—"Who is this Jesus Christ?"

All day and for many days, Adoniram preached at the Buddha's knees. Lifting his eyes from the immediate worshipers, he saw the broad platform crowded with scores of devotees; women in rose silk tameins, men in green and purple, little children, brown and half naked, all holding flowers in their clasped hands and making their obeisance to the memory of the dead Gautama. Lifting his eyes beyond these, he saw the Burma which always made his heart ache with beauty: the little town set with palm and tamarind, thick-dotted with the lotus-bud domes of pagodas, and the majestic river red and silver beneath the glorious hills, all bordered by wide paddy fields so unbelievably green when the rain ceased and let the unbelievable blue of the sky show through.

Christ was standing at Buddha's very elbow, looking into the serenely withdrawn eyes, looking with gaze that was agonized for Burma's agony. Surely, surely, the Burmans must see, must welcome Him.

But they dared not! Adoniram and his disciples distributed a thousand tracts. Maung Ing told him that everywhere the people were gathered round those who could read, listening to the message. Yet they dared not ask the teacher to explain, to offer salvation. And even the distributing of the tracts was stopped when the viceroy had Adoniram brought to the hall of justice and informed him that the lord of white elephants had ordered the teacher to leave Burma.

"But why, O dispenser of justice?" demanded Adoniram, looking from the viceroy to the rotting walls of the court room, alive with lizards.

"You are looked on as a spy, Maung Judson. Nothing you can do will persuade the golden voice that you are otherwise," replied the viceroy in soft tones that were more venomous than harshness would have been.

Adoniram listened to the rain pouring over the thatch

and watched a lizard snap at a foolhardy fly which had landed on the viceroy's mat.

"The lord of life would permit another missionary to come to Prome, am I to understand?" asked Adoniram.

"I know only what my order says, foreign teacher," answered the viceroy, pulling at his ropelike chin-beard. "I would guess, though, that the English representative at Ava could get another teacher introduced at court, if *you* will leave Burma."

"I will not leave Burma," replied Adoniram, buttoning his black coat around him and standing very erect. "I will leave Prome if you insist on carrying out his majesty's order. But I shall continue to teach as close to Prome as I can."

"We shall see!" grunted the viceroy. "You will leave Prome to-morrow."

Adoniram walked from the room with his head high, slipped on his shoes in the veranda and raised his umbrella. He would leave Prome, yes, but only to go up to Ava and interview the British resident, Major Burney. He was expecting two new recruits from America to reach Moulmein this fall. He would arrange for one to go at once to Ava, if he proved to be of possible material. A good man could learn the language as well in Ava as in Moulmein and during this two or three years of learning he could act as Christ's resident in the Burmese seat of government. Surely Christianity could have its representative as well as England!

Full of this new idea he reached the zayat where he found that Wade had sent up a disciple from Rangoon with letters. One was marked urgent. This Adoniram opened with a shudder of apprehension. Who was dead now: George Boardman? But it did not contain the worst news, although bad enough.

Jonathan and Deborah Wade were both desperately ill with dysentery. Jonathan had taken his wife across to Moulmein to consult Dr. Richardson and had been advised that the pernicious form of the disease which afflicted them

AT THE FRONT AGAIN

could be cured only by a two years' change of climate. To remain even in Moulmein would mean death in a few weeks; Rangoon would kill them in a fortnight. Wade asked permission to leave for America at once, in fact had left, but would wait in Calcutta for Mr. Judson's approval.

With this letter was one from Cephas Bennett. George Boardman had gone back to Tavoy to die in the jungle with his Karens. Sarah and Georgie had gone with him.

By a curious turn of fate, Adoniram was suddenly the only white man left in all the missionary organization who could preach to the Burmans. The trip to Ava must be put off. He would not return to Moulmein but if the authorities forced him, he'd return to Rangoon.

He gathered his disciples about him and gave them their orders, then led them aboard the boat.

They landed the next morning at a town ten miles below Prome. Adoniram repaired at once to the chief pagoda and, taking his station beside a Buddha, preached while his disciples scattered through the village and the surrounding paddy fields and distributed tracts. For two days the people listened wistfully. On the third, a golden boat drew up to the shore and a messenger from Prome ordered them in the king's name to leave.

Adoniram obeyed as slowly as possible, the people watching while his boat was launched. As he clambered aboard a tall young Burman called in a clear voice, "Don't be discouraged, great teacher! You have planted a seed that will grow like a banyan tree. Mark me as your disciple. I pray to God every day. I and my children and my children's children will give His word in the books you gave us, houseroom forever."

And Adoniram knew, with a great uplifting of his heart, that the young man's words were prophetic. It was the written Word that could save Burma.

His method was simplicity itself. He stopped about every ten miles, or as near that interval as villages appeared, to sow the immortal seeds. Each village countenanced him until the king's order came, and then he left, always as tardily as possible. He was falling back but he was fighting every step of the way.

Just as the rains were finished, he reached Rangoon. The town was bursting with loveliness of flower and leaf. Adoniram had renewed his courage in Prome and he went directly to the zayat at the old mission. It was quite different, thank God: just a little house on stilts set in a clearing. All the rest of the mission property had been claimed by the jungle. Only the Shwé Dagôn was familiar. Here Adoniram settled himself to hold the final line of defense. He and Maung Ing took turns occupying the teacher's mat. Maung Ing was not much of a preacher but people liked his fat, comfortable face and there were many who remembered him in the vicinity. Mr. Beg Pardon swung under the eaves.

All his spare time Adoniram gave to working on the Bible. He was more convinced than ever that a Bible in every Burmese village with a single native convert, could do more than a thousand white missionaries scattered over the country. As if to corroborate this, a Burman came to the zayat one day in December and asked to be baptized. He proved to be the first man to whom Adoniram had given a copy of the first gospel translation twelve years before. The man had converted his village of three or four families. He asked for more tracts and got them and Adoniram in January baptized him in the rush-choked lake under the Shwé Dagôn.

It was lonely, of course, in spite of the fullness with which Adoniram immersed himself in work and it grew bitterly hard to crush back the familiar sense of frustration as Rangoon's old gloom closed in on him. Maung Ing was sick for some weeks during the winter months and Adoniram taking his place on the mat in the little veranda found the many hours during which no inquiries came quite insupportable. He turned again to Jeanne Marie, giving the autobiography a careful reading from cover to cover. He had just finished

AT THE FRONT AGAIN

the book when he received the first letter from Sarah Boardman which she had sent him since early fall.

George was dead. He had gone on a litter for his last preaching expedition among the Karens and had died, as he had wished, on the firing line.

"I need not tell you, dear Mr. Judson," wrote Sarah, "that my days are black, just now. No one knows the ways of grief so well as you. Beauty has gone out of life for me now. I can only spend my day trying to etch his dear features, his dear voice, on my memory so that I never can forget. I pray that God will enable—"

Adoniram was deeply moved. Boardman had been a superb missionary. He would have mourned the young man for that even if he had not loved him for the sweetness of his character. And it hurt Adoniram inexpressibly to think of Sarah's sufferings. But when he wrote her, he wrote from the standpoint of one into whose soul the iron had entered.

"My dear Sister: You are now drinking the bitter cup whose dregs I am somewhat acquainted with. I venture to say it is far bitterer than you expected. It is natural for people to cling to the dead and to fear they will too soon forget the dear objects of their love. But don't be concerned. I can assure you that months and months of heartrending agony are before you, whether you will or not. I can only advise you to take the cup with both hands and sit down to the bitter repast which God has appointed for your sanctification. As to your beloved, you *know* that all *his* tears have been wiped away and that little Sarah has found her father. What more can you desire for them? Yet take your bitter cup in your hands and sit down to your repast. You will learn a secret—that there is sweetness at the bottom. You will find heaven coming near to you and familiarity with your husband's voice will be a connecting link drawing you almost within the sphere of celestial music.

"I think from what I know of your mind that you will not desert the post but remain to carry on the work which he gloriously began. The Karens of Tavoy regard you as their spiritual mother.

"As to little Georgie, you cannot, of course, part with him at present. But if you should wish to send him home, I pledge myself to use what little influence I have to procure for him all the advantages of education which your fondest wishes can desire. Or if you should be taken away and should commit him to me, I hereby pledge my fidelity to treat him as my own son.

"I hope you will feel no uneasiness or think it necessary to make any inquiries about your support. By our regulations, a widow is entitled to seventy rupees a month and a child ten rupees.

"I shall be with you in my prayers, dear lady of Tavoy."

He did not write this letter easily. It was difficult not to let her see how keenly he felt her trouble. He tore up several attempts before completing the one he finally sent her and for a week after it was gone by special messenger, he was unsettled in his work. During this period he wrote a long letter to the secretary of the Baptist Board. He told of George Boardman's death in words of poignant sympathy. But he added the plea he had made so often before, that they refrain from sending men of a consumptive tendency to Burma. And then he once more begged them to send men and more men to answer "the heart-melting, soul-stirring cry of the varied population of this great country, 'come and save us, come to our rescue, ye bright sons and daughters of America, come and save us for we are sinking into hell!'"

CHAPTER XXXIV

RAIN IF THOU WILT, O SKY!

ABOUT two weeks after the news of Boardman's death reached Rangoon, Maung Ing observed the copy of Madame Guyon lying on the mat from which Adoniram had been preaching the day before. It had lain there all night. Always before when the precious book was not in the teacher's hands it had been returned to the sandalwood box. Maung Ing reproachfully called the teacher's attention to this unprecedented neglect.

"Thank you, Maung Ing," said Adoniram, absent-mindedly. "Just put it in its place for me."

Wonder in his round face, the Burman obeyed. He never before had been permitted to touch the volume. And he was still more bewildered when he observed that the teacher did not read this constant companion of years, for many weeks.

Adoniram was quite unconscious of the fact that he was neglecting his favorite. He was wrestling with a new problem based on the fact that from the moment he had received Sarah Boardman's letter, Sarah had not been out of his mind. He was not in the habit of lying to himself and so, after a few days, he admitted that his interest in Sarah was keener than any he'd felt in any human being since Ann's death.

He was taking his evening prowl along the Pagoda Road when he made the admission, hands clasped behind him, for once unheeding of the worshipers as they came and went. It was going on to six years since Ann had been laid under the hopia tree. During all that time it never had occurred to him as possible that he could care for a woman again. The thought of putting any one in her place was intolerable now. His love for her was unabated. And yet, Sarah Boardman haunted him: not crowding out Ann but with Ann. *Did he want to marry Sarah Boardman?*

No, decidedly not, he assured himself. And yet—the thought of that gallant soul drinking her bitter cup alone in Tavoy had crowded out Jeanne Marie Guyon. Was this wrong?

For two years he had mortified his spirit, had sweated blood to teach it that there was no finding God, save by sloughing off every personal happiness, by denying self. He had fulfilled all Madame Guyon's precepts but he had not found God, he had not answered a single question that tormented him. He had lived housemate to sorrow, intimate to despair, for six years. He had denied himself everything save what would keep his unquiet body from actually succumbing to death. Yet he had not beheld God in grief nor in hunger. God was not in the wind nor in the earthquake nor in the fire that had devastated his heart and mind ever since that dread day when he had been thrust into the Hand-shrink-not.

Would it be fair now to seek Him in another road than the road of loneliness? Would God understand? Would Ann understand—darling, darling Nancy—? A great sob burst from him.

He had paused at the foot of the war-scarred arcade that led to the Shwé Dagôn. On sudden impulse he began to ascend the stairs. The people did not protest as so long ago they had protested. They knew him now and, though those in authority were against him, the common folk understood and loved him.

He mounted up and up, under the grandly carved arches and out on the great platform with its Buddhas, its banners, its sweet, deep gongs and its magnificent gold spire touching the evening sky. He threaded his way among the worshipers and leaned on the balustrade that edged the platform. The beautiful country of the delta unrolled below him, waters mirroring the crimson and orange of the heavens. Whatever God thought of beauty as a possession for men, He had left none out of the world He had given Burma. Adoniram gazed with parted lips, enchanted by loveliness. And without volition on his part something touched the elbow of his understanding.

" 'Whatsoever things are just, whatsoever things are pure, whatsoever things are lovely—think on these—' "

And for six years, horror had ruled in Adoniram's inner thinking.

"Ann! Ann!" he whispered, "did I wrong your happy spirit in putting Madame Guyon in your place?"

Ann, with her beauty and her frank love of beauty, or Adoniram, sitting on the edge of the grave in the rotting jungle of Moulmein, which was right?

Darkness was closing swiftly. The enormous red moon was rising above the pagoda lake. Remotely above his head sounded the chimes on the sacred umbrella. The scent of blossoms and fruit in the hands of the worshipers was borne to him subtly on the evening air. Far in the jungles to the north a tiger called and in the ruined terraces below the crickets dreamed.

Beauty! For the first time in many years, Adoniram opened his heart and permitted beauty to enter freely.

After an hour or so, he descended the dark stairway and slowly made his way home. There, sitting on the veranda with the moonlight making a glory of the casuarina tree and the nightingale as of old sighing of his love, he told himself that he was going to try to win Sarah Boardman to be his wife. He did not delude himself with thinking that he could give her what he had given Ann. He would not wish to. Nor could Sarah give any one what she had given George. But might they not, if Sarah could be won, build on the ruin of their first homes a second that would have dignity and sweetness and usefulness to God and man?

It would be long before Sarah could contemplate the idea

with anything but aversion. Perhaps she never would contemplate it. But in the meantime, he would do his utmost to make her see that such a union could bring happiness to her.

And thus, Madame Guyon was left to mildew in her sandalwood chest while faintly through the black mists with which she had helped so long to darken Adoniram's mind, there pierced a faint, uncertain shaft of light. Very faint, for Adoniram had little on which to feed his new interest in happiness. He wrote regularly to Sarah, receiving replies from her only at long intervals. She was in the jungle, winning Karen converts, and wrote entirely of these. But one of the lessons Burma finally had taught Adoniram was patience. He had been born persistent.

He remained in Rangoon, working indefatigably on the Bible, fighting illness and seeking conversions. But the hostility toward the mission increased until, as Adoniram wrote Sarah, "to get a new convert was like pulling the eye tooth of a live tiger." He made this comment when he compared his tiny list of five baptisms for the year with the one hundred and thirty-six made at Moulmein and with Sarah Boardman's seventy-six at Tavoy. But, at that, he was proud of his list. It had been won from the very heart of Buddhism.

Early in 1833, the devoted Americans sent their response to Adoniram's Macedonian cry. Word reached him in Rangoon that six missionaries had arrived at Moulmein,—the Masons, the Joneses and the Kincaids. Adoniram knew then that he'd have to go over to Tenasserim long enough to study his recruits and place them. He left Pastor Thah-a and Maung Ing in charge at Rangoon and in July crossed to Moulmein. By August, he had measured his people and made his plans. Mr. and Mrs. Mason would go to Tavoy. Mr. and Mrs. Jones to Siam. In the Kincaids he saw the material for which he had hoped for making the reëntry to Ava. He decided to keep them with him at Rangoon for training and while he communicated with Major Burney at

Ava. The Bennetts must carry on at Moulmein until the Wades returned.

The Masons departed and the Joneses. But before Adoniram and Mr. and Mrs. Kincaid had left for Rangoon, came a letter from the Baptist Board which gave Adoniram one of the most difficult hours he ever had endured in his life. The Board requested him to remain in Moulmein where his health was secure and complete the translation of the Bible. No one on earth could do this job but he, they told him. His translation thus far, the scholars who knew had apprised them, was the finest ever made of the Bible into an Oriental tongue. His letters had fully persuaded the Board that the Bible in Burmese was the ultimate solution of the Christianizing of Burma. Ergo, Mr. Judson would kindly cease to jeopardize his life and proceed on his marvelous work of scholarship.

At first, Adoniram told himself flatly that he could not, he would not, obey and he wrote this to Sarah Boardman. The effect of this was to bring Sarah to Moulmein at once. She arrived on a rainy day in late summer, when Adoniram sat alone in the little study that had been partitioned off for him from the general living room. He looked up from a letter of vehement protest he was preparing for the Board, to see her tall figure in his doorway.

He rose precipitately, staring at her. She wore an indigo linen riding dress which had been cut off to ankle length. It was unadorned save for the flat linen collar at the neck. On her golden head was a small rice-straw riding hat, strapped under the chin. This he took in at the first quick glance, then his eyes focused on her face. She had suffered. Aye, she had suffered! The Tavoy jungle had robbed her of her pink and whiteness, but grief had etched the shadows round her eyes and taken from the uptilt of her lips, had given her glance the expression of one who had wrestled with life and death.

"I came, at risk of offending you, to protest, Mr. Judson," she said.

He smiled. "Aren't you going to greet me, after three years' absence?" he asked. "Where are your manners, dear lady of Tavoy?"

"In the jungle with the Karens, undoubtedly," she replied, suddenly returning his smile as she shook hands.

He placed a chair for her. She unfastened the chin strap and tossed the hat to his desk,—his orderly, old maidish desk which no one was permitted to touch but himself. He laid his hand on the soft straw with a little sense of warmth and happiness.

Sarah wasted no more time on preliminaries. She leaned toward him. "You will not go back to Rangoon?" Her low voice was full of pleading.

"I thought," he replied, "that in my letters I'd made clear to you what Rangoon means to the cause of Christianity."

"The Bible means more," she exclaimed, "your life means more. What can I say to you to make you see how much more!"

He did not speak for a moment. It was essential that his decision be made on absolutely impersonal grounds. He was not at all sure that he could do this with Sarah sitting opposite, making an impassioned plea, although, alas, she meant to be impersonal enough!

She affected him as no one ever had affected him before. The only near analogy in his experience was the affection he had felt as a boy of fifteen, for a schoolmate. Young Geoffrey had been just such an intrepid, brilliant spirit as Sarah and Adoniram had loved him with all the enthusiasm of his ardent nature. As he had cared for Geoffrey, he cared for Sarah. He would not for the present permit himself to think of her as a woman.

So now he answered her as he would have answered that close friend of long ago.

"Don't harp on my health, Sarah Boardman. I'm sick of the silly subject."

"I'm not!" replied Sarah. "It's of prime importance to Burma, I assure you, no matter what that absurd Madame Guyon has to say about the sacred necessity for you to have the jungle illness."

Adoniram chuckled. Since Ann's death, no one had talked to him, man to man. Once he had been stiff on the matter of respect for the cloth. Now, as the acknowleged leader of a great religious experiment on which the eyes of the world were turned, he longed for a familiar hand on his shoulder and a familiar voice that would chide him and laugh at him.

As if she read his thoughts Sarah went on. "Mrs. Bennett lent me the copy of Lady Guyon's biography you got for her a year ago. If anything could detract from your nobility in my eyes, Mr. Judson, it would be the fact that you allowed her to influence you so terribly."

"She's been of supreme value to me," remonstrated Adoniram. "She came to me at a time—" He paused. Had she been of supreme value? Had she led him toward God—? He moved his shoulders uneasily and added sadly: "I know nothing. Less than nothing. But I laid her aside shortly after dear George's death and I've not looked at her since. If I've been wrong, God forgive me."

"May she rest in peace!" cried Sarah. "Now, I know there's a chance to save your life. Lord teacher, will you tell me what can be more important than the translation of the Bible?"

"In the long view, nothing," answered Adoniram. "But immediately, to train Brother Kincaid to plant a church in Ava, and to hold the church in Rangoon until that's accomplished. In Rangoon, I can translate also, you know."

"You know that nothing can kill the church at Rangoon now," urged Sarah. "Consider! After the war it looked as if it were utterly destroyed. You mourned that the flourishing young tree had been cut off to the root. And so it had. But like a young tree, the roots didn't die. They put up new shoots. First Maung Thah-a, and then the man you wrote me of, to whom you'd given the Gospel of St. Matthew so many years before. Don't you see that you and Mrs. Judson had planted deep and forever long before the war drove you out? A hundred years from now there'll still be your church in Rangoon."

"But why handicap it by not keeping a white clergyman there who can preach in the tongue?" protested Adoniram, moved though he was by her argument. "Do you realize that you and I are the only whites preaching in the vernacular in Burma or the provinces, to-day? Must I stop preaching and leave you to carry on alone?"

She tapped the desk thoughtfully with her long tanned fingers, then nodded her golden head. "I have it! Take Mr. and Mrs. Kincaid to Ava yourself and establish them there as only you can!"

"My original plan was to apparently settle with them in Ava and then bargain with the king to leave if he allowed the Kincaids to stay," said Adoniram. "But I proposed to continue in Rangoon as a perpetual menace and threat. I know the lord of white elephants. He's a recalcitrant child."

"How much longer will it take you to complete the translation, lord teacher?" asked Sarah.

"Another year, if I escape the autumn attack of fever, to finish the first draft of the whole ready to put in Bennett's hands for printing. This we may distribute at once. But it will require ten years for me to revise the whole as I would wish it to remain. Could you who understand ask me to give up Rangoon for a decade if I live that long?"

"No!" replied Sarah, "but, dear teacher, I ask you to give it up for a year. Take the Kincaids to Ava, now. Then return here and finish the sacred task. Rangoon is only twenty-four hours away. You can manage to be a menace and a threat to Bagyi-daw from Moulmein, I'm sure."

Was he making his decision, impersonally? Adoniram jumped to his feet and began to pace the floor. Sarah rose and paced with him, shoulder to shoulder in understanding silence. After five minutes he paused and faced her.

"You know, don't you, that you have a great influence over me? I find it impossible to remember how much I'm your senior in years and experience."

"I'm glad and proud and unworthy," she replied, meeting his gaze, earnestly.

He turned abruptly away. She, at least, was impersonal.

"After all," he said suddenly, "I have no choice. I must obey the Board or never again dare to try to exact obedience from my associates here."

Sarah nodded. "When do you leave for Ava?"

"Good gracious!" ejaculated Adoniram. "Not for a quarter of an hour, at least! I'd like that time to see young Georgie and to tell you how proud I am of you. How many other women preachers are there in the world?"

"It's not so much my preaching that counts with the Karens. They're very simple. They know I love them and they let me give them my faith. Is there some one around to get your things ready for the trip? I'm not much of a housewife, you know, but I'll mend up things or pack or—"

Adoniram's heart leaped. Impersonal, this? But he answered carelessly, "Oh, I've done my own mending since I was a boy. It distressed Ann so much when we were first married. She felt it was an aspersion on her perfect New England housewifery. And I've packed for myself for seven years, now."

"I see," was Sarah's comment, a little formal.

She moved toward the door. "I'll find Georgie."

Adoniram followed. Georgie was playing with Elsina Bennett, under the banyan tree. He was standing on a box, preaching with Elsina and Fidee as a much amused congregation. He was a beautiful boy of five, but very delicate.

"I suppose I must make up my mind to send him to America next year," said Sarah with a heavy sigh. "He's not growing physically and he's getting too much of the natives."

"We'll find a family there for him," nodded Adoniram. He played with the children for a short time and then went off to write a docile letter to the Board.

The next day he left for Ava with Kincaid. Mrs. Kincaid was to follow when a place had been prepared for her.

His liking and respect for the young missionary increased all the way up the Irrawaddy. Eugenio Kincaid was a man of education and of a virility, physical and mental, greater than that of any man Adoniram had as yet welcomed to Burma. He had the natural suavity of manner which was indispensable in the diplomatic position he was about to occupy. And he had clenched Adoniram's faith in him by refusing the offer recently made by the Board to send missionaries out for a limited period. Adoniram thought the limiting of the period extremely unwise and when young Kincaid said with quiet emphasis that he was in Burma for life, Adoniram knew that his missionary zeal was founded on a rock.

The trip up the river was exceedingly uncomfortable but this was overshadowed by the discovery that the visit to Prome was already showing its harvest. At every stopping place south of the old town, Burmans in groups or singly came to the missionaries and asked to be baptized. They all had in their possession one or more of the tracts. Many of them remembered vividly whole sentences from Adoniram's preaching. Young Kincaid, struggling to understand the difficult tongue and watching the eager devotion of these people to Adoniram, was having an unforgettable object lesson in the highest type of missionary work.

They reached the golden city late in October and went at once to the house of the British resident. Major Burney was a little aghast at the plan Adoniram presented to him, but promised to do what he could to get the two an audience with Bagyi-daw. In the meantime, in true British fashion, he was extremely hospitable and made them move from their boat into his house.

Late on the afternoon of their arrival, Adoniram walked out on the road to Amarapura, moving sadly enough. Ava was agony to him, try as he would to treat the place casually. But he wanted to see the zayat and the lotus lake once more. These, at least, were not associated with Ann. He found them unchanged, in the sunset glow. He was standing quietly by the zayat, thinking of young Colman and of the gaing-ôk, when a mount of the king's guards galloped up the road on their stirrupless ponies. They shouted to all and sundry to hide their eyes for the lord of light and air was approaching. The few passers-by immediately threw themselves on their faces. But Adoniram, looking at the approaching elephants, doffed his hat and, with a little smile, remained standing. He knew his Bagyi-daw.

Through the dancing orange dust, under the towering palms came his majesty's elephant. Bagyi-daw was perched on his back, shaded by the nine royal white umbrellas. Adoniram ignored the horrified shouts of the retainers and, looking up, caught the golden eye and bowed profoundly. Then he smiled. Bagyi-daw gave an order and the elephant with the half dozen that followed halted.

"What brings you to the golden city, O friend of our enemy?" shouted his majesty, angrily.

"My religion brings me, lord of righteousness," replied Adoniram promptly.

"I ordered you to cease teaching in Burma," snarled Bagyi-daw. "Do you long for another taste of the death prison?"

"O lord of the air," Adoniram's face was lifted, for the king's perch was very lofty, "O lord of the air, your Buddha died comfortably as a man may die, recumbent on his mat, with his spirit slowly withdrawing from a body left whole. The Jesus Christ who gave me my religion died as only God could die, giving Himself voluntarily to crucifixion on a cross, His spirit torn from a body in agony. Since that time the Cross has been the emblem of the one religion by which man may save his soul. It is an emblem that no white man can see without awe, an emblem that no white man will see desecrated."

Bagyi-daw moved his head impatiently but permitted Adoniram to finish.

"You will remember, O lord of righteousness, that when I made the peace for you, I was able to do so because it was borne in on your celestial mind that always I kept my word. Always I spoke truth, for Christ's sake. You remember, O gracious majesty?"

"I remember," muttered the king, sullenly.

"I have come to Ava to say this to your golden ears with my head below your golden feet in all humility. I brought the Cross to Ava. So long as I live I will not leave Ava unless I leave here a teacher like myself upholding the Cross."

Bagyi-daw's face brightened. "You are the only one Buddhism has to fear, O friend of the unspeakable enemy. Dr. Price, what was he—a fool who cut wens and preached sermons in a ridiculous vernacular. What trace has he left behind of your Cross? Many, many whites have brought your Cross to Burma. For you alone will it take root. O foreign animal, if you will give me your promise not to return to Ava as long as I live, you may bring three or thrice three teachers here in your stead."

"I have with me a young teacher whom Major Burney will bring to the golden presence, if you permit. On the hour you welcome Maung Kincaid to your protection that hour I leave for Rangoon."

"For Moulmein," said Bagyi-daw.

"For Moulmein for one year, then Rangoon, O lord of righteousness, but not Ava so long as your golden reign shall hold and you permit one of my brothers to teach here."

"That is your promise?" asked Bagyi-daw.

"That is my promise!"

"Bring him to me at the monk's begging time!" The king laughed uproariously. "See how I protect the children of Buddha?" He ordered the parade to be on its way.

So simply as this was it done. So simply!

By mid-morning, on the following day, Bagyi-daw had granted Mr. Kincaid the right to purchase a bit of ground in Ava and Adoniram's boat was getting under way on the Irrawaddy.

In two months' time he was back in Moulmein.

CHAPTER XXXV

SPLENDOR OF GOD

ALONE in his little study Adoniram now put all of his enormous intellectual drive into the task set by the Board. The work was exacting and exhausting to a degree and when he found that the fine shades of the translation were suffering because of brain fag, he would gather together several of the disciples and go into the jungle along the Salween River to preach to the Karens for a week or so. But his usual relaxation consisted in writing on his diary letters to Sarah and the secretary of the Baptist Board each evening and afterward a stroll, with panting old Fidee.

He always took his walk up Sir Archibald's road and along the hill where occasionally he met the gaing-ôk. The old man had given Adoniram back to what he called the senses.

"I never really hoped about you," he admitted sorrowfully one evening when the two sat together near the recumbent Buddha, watching the myriad bats blacken the pale pink sky.

"You call my religion sad," returned Adoniram. "But I call yours empty, utter negation. I suppose, after all, life was given us to live, O lord of dreams."

"Ah, but what is life?" asked the old man, looking like an ancient Buddha himself in the twilight.

Adoniram sighed—the old, the eternal question! But for the first time since Ann's death, he thought of it without a feeling of helplessness and blind groping.

"It must be something very precious," he said, slowly, "because God gave it to His Son as a supreme experience. And as one of God's possessions it's not to be scorned. 'For as the Father hath life in Himself so hath He given to the Son to have life in Himself.'"

"If one grants God, yes," mused the gaing-ôk.

"Once you were all but willing to grant God," exclaimed Adoniram.

The old Buddhist looked at him wistfully. "What is life?" he urged.

"Life," replied Adoniram, "is knowledge. It is not escape. It is not running away to a hermitage. It is knowing what Christ knew. And He turned his head from nothing except causing suffering in others. He said 'I am life.'"

"Words! Magic words, I admit, but merely toys—a football tossed by the mind's knee higher than the old Moulmein pagoda."

"Words are the soul's antennæ," Adoniram was not heeding the old man's scorn. "We can only know what they seek out for us. I've been seeking stupidly, looking beyond when the answer is to my hand. When Christ said, 'I am life,' He told me all. And He spent no time save the forty days, in mortifying the flesh. If I slough off all that interferes in carrying the Gospel, that is enough."

"Words!" scoffed the gaing-ôk. "Excuses, I don't doubt, for going back to marriage."

"O hungry one for God," said Adoniram, "ever since I made up my mind that I might dare have a home again, the gibbering, festering memories of the Hand-shrink-not have ceased to stand at my elbow, snatching at my mind whenever it was empty for a moment. Riddle me that."

"The only escape from thirst is the annihilation of desire," returned the gaing-ôk.

"You're consistent, anyhow," smiled Adoniram, rising, "which I'll admit I am not."

"Come and see my new find, a copy of Lord Buddha's sermons, authenticated by himself," urged the old monk.

Adoniram sighed but shook his head. "Nay, in that I am consistent. I shall never again give my mental interests to any but the mission work."

In the gloaming they smiled at each other and parted.

Yes, Adoniram was returning to spiritual health. He recognized the fact himself, although he often wondered wistfully what would become of this new-found normality if Sarah refused him after the enormous drive of the translation was completed. For this was the great risk he proposed to take after the last word was transcribed.

On and on he drove through the supremely moving books, Esther, Ezra, Nehemiah, twenty odd verses a day. And at last, Malachi—on the 31st of January, 1834 . . . "and the Lord whom ye seek shall suddenly come to His temple . . ."

It was sunset when Adoniram wrote the last word and softly laid down his pen, while he gazed unbelievingly at the piles of manuscript. From the zayat at the gate he heard Cephas Bennett's voice in words of deepest felicity. "If there be therefore any consolation in Christ, if any comfort of love, if any fellowship of the spirit, if any bowels and mercies, fulfill ye my joy—having the same love—"

Adoniram slipped to his knees and bowed his head on the last sheet of his work.

The monastery gongs boomed softly. The scent of roses was wafted across his desk and at last roused him from thoughts too deep for words. He rose and again took up his pen. In this supreme moment, Sarah must share since Ann could not.

"Thanks be to God, I can now say I have attained! I have knelt down before Him and with the last leaf in my hand, and imploring His forgiveness for all the sins which have polluted my labors and His aid in future efforts to remove the errors and imperfections which necessarily cleave to the work, I have commended it to His mercy and grace. I have dedicated it to His glory. May He make his own inspired word now complete in the Burmese tongue, the grand instrument of filling all Burma with songs of praise to him. Amen."

He was very weary and the Bennetts urged him to take a sea voyage to Calcutta for a rest. But Adoniram, while he admitted that he needed the rest, had no desire to visit Calcutta. He would go to Tavoy for his holiday.

Nobody thought of Tavoy as a vacation spot but Adoniram laughed and set off by boat down the glorious island-set coast with the noble chain of heavily forested mountains running its length which made most of its shore uninhabitable. To avoid three or four days' delay in going round Tavoy Point and up the river to the town, Adoniram had himself and a coolie set ashore when their southing brought them to a tiny village about eight miles' walk eastward across the mountains to Tavoy.

The going was rapid for a mile or two, through a strip of cultivated lands; pineapples and oranges. Then they entered the mountain path and slowed the pace. The air was heavy with the fragrance of innumerable flowers. The mighty trees were festooned with vines. There was a bird chorus from every covert. Adoniram paced steadily, his heart beating heavily not only from the rapid lift of the mountain but from apprehension. He was about to try once more for happiness.

At the summit there was a water pool and here they paused for the noonday meal. While the man cooked the rice, Adoniram walked over to view the descent on the other side. It curved sharply just below him and he heard unseen footsteps—a moment later, a child's voice— He stood transfixed by the familiar tones of it.

A moment later, Sarah Boardman, holding Georgie's hand, rounded the curve. She was followed by two or three Karens, leading ponies.

The little boy shrieked his surprise and welcome, but Adoniram and Sarah clasped hands in silence.

"We were coming to see you to thank you for making the Bible!" shouted Georgie.

"May I invite you to dinner, if there is enough in my larder?" asked Adoniram with a smile.

"Yes, lord teacher, if you will allow me to add my rice to yours," replied Sarah.

She was a little more tanned, a little thinner, with eyes that knew a little more of loneliness. She wore the shortened blue linen riding dress that so became her and was so useful in her work. They chatted commonplaces at the meal, deciding to return in the afternoon to Tavoy, where Adoniram's inspection and advice, Sarah declared, really were needed. After a little rest, they began the descent, young George on a horse drawing ahead with the Karens. When his mother would have protested, Adoniram said:

"Don't you trust him with them?"

"Oh, yes," replied Sarah, "but—"

"But—let us have just the little time alone then. It will be impossible after we reach the mission," pleaded Adoniram.

She flushed but seated herself on a great red rock by the trail and gave him her clear gaze as he stood before her.

"Do you remember," he asked, "the many times that you have insisted that always there is beauty in life—that God wills it to be so?"

She nodded.

"I still think," he said, "that for myself—I don't pretend to judge for any one else . . . but for myself many of the sacrifices I made were essential. I was drunk with the love of sociableness. It was necessary to make an absolute stop, all or nothing. I couldn't trust myself. As to the hermitage—"

Sarah raised her hand. "Don't, lord teacher, I can't bear to think of that time. Let me tell you instead how great your service to mankind in the translation—"

In his turn, Adoniram interrupted. "I deserve no praise. If Ann in heaven and you on earth think I've done my duty and God finds it useful, that's enough. Sarah, it's eight years since darling Nancy left me and three years since that saint, George, left you. What do you think they would say up there in the celestial blue, if I asked you to be my wife?"

Sarah's cheeks flushed again deeply. "You know," she said quietly, "that one gives to first love when it ripens into marriage an ecstasy that never comes again."

"Yes, I know," agreed Adoniram gently.

"And if they had lived," Sarah went on, "that ecstasy would have been continuing now in an indescribable happiness."

"Yes, it would." Adoniram's eyes were tear blinded. He brushed the drops aside with his hand. "My feeling for you is utterly different from any I've ever experienced before, but, dear Sarah, it's very strong and deep and draws on the best there is in me."

Sarah smiled, uncertainly: "I think I told you once that George and I had loved you since we were school children." She looked from the wistful beauty of his hazel eyes to the glimpse of the perfect valley below, palm and pagoda set, rioting in color. "But, dear lord teacher, I can't follow where you go in mysticism. I'm afraid it would come between us. And unless our spirits see eye to eye, we never can rebuild our shattered lives."

"You mean—?" he asked in a low voice.

She kept her eyes on the far valley. "I mean, if you keep up your terrible lonely effort to see God's face, you'll go mad. No human being can endure the struggle."

"You bargain with me?" he protested, passionately. "You ask me to give up my soul's birthright—?"

She turned and said gently: "You *know* I couldn't do that—I'm not a fool and I'm not wicked, at least not consciously wicked. I want to save your reason, dear lord teacher, by asking you to leave to God the things that are God's. And unknowableness is His. I want you to find peace."

" 'Whatsoever things are true, whatsoever things are just, whatsoever things are lovely,—think on these—and the peace of God shall be with you.' " Adoniram repeated the words slowly and with new understanding. "Sarah, I'll try, with all my soul, I'll try to think only on these things. And when that overpowering craving comes to know Him—for it will come again and again—instead of turning to loneliness and starvation and horribleness, I'll think on what Christ said. For He knew that our poor minds couldn't yet grasp God and so He told us, *I am the way and the truth and the Life.*"

He fell silent while his mind harked back over all the spiritual struggle his soul had known since first he came to Burma. Sarah waited, motionless, a little pale, a little sad. Finally he said:

"Love has always been my spiritual solvent. I am not fit to go on without it."

"God *is* love." Sarah's low voice thrilled his heart.

He drew a deep breath. He had given up happiness forever, yet now such a rush of happiness flooded him that his very body shook. It was not happiness as the young man Adoniram had known it, flawless, full blooded, ecstatic. It had little of the body in it. But it was the happiness of the disciplined soul, built on a life seared with scars the Cross had worn there.

The forest murmured about them in inexpressible beauty. One might not see His face but one could see His splendor and love it unafraid.

"Will you trust me now, Sarah?" he asked, humbly.

She looked into his face. "Yes! with all that I am and all that I hope to grow into, to be worthy of you, Adoniram."

"Don't grow beyond me!" he exclaimed, smiling as he drew her to her feet. They were of the same height and after a moment's clear gazing, eye level with eye, they kissed and then, arms about each other went slowly down into the lovely valley.